CHICAGO PUBLIC LIBRARY

R0L0077 14223

D0463610

Brazil: A Study in
Development Progress

The Committee on Overseas Development of the National Planning Association has been sponsoring a series of studies of development progress. The purpose of the series is to explain how certain developing nations have been able to achieve and sustain high rates of economic growth with resulting improvements in the real incomes of their people. The Committee recognizes the limits on the transferability of one country's experience to another. Nevertheless, development involves coping with many of the same problems by choosing from among the same variety of means. Countries can learn from each other's experiences with respect both to the choice of particular means and to the specific ways in which they are implemented.

This study of Brazil's development provides important insights into the factors responsible for the economic growth and improved living standards of the country. The study is the fourth in the series, and we believe that, like the others, it makes an important contribution to our knowledge of the realities of economic and social progress.

On behalf of NPA, I wish to acknowledge the generous contributions received from the Tinker Foundation and other donors toward the cost of the Brazil study. However, these donors and NPA's Committee on Overseas Development are not responsible for the data, analyses and conclusions in this study, which are solely those of the author.

Rodman C. Rockefeller
Chairman, Committee on Overseas
    Development
National Planning Association

The first three books in the series were published by and are available from the National Planning Association, 1606 New Hampshire Ave., N.W., Washington, D.C. They are *Central American Regional Integration and Economic Development; Mexican Economic Development: The Roots of Rapid Growth*; and *Tales of Two City-States: The Development Progress of Hong Kong and Singapore.*

Brazil: A Study in Development Progress

Stefan H. Robock
Columbia University

Lexington Books
D.C. Heath and Company
Lexington, Massachusetts
Toronto   London

REF
HC
187
.R612
cop.1

Library of Congress Cataloging in Publication Data

Robock, Stefan Hyman

Library of Congress Cataloging in Publication Data

Robock, Stefan Hyman, 1915-
  Brazil: a study in development progress.

  Includes index.
  1. Brazil—Economic conditions—1945. 2. Brazil—Social conditions.
3. Brazil—politics and government—1954. I. Title.
HC187.R612   330.9'81'06   75-18348
ISBN 0-669-00134-1

Copyright © 1975 by D.C. Heath and Company.

All rights reserved. No part of this publication may be reproduced or
transmitted in any form or by any means, electronic or mechanical,
including photocopy, recording, or any information storage or retrieval
system, without permission in writing from the publisher.

Published simultaneously in Canada.

Printed in the United States of America.

International Standard Book Number: 0-669-00134-1

Library of Congress Catalog Card Number: 75-18348

NOV 3 - 1976
BUSINESS & INDUSTRY DIVISION
THE CHICAGO PUBLIC LIBRARY

R06007 14223

Contents

List of Figures

List of Tables

Preface

When the National Planning Association (NPA) invited me to undertake this study, I was pleased to accept. I shared the view of the NPA's Committee on Overseas Development that Brazil's development experience merited the attention of policy makers and opinion leaders in other countries. Furthermore, I felt that my particular mix of Brazilian background would enable me to contribute toward a better understanding of Brazil's "economic miracle."

I have been involved in Brazil for more than 30 years and I have lived in the country for a cumulative total of about six years over this period. My acquaintance with Brazil began in 1943 when, as an officer in the United States Navy, I was stationed for a year at various air bases in the Northeast. My involvement as an economic adviser to Brazil, however, dates from 1954. In that year, while serving as chief economist of the Tennessee Valley Authority, I was invited by the Brazilian government through the United Nations to work in Brazil as an adviser on the development of Northeast Brazil. This mission, which lasted for two and one-half years, was followed by a series of shorter assignments over subsequent years as an economic consultant on a number of national and regional development programs.

Since 1964 I have worked with ELETROBRÁS, the government holding company in the electric power sector, on long-range power market planning, with the minister of the interior on regional and resource development, and I have returned to the Northeast on several occasions to advise the Bank of Northeast Brazil. I have participated in management training programs of the Columbia Business School—João Pinheiro Foundation project in Minas Gerais, and I have acted as consultant to a number of foreign business firms on their Brazilian projects.

This elaboration of my Brazilian experience and my continuing involvement with Brazil may help to explain why my perceptions and analysis of the Brazilian experience may differ from those of other observers and analysts. Having been involved in Brazil's development efforts over two decades—during the Vargas, Kubitschek, and Goulart regimes as well as during the post-1964 military governments—I have been especially sensitive to the historical antecedents of the last decade's economic and political events. Having lived and worked in Brazil's Northeast problem area, I can view this vast country through a wider angle lens than would have been possible had I worked only in the Rio de Janeiro and Brasilia offices of a government agency or in the industrial center of São Paulo.

Still another characteristic of my involvement with Brazil is that my relationship with the country has always been as an independent professional consultant rather than as a representative of a foreign government. As a United Nations adviser and as an individual consultant to the Brazilian government, I have been fortunate in being accepted into the inner councils. My access to information and people has also been facilitated by the fact that, in my first United Nations assignment, I was forced by circumstances to initiate a series of training programs as a means of developing staff assistance for my work. Over the years many of the Brazilian trainees with whom I was associated have moved into positions of major responsibility. As long-time friends and professional colleagues, these Brazilians have been willing to share with me the background information and insights that normally are not easily available to foreigners.

In brief, my background influenced this study in that I have had good access to information and people, personal familiarity with the problem area of the Northeast and the historical perspective. At the same time I have tried to remain objective and resist the natural personal bias that comes from being both fond of Brazil and an intermittent participant in the phenomena being studied.

Now a brief word about the readers for whom this book has been written: The book is directed primarily toward development officials, scholars, and businessmen outside of Brazil. But I am hopeful that my Brazilian friends will also find it informative. It is certainly immodest for an outsider to presume to tell Brazilians about themselves. Yet, sometimes an outside observer who is familiar with, but not a regular participant in, the Brazilian development effort is able to identify trends, forces, and implications that are not easily perceived by those who are continuously involved in the development process.

The individuals in Brazil who assisted me are so numerous that I cannot mention all of them. During my field work many former and present government officials were kind enough to make time for me in their crowded schedules. Among these were the president of the Central Bank, Paulo H. Pereira Lira; minister of planning, João Paulo dos Reis Velloso; minister of finance, Mário Henrique Simonsen; minister of industry and commerce, Severo Fagundo Gomes; president of the Fundação Instituto Brasileiro de Geografia e Estatística, Isaac Kerstenetzky; former minister of mines and energy, Antonio Dias Leite; former president of the National Housing Bank, Rubens Vaz da Costa; former president of the Furnas government electric power company, John Cotrim; and former superintendent of the Planning Ministry's Institute of Research, Annibal Villanova Villela.

I am also indebted to members of the NPA Committee on Overseas Development who critically reviewed my manuscript. I owe special thanks to Theodore Geiger and Frances Geiger of the NPA staff for the encouragement, professional and editorial assistance, and technical guidance that were unselfishly given throughout the project; and to Olga Bilyk, who so pleasantly and efficiently provided the administrative and secretarial services at NPA in Washington.

I benefited immeasurably from the assistance, comments, and suggestions of many people, including my colleague Professor Nathaniel Leff, but I should make clear that I assume full personal responsibility for the final results of this effort.

Finally, I must give special recognition to George Browne, who used his profound knowledge of Brazil and his editorial skills to provide highly professional assistance on my manuscript; to my wife, Shirley Robock, who reviewed several drafts of the study and made valuable suggestions from her own perspective of Brazil; and to Mrs. Ana Rancier, who processed the many versions of my draft manuscript with patience, efficiency, and good cheer.

MAJOR REGIONS OF BRAZIL

RORAIMA (TERR.)

AMAPÁ (TERR.)

EQUATOR

Amazon River

Manaus

Belém

NORTH

AMAZONAS

PARÁ

MARANHÃO

Fortaleza

CEARÁ

RIO GRANDE DO NORTE

NORTHEAST

PARAÍBA

PIAUÍ

Recife

PERNAMBUCO

ACRE

RONDÔNIA (TERR.)

São Francisco River

ALAGOAS

SERGIPE

GOIÁS

BAHIA

Salvador

CENTRAL-WEST

FEDERAL DISTRICT

Brasília

MATO GROSSO

MINAS GERAIS

SOUTHEAST

ESPÍRITO SANTO

Paraná R.

SÃO PAULO

RIO DE JANEIRO

PARANÁ

Rio de Janeiro

São Paulo

Curitiba

SOUTH

SANTA CATARINA

RIO GRANDE DO SUL

Porto Alegre

0   300   600 km

CLB

That Brazilian Economic Miracle

Economic success stories are popularly called "economic miracles." Since the end of World War II there have been the German and the Japanese economic miracles. More recently Brazil's high level and sustained rate of economic growth has been labelled the "Brazilian economic miracle."

A miracle is an event that apparently contradicts known scientific laws and is hence thought to be due to supernatural forces. When asked about the Brazilian economic miracle, a former minister of finance, who played a central role in guiding Brazil's development efforts, explained with a typical Brazilian sense of humor, "The German economic miracle, as we later discovered, was largely due to massive foreign aid under the Marshall plan and a highly developed scientific and industrial infrastructure. The Japanese economic miracle has been explained by high rates of savings, a well disciplined and industrious labor force, and large amounts of postwar foreign aid. Now there is the Brazilian economic miracle. And anyone who knows Brazil and the Brazilians must conclude: This is the *real* miracle."

Humor aside, there is much truth in what the minister said. Known scientific laws are not really contradicted when two former world powers with relatively advanced economies are able to recuperate with the assistance of external aid and then continue for some time with unusually high growth rates, or when an oil-rich country like Iran can achieve rapid economic progress. But when a less developed country, in the stereotyped "mañana land" of Latin America, bursts forth with a spectacular and long-sustained growth record, without the help of large oil discoveries or large amounts of foreign aid, the event apparently contradicts known scientific laws and comes as a surprise to people within, as well as outside, Brazil. In statistical terms, the evidence of "the miracle" has been an economic growth rate averaging 10 percent a year in real terms from 1968 through 1974.

Why has Brazil's recent extraordinary economic performance attracted so much attention, aside from being an unexpected event? As anyone who understands the magic of compound interest or geometric growth rates is aware, an amount subject to 10 percent compounded annually doubles in seven years. In more dramatic terms, over the seven-year period from 1968 through 1974 Brazil increased its national output by an amount equal to its total cumulative economic growth over all the previous centuries of its history. Such a performance has been matched by relatively few countries among the advanced industrial economies, the Socialist countries, or the less developed nations.

1

Other economic results make the Brazilian achievement even more impressive. The growth record was achieved concurrently with a drastic reduction in domestic inflation. The international oil crisis and the world recession of the mid-1970s created serious problems, but it appears that Brazil will be able to continue its development drive at a rapid, though probably reduced, rate.

The Importance of the Brazilian Experience

Why is the Brazilian experience important and to whom? Not surprisingly, the attention of United States, Japanese, Canadian, and European multinational companies seeking business expansion opportunities has been attracted to Brazil. Many officials of other developing countries have been scrutinizing the Brazilian model for policies and practices that they might use in their own national efforts to accelerate economic growth. Academic scholars, also, have been drawn to the Brazilian case as a source of new insights into the process of political, social, and economic development.

The Brazilian case, however, has broad international importance beyond these special group interests. In a world where the supply of natural resources is becoming scarce relative to growing world demand, Brazil stands out as one of the few areas with vast potential for increasing the supply of strategic minerals and renewable natural resources. It has only begun to tap its large mineral deposits. It can massively expand agricultural output through bringing new land into cultivation and through increasing productivity on presently cultivated land. It has immense untapped forest resources that can be managed to add fabulous amounts to world supplies.

The newness of the Brazilian economic miracle has meant that the press has been the principal source of information on Brazil for most foreigners. In the foreign press Brazil has received both glowing eulogies and bitter criticism. Business journals by and large have accented the positive features, emphasizing the business opportunities created by rapid growth and the political stability maintained by a military authoritarian government. Other journalists, frequently joined by scholars, question the ethics of economic development in an environment that curtails civil liberties and permits the torture of political prisoners. The critics generally quote a recent military president who observed that Brazil is doing well, but the people are not.

The Brazilian experience is sufficiently significant to warrant a more comprehensive analysis that allows the observer to evaluate the economic achievement against the political and social cost. Brazil's development progress gives it a chance of becoming one of the first major countries to cross the wide chasm separating the less developed and the developed countries. If it achieves this distinction, while improving the economic, political, and social quality of life for its people, Brazil will be a source of encouragement and hope for billions of the world's population that still remain in poverty.

Scope of the Study

To contribute toward better understanding of Brazil as a case study of development progress, this book attempts:

1. To provide a long-term overview of Brazil's development efforts and accomplishments
2. To examine in greater depth the evolutionary patterns in key economic, social, and political sectors
3. To explain the motive forces and sources of growth
4. To identify the major problems Brazil faces in the future
5. To suggest the lessons other countries might derive from the Brazilian experience.

Some Limitations

The easiest task is to describe what has happened in terms of overall trends and in key sectors. A more difficult task is to explain why certain events happened, and how specific difficult goals were achieved. It may be trite—but still true—to state that the process of development is complex and poorly understood. It involves many intangibles, such as cultural patterns and social values. It has political and human, as well as economic, dimensions. The development process must be examined in a long historical frame. It depends on uncontrollable external factors as well as internal forces that are more susceptible to control. An explanation of the "why" and the "how" must inevitably involve some speculation, be influenced by the experience and perspective of the analyst, and is certain to evoke differing views.

It is inherently impossible to expect widespread agreement as to whether certain features of the Brazilian experience are "good" or "bad." There are no universally accepted standards against which such an evaluation can be made. Any attempt at objective evaluation, therefore, should recognize the point of the well-known story about the economist who, when asked "How is your wife?" replied, "Relative to what?"

The people of Brazil, in common with the people of all other countries, have constantly been making choices among imperfect but realistic alternatives rather than between perfect and idealistic models. In making these choices societies must always make trade-offs. In the political area, for example, many Brazilians believe that there has been a favorable trade-off in which the people gave up some civil liberties and part of their political franchise in order to secure economic growth. Others feel that the trade-off was not necessary, or that the gains were not worth the losses. But this subject becomes one of the "what might have happened" issues that are impossible to resolve.

In any event, if the political process becomes more open for dissenting views and free debate, and if violations of civil liberties are reduced, as seems to be happening currently, most Brazilians might agree that the unfavorable political events of the past were not an unreasonable price to pay for the achievements of a decade of military rule.

The political example illustrates the fact that this book leaves many important questions unanswered. Not only has the author been constrained by limitations of space and time, but many important questions can only be answered as the future unfolds. One area of present controversy is the way in which the fruits of economic growth have been distributed. The government has indicated its desire to increase the participation of the lower-income people and regions in the fruits of economic growth. If it is successful the criticism of past trends will be muted.

A final but necessary point relates to the perspective or bias of the author. On numerous occasions over the past 30 years the author has lived and worked in Brazil, particularly in the Northeast. As a result of this personal experience he can make many comparisons of the current situation with Brazil's own past. Also, Brazil is a seductive country. It is hard to resist its beauty, its people, its accomplishments, its way of life, its "grandeur." It is also impossible to ignore its warts.

This account considers both aspects of the country but may not resolve many of the controversial views provoked by the Brazilian experience. Nevertheless, it aspires to enlarge the understanding of what has been happening in Brazil and thereby contribute to a better-informed appreciation of that country as an important example of development progress.

The Brazilian Setting

The Brazilians are great people for making fun of themselves. One story that was going the rounds a few years ago was about God and an archangel on the third day of creation. When the Lord finished making Brazil, he couldn't help bragging a little to one of the archangels. He had planted the greatest forests, laid out the world's biggest river system, and built a magnificent range of mountains with lovely bays and ocean beaches. He had filled the hills with topaz and aquamarine and sowed the rivers with gold nuggets and diamonds. He had arranged a climate free from hurricanes and earthquakes and a soil that would grow every conceivable kind of fruit.

"Is it fair, Lord," asked the archangel, "to give so many benefits to just one country?"

"You wait," said the Lord, "till you see the people I'm going to put there."

The humor of the story is in its irony. For centuries the development of Brazil has been held back by its inconvenient geography. The rivers run the wrong way. The mountains are in the wrong places. The steep coastal range has been a formidable barrier to penetration of the interior. The rain forests and climate of the Amazon North have been persistently unfriendly to colonization. The Northeast bulge is subject to periodic droughts. Until the coming of air transportation it literally took months to travel from one part of the country to another. The fact is: the chief asset of Brazil is the Brazilians.

In its drive for development Brazil has had to overcome many obstacles imposed by certain features of the physical environment. At the same time other aspects of the environment have greatly aided Brazil in fulfilling its development aspirations. An understanding of the Brazilian development experience requires an appreciation of the physical, social, and political setting within which economic policies and institutions have evolved.

Size

One of the most favorable features of the Brazilian setting is the enormous size of the country. Brazil is the fifth largest country of the world, surpassed in area only by the Soviet Union, the United States, mainland China, and Canada. Its 3.3 million square miles occupy nearly half the area of South America. Before Alaska became a state and its vast area was calculated as part of the United

States, it was common to refer to Brazil's size as greater than that of the United States by another Texas.

In population as well as area Brazil is a major nation. With slightly more than 100 million people, Brazil is the world's seventh most populous country. Over the last decade the population has been increasing at the relatively high rate of almost 3 percent annually.

In terms of development, size means that Brazil has the potential of a massive internal market. It means that Brazil does not have a feeling of great population pressure, nor does it sense an urgent need for population control policies. Size also increases the chances that a country will have within its borders a wide variety of natural resources in reasonably large quantities. At the same time size magnifies the problem of internal communication and transportation and contributes to great social and political diversity.

Geography

The geography of Brazil has limited in many ways the country's development potential and made the development task more difficult. Brazil is essentially formed by a slightly tilted plateau, of which the highest edge, known as the Great Escarpment, overlooks the Atlantic Ocean, while inland the ground falls off gradually in a northwesterly direction toward the vast plain of the Amazon. The Great Escarpment, a steep shelf extending southward for 2,000 miles from Salvador, Bahia to Porto Alegre in the state of Rio Grande do Sul, rises in a series of steps forming parallel ridges that effectively separate the seacoast from the interior. Northeast of Rio de Janeiro the escarpment reaches a peak of almost 10,000 feet.

A visitor, approaching the cities of southern Brazil and observing a mountainous wall rising almost from the sea, can easily form an impression of rugged topography. Actually, only 3 percent of Brazil's area exceeds 3,000 feet in altitude. But the location of the mountain ranges has acted as a serious development barrier. In particular, the Great Escarpment has made the construction of railways and highways into the interior, as well as along the coast in the heavily populated Southeast, difficult and costly.

Transportation difficulties have been further aggravated by the flow pattern of Brazil's rivers. Only a few rivers cut through the coastal mountains to the sea. The principal rivers of the Southeast flow away from the coast and eventually empty into the tributaries of the Rio de la Plata and thence into the Atlantic Ocean between Argentina and Uruguay. Only the Amazon in the north can be navigated far into the interior. River transportation, therefore, has not played a significant role in Brazil's development.

Unlike the United States and Canada, Brazil has no Pacific Coast as a westward objective for expansion. The "Go West" inspiration that sparked the settlement and development of the United States and Canada, and that was stimulated by the various attractions of the Pacific coast, has not been a similar force in the development of Brazil. In Brazil westward movements—originally inspired by the search for gold and diamonds—did not result in permanent farm settlements because grasses proved too poor for cattle, and the land did not serve for crops.[1] Contrary to widely held impressions outside Brazil, the central and southern interior that Brazil has been so anxious to settle is not jungle. The tropical jungles are in the Amazon River basin of the far north.

Still other physical features such as climate, poor soils, and tropical vegetation have retarded the development of the vast Amazon region. The six states and territories of the Amazon North have 42 percent of Brazil's total area but are inhabited by less than 4 million people.

In spite of Brazil's long standing determination to populate its "hollow interior" through such major efforts as the recent establishment of Brasilia about 600 miles from the coast, the principal concentrations of population and economic activity are along the coast. The size of the country, the geographical variations in resources, and historical factors have separated Brazil into regions with widely different characteristics. Regionalism has been and continues to be a strong force in economic policies and in Brazilian politics.

To complete the geographical picture, a brief comment on climate is necessary. Although Brazil's climate varies less than might be expected in view of its great size, Brazil has many physical environments. There are the humid Amazon lowlands, the semiarid Northeast, the eastern highlands, and the southern Pampas—to mention only some of the climatic contrasts in this huge country.

Most of the country, however, lies within the tropical zone where factors such as prevailing winds, rainfall, distance from the ocean, and differences in altitude combine to vary the climate from tropical to temperate. Frost occurs with some frequency in the three southernmost states. But in the North and Northeast high temperatures rarely approach the levels reached in Africa or North America. The Amazon region has heavy rainfall and high relative humidity. Along the coast the heat is somewhat tempered by trade winds and proximity to the sea. Rainfall throughout the rest of Brazil is adequate in most agricultural areas except for a small subregion in the Northeast where irregularity rather than the amount of rainfall characterizes the notorious Drought Polygon.

Natural Resources

The popular description of Brazil as rich in resources is only partially accurate. Much of Brazil's resource potential is still unknown. As resource surveys require large investments, much of the vast territory of Brazil has not yet been systematically explored. In fact, there are regions of northern Brazil for which no surface maps are available. Based on present knowledge, Brazil's resource endowment has both great riches and serious deficiencies.

Minerals are found throughout Brazil. Until major mineral deposits were recently discovered in the Amazon, the principal zone of deposits was in a north-south mountain range running through the state of Minas Gerais. The state's iron ore deposits are among the richest in the world and in 1974 produced 60 million tons of ore as compared with US production of about 80 million tons.

In 1967 the Serra dos Carajás iron ore deposits were discovered deep in the Amazon by the U.S. Steel Corporation. These deposits have reserves of 18 billion tons of iron ore with 66 percent iron content. The Serra dos Carajás is located far in the interior, and about US$500 million is being spent to construct a 950 kilometer railway linking the mine and a location, Itaqui, near the capital city of São Luis in the state of Maranhão, where a huge port is being built. The port is scheduled to be completed in 1979, when annual exports of 12 million tons are projected, rising to 45 million tons in 1985.[2] The massive investment required for this project is estimated at more than US$1.4 billion.

Manganese is currently Brazil's second most important mineral product. Manganese deposits are found near the Bolivian border and in the far north. Major new bauxite deposits in the Amazon region were identified in the late 1960s by a Canadian company and are in process of being exploited. Other minerals found in significant quantities include tin, copper, lead, zinc, nickel ore, phosphate rock, gypsum, thorium, quartz crystal, gem stones, industrial diamonds, graphite, chromium, tungsten, and gold. The tin reserves near the Bolivian border are estimated to be larger than those of Bolivia. Brazil's first important copper deposits were only recently discovered in the state of Bahia, but negotiations have moved slowly to exploit this new resource.

On the negative side, fuel resources are sadly deficient. The only producing coal deposits, located in the far south, are of poor quality and of limited use for making metallurgical coke. The recent discovery of extensive lignite deposits in Amazonia, however, may improve significantly the coal resource situation. Brazil's known oil reserves, located mainly in the northeastern state of Bahia, are far from adequate for supplying Brazil's petroleum needs. Petroleum exploration and production in Brazil is monopolized by the government enterprise, PETRO-BRAS, which has been investing large sums over many years to find major new sources of oil, but with only modest success. However, the 1974 offshore discoveries near Campos in the state of Rio de Janeiro and farther north near the state of Sergipe are estimated to double Brazil's reserve and to yield about 200,000 barrels per day, starting in late 1977. In the energy field Brazil has been importing 65 percent of its metallurgical coal requirements and about 75 percent of its rapidly growing crude petroleum consumption.

Offsetting these deficiencies, Brazil's hydroelectric potential is among the largest in the world, estimated at about 150,000 megawatts of which only a small fraction (about 7 percent) has been utilized so far, in part because of its remoteness from consumption areas. More than 50 percent of this total potential is located in the more industrialized South, Southeast, and Northeast and has been surveyed in some detail. The remainder is mostly located in the Amazon region.

Until the 1960s many of the best sites for hydroelectric development were considered too remote from the centers of population. But rapidly growing power requirements and technological advances, which permit long-distance transmission of large power loads with tolerable losses, have made it economically feasible in the last decade to develop several major power sites in the interior. The most ambitious project, the Itaipu dam on the Paraná River where it borders Brazil and Paraguay, will be the biggest hydroelectric plant in the world when it becomes operational in the early 1980s.

Of Brazil's 279 million hectares of arable land, 88 million are unexploited, and much of the remainder is exploited only extensively. Thus, Brazil probably has the largest still unused, accessible fertile land area in the world. In the case of forests, some readily accessible hardwood stands are in the coastal regions. The pinewoods in the southern state of Paraná have been cut severely. Access to some 250 million hectares of tropical rain forest in the Amazon is now being made practical by the government's new program to build highways in that area.

The soils of Brazil have been the subject of scientific study only in recent decades, and detailed information on the characteristics of Brazilian soils is still scarce. A traditional view is that tropical soils are poor and vulnerable to erosion and lixiviation (the depletion of fertilizing substances from the soil). Some observers, however, dispute this negative evaluation and suggest that this error has arisen because of the common failure when agricultural techniques developed in temperate and cold countries are applied in the tropics.[3]

Brazil lacks large areas of superior soils, such as are found in the Ukraine, the North American Great Plains, Manchuria, and the dry Argentine Pampas. Nor does Brazil have large areas of nonagricultural soils, as are encountered in these same countries. The soils of the forest areas of the Amazon are little known, but great areas of superior cattle-raising land and some good quality red soil areas have been recently identified. The coastal areas of the Northeast, South, and Southeast have relatively fertile soils. The vast areas of the central plateau, however, have proven difficult or impossible to use for agricultural purposes by conventional methods and present a major technological challenge that may be overcome.[4]

The People

A nation's human resources can be its most valuable means of achieving social and economic development goals, as has been so dramatically demonstrated by a country like Japan with virtually no natural resources. Unfortunately, for centuries Brazil failed to give a high priority to investment in its human resources, with the result that much of the potential of its large and diverse population has long been seriously underutilized.

The Brazilian people come from three major racial stocks of the world: the Mongoloid American Indian, the African Negro, and the Caucasoid European. To the already heterogeneous population composed of these three original strains and of which the white Portuguese component was already a composite of many elements, the nineteenth and twentieth centuries brought millions of Europeans, mainly Italians, Germans, Poles, Portuguese, and Spaniards, and the twentieth century added large contingents of Lebanese and Japanese. The Japanese component, estimated variously to number from 500,000 to 1 million including first and second generation Brazilians, represents the largest group of that ancestry living outside Japan. As T. Lynn Smith, the noted American sociologist, has observed, "If the United States is described as a 'melting pot,' Brazil must be considered a caldron. No other country has had for four hundred years such large numbers of white, red, and black people thrown into so close physical and social contact with one another."[5]

Despite its diverse population Brazil has achieved a remarkable degree of cultural unity. Except for a handful of people, such as the tribal Indians deep in the Interior of the North, all Brazilians speak Portuguese. Differences in accent between one region and another are less noticeable than those between a Bostonian and a person from the Deep South in the United States. Everywhere, Brazilian Portuguese contrasts with that of Portugal in the distinctive usage of words, syntax, pronunciation, and slang. "There is a strong and deep feeling among Brazilians of all racial backgrounds and national origins that they form a 'people' and a nation. They share common ideals, common tastes, common problems, common heroes, a common past, and a common sense of humor."[6]

Few other nations have the religious unity of Brazil; 92 percent of all Brazilians profess Catholicism, although their religion is tempered by spiritualistic elements. Spiritism or Macumba, as it is popularly called in Brazil, is widely practiced. The primitive cult brought by the slaves from Africa two centuries ago has been transformed by Brazil's natural ecumenism into a thoroughly middle-class religion that exists as a subculture in relative harmony with formal Catholicism.

Brazil imported African slaves as early as the sixteenth century. On the eve of independence (1822) it was estimated that about half the population of about 3.8 million was black. Before the slave traffic was finally stopped about 1850, several million more had been brought into the country.[7] Although recent data on the color composition of the Brazilian population are not available, the 1950 census classified 11 percent of the total population as black and 27 percent as mulatto *(pardo)*.

As the dominant group in colonial times, the Portuguese were able to impose their European culture on the African slaves and on many of the aboriginal people. In turn, the Indians and Africans exerted a strong influence upon their European masters, as did the new physical environment. Thus, Brazil's culture is not simply a Portuguese way of life transferred to a new country, "but a unique development of diverse heritage molded into a distinctive whole."[8]

Social Structure

Traditionally, Brazil had two well-defined social classes, and there was relatively little mobility between them. The upper class consisted of landowners, merchants, professionals, government officials, and bureaucrats. The lower class was the manual laborers and artisans. The son of a poor man remained poor, and the son of an illiterate remained illiterate. People were conscious of their class and tended to marry within it, thus perpetuating class solidarity.

Since World War II, however, the traditional Brazilian class structure has been changing in a significant and rapid fashion, and the sharp class lines of the past have become increasingly blurred. Brazil has become a highly dynamic society in a state of rapid flux with considerable social and economic mobility based on educational achievement and changes in occupational and economic status.[9] The traditional lower class has split into two groups: agricultural peasants and farm workers as one subgroup and a rapidly expanding urban lower class of service and factory workers. A new urban upper class whose power stems from the ownership of business enterprises has been melding with the traditional elite to form, along with the military, a new dominant segment of Brazilian society.

Even more significant, a large and rapidly growing middle class has emerged in Brazil. This new middle class, consisting of salaried professionals and white collar workers, has become particularly important in the large cities. Government employment, which has been expanding tremendously at federal, state, and municipal levels, has been one of the most important paths to membership in the middle class. The rapid growth of industry and commerce has created many white collar jobs and thereby greatly enlarged the middle class. Furthermore, job opportunities for professionals and technicians have increased with the expansion of the population and the greater purchasing power of the people.

Still another feature of Brazil's dynamic social structure is the changing role of women. Recent years have seen a dramatic increase in the participation of women in education and in employment categories previously reserved for men. The 1972 National Household Sample Survey, for example, reveals that of Brazil's population ten years and over almost a million more women than men are attending school (5.4 versus 4.5 million). Other data show that women comprised 47 percent of the university enrollment in 1972 as compared with 37 percent in 1969, only three years previously. The 400,000 women attending universities have entered into all fields of advanced study.[10]

In employment women comprise 29 percent of the labor force in Brazil as compared with about 35 percent in the United States. The employment of females is still heavily in the service fields, including domestic service, but their participation in industrial, governmental, commercial, and professional employment is growing.

Because Brazil is a multiracial country in which race and class are historically and functionally interrelated, one of its most cherished national themes is that it is a racial democracy. Although there has been no legal form of discrimination or segregation in Brazil since the abolition of slavery in 1888 significant color prejudice does exist. For Brazil as a whole the old Brazilian rule of thumb still stands: The darker the skin the lower the class and the lighter the skin the higher the class.

The existence of color prejudice does not mean that Brazilian racial democracy is a myth. As Charles Wagley has observed, "The emotional tone surrounding color prejudice is generally light-hearted and amused." Race prejudice in Brazil is based on appearance rather than on racial origin. Perhaps the most important difference between race relations in the United States and in Brazil is that color is only one of the criteria by which people are placed in a social class. Other considerations such as income, education, family background, and personal charm are used in addition to color as multiple criteria for determining a person's position in the social hierarchy.

Political System

Brazil was governed as a colony of Portugal for more than three centuries after its accidental discovery in 1500 by Pedro Álvares Cabral who was sailing a westerly course on his passage to India to take advantage of the northeast and southeast trade winds as instructed by Vasco da Gama. In 1808 Brazil suddenly found itself the head of the Portuguese empire instead of being an exploited colony. Napoleon's armies were sweeping Europe, and when the French advanced to Lisbon the ruling Braganças embarked on a fleet and took off for Brazil. For 14 years, Dom João VI reigned in Rio de Janeiro as head of the Kingdoms of Portugal, Brazil, and the Algarve.

When the Branganças were restored to the Portuguese throne after Napoleon's abdication, the Brazilians refused to go back to colonial status and declared their independence in 1822 with João VI's son Dom Pedro I as emperor. When he failed to suit the Brazilians they sent him back to Portugal in 1831 and chose his son Dom Pedro II, still a small boy, to succeed him. Dom Pedro II ruled for more than 50 years with great success but was forced to abdicate in 1889 in favor of a federal republic. One of the contributing factors was the freeing of slaves in 1883. The transition from monarchy to republic took place virtually without bloodshed. Since 1889 the political history of Brazil has been a search for a governmental formula to replace the imperial regime.

As a republic Brazil passed through a variety of stages. The early republic, though formally a democracy, was a period of rule by a small oligarchy. From 1930 until 1945 Brazil experienced a dictatorship under Getúlio Vargas, who established by a new constitution in 1937 a form of government called the *Estado Novo* (New State) patterned somewhat after the Italian corporate state. In 1946 Brazil returned to a democratic form of government with wider participation by the population than before. In 1964, after a period of political turmoil, the military took over the government and have continued to exercise the ultimate political power in Brazil. The governing document of the republic is still the Constitution, which provides for indirect election of the president. Under the present system four generals have served as presidents, and although the formality of indirect elections has been observed, the choice of a military leader as president has been made within the military circles.

The striking feature of the Brazilian search for a viable political form has been the great amount of political continuity and the minor degree of violence that has occurred in Brazil compared to most of the Spanish countries of Latin America. There have been numerous local and sometimes bloody wars in Brazil during the years after independence. Yet, there was no nationwide war to achieve independence. The major historical events—the abolition of slavery, the overthrow of the empire, the coup when Vargas took over as dictator, the attempted secession of the state of São Paulo in 1932, the political crisis in 1954 that caused Vargas to commit suicide, the military coup in 1964 that removed President João Goulart from office, and other political crises—took place peacefully and with little or no bloodshed. The essentially peaceful though turbulent history of Brazil's political life is perhaps unparalleled in the Americas. Brazil has demonstrated a knack for political moderation that is part of the Portuguese inheritance and different from the Spanish tradition of its Latin American neighbors.

Notes

1. See Vianna Moog, *Bandeirantes and Pioneers* (New York: George Braziller, 1964) for an interesting study of the contrasting settlement patterns in Brazil and the United States.

2. Antônio Dias Leite, *Política Mineral e Energética* (Rio de Janeiro: Fundação IBGE, 1974), p. 71.

3. *25 Years of the Brazilian Economy* (São Paulo: Banco Moreira Salles, S.A., 1967), p. 34.

4. See Rui Miller Paiva, Salomão Schattan, and Claus F. Trench de Freitas, *Brazil's Agricultural Sector* (São Paulo, 1973), pp. 253-74.

5. T. Lynn Smith, *Brazil: People and Institutions* (Baton Rouge: Louisiana State University Press, 1963), p. 51.

6. Charles Wagley, *An Introduction to Brazil* (New York: Columbia University Press, 1971), Revised Edition, p. 5.

14

7. George Wythe, *Brazil: An Expanding Economy* (New York: The Twentieth Century Fund, 1949), p. 24.

8. Wagley, *Introduction*, p. 9.

9. Wagley, *Introduction*, pp. 91-133. See also Phillipe C. Schmitter, *Interest Conflict and Political Change in Brazil* (Stanford, California: Stanford University Press, 1971), pp. 43-45.

10. Rubens Vaz da Costa, *A Participação da Mulher na Sociedade Brasileira* (São Paulo, 1974), Mimeo.

The Drive for Development

With their penchant for self-deprecating humor, Brazilians for many years explained to foreigners that, "Brazil grows at night, when the Brazilians are asleep and can't get in the way." If this explanation were true one would have to conclude that Brazilians have been good sleepers for several decades, and that their sleeping ability has been steadily improving.

Although historical statistics are sparse and use of them is somewhat precarious, they show that since 1920 Brazil has experienced a steady, sizeable, and ever-increasing rate of economic growth; that recent spectacular results have been a continuation and an acceleration of long-term trends, temporarily interrupted by a brief hiatus; and that rapid industrialization has been the leading edge in Brazil's successful drive for development. Before Brazil set out on its recent road to development, however, it was caught for many centuries in a series of boom and bust production cycles based on ever-changing dominant agricultural or mineral products for export.

Some Past History

Brazil's colorful economic history extends back to the early 1500s. In fact, sugar plantations with slave labor were well-established in Brazil before the colonial settlements of Jamestown and Plymouth were founded in the United States. Until the twentieth century Brazil's economic history was characterized by a series of production cycles during which Brazil occupied the leading position in world production of dyewoods, sugar, gold, diamonds, rubber, cacao, and coffee and then lost its primacy in all except coffee. As one historian has observed, "Brazil's economic history is a series of sensational accomplishments, characterized by a sequence of amazing fluctuations. It is, in fact, the story of the appearance and disappearance of entire economic systems on which a nation bases its existence. Its chief characteristic is the constant change in the nature of the product, which we may term the 'king-product.' "[1]

The production cycles have no precise beginning and ending dates. They were linked together, and their influence often continued to persist after the peak periods had passed. The approximate time periods during which the "king products" dominated the Brazilian economy are as follows:[2]

Brazilwood cycle	1500 to 1550
Sugar cane cycle	1550 to 1700
Gold cycle	1700 to 1775
Rubber and coffee cycle	1850 to 1930

Shortly after Brazil's discovery in 1500 the principal economic activity was the cutting and export of brazilwood, a product that gave the country its name and from which a red dye was extracted. Brazilwood came from a relatively narrow strip of land along the coastline. Within several decades all the dyewood in accessible areas was exhausted, and interest in the trade declined.

Sugar cane was brought to Brazil, probably about 1530, from other Portuguese possessions and for more than three centuries continued as Brazil's most important product. Sugar production for export served to colonize the vast Northeast region, where a colonial society of great wealth and prosperity developed with the characteristic social classes of plantation masters, slaves, and sharecroppers. Sugar was one of the principal factors leading to the Dutch invasion and domination of Northeast Brazil during the first half of the seventeenth century. It was the motive for Brazil to import African slaves, who contributed so significantly to the country's ethnic, cultural, and spiritual formation. It was the source of political power in a system where "sugar barons" dominated politics from Independence up to the Republic.

Cattle were introduced into Brazil in the first half of the seventeenth century, serving first as an auxiliary activity to sugar and later as a primary activity stimulating the occupation of interior lands and the march to the hinterland. Tobacco cultivation is credited to the Indians. In spite of the early persecution of tobacco users for a "diabolical and infernal practice," the pleasure of the vice spread to Europe and, in the seventeenth century, tobacco exports from Brazil reached significant levels.

The gold cycle began toward the end of the seventeenth century, when the "bandeirantes," or armed bands of explorers, discovered gold in the state of Minas Gerais. The gold rush that followed attracted people from all parts of the country and from abroad. The discovery exceeded all expectations, and by the middle of the eighteenth century Brazil became the world's leading producer of gold. Most of this fabulous new wealth, in the words of a Brazilian historian, was consumed "by the uncontrolled expenditures of the Portuguese Court."[3] Brazil's portion amounted to some personal fortunes, the sumptuousness of several churches, and the founding of numerous towns. The historic function of the mining cycle consisted in the widening of Brazil's economic frontiers, moving the country's borders to the extreme west and south. The decline of the cycle, which lasted for close to a century, almost coincided with the emergence of "King Coffee" in the Brazilian economy.

Coffee was first introduced into Brazil in 1727, brought from the French colony of Cayenne. The first plantings were in the north, but coffee production steadily moved to the south where the states of Rio de Janeiro, São Paulo, and later Paraná successively became the major producing areas. The prosperity cycle due to coffee exports began about 1850. Coffee exports averaged close to 3,000,000 bags of 60 kilograms each during the 1850s and expanded steadily to about 13,000,000 annually by the first decade of the twentieth century.[4]

As coffee trading was essentially a commercial activity, it gave birth to the "paulista," or South American "yankee" type, with important implications for the development of commerce and industry. Coffee attracted large-scale foreign immigration, developed railways, stimulated urbanization, and greatly enlarged the demand for manufactured consumer goods. In brief, it created resources and a domestic market that favored the growth of indigenous industry.

Coincident with the later phases of the coffee cycle, rubber production had its boom in the extreme North, causing the rapid enrichment of that region. Rubber exports skyrocketed from 7,000 tons in 1880 to a peak of 42,000 tons in 1912. From that time on Brazilian production began to decline as a consequence of competition from Malaysian rubber. During World War II the production of natural rubber recovered to about 30,000 tons a year and currently continues at slightly above that level.

Cacao, or cocoa beans, assumed importance about the same time as the rubber boom began. Production was concentrated in southern Bahia. Cacao exports steadily mounted from about 1,700 tons in 1890 to a level of about 65,000 tons in 1920. Thereafter, Brazil's world dominance was again lost to foreign competitors in Africa, mainly Ghana and the Cameroons, even though production continued to rise to current levels of 150,000 to 200,000 tons a year.

In Brazil's long history of ever-changing production cycles, none ever assumed the character of a broadly based development drive. The cycles created economic islands in the various regions of the country, which were isolated from each other and which prospered during different time periods. The result was a dispersed colonization, an expansion based on exports of raw materials, and little national economic integration. The cycles of limited duration, such as gold and rubber, after periods of grandeur and splendor, left behind immense vacuums, causing stagnation and economic recession.

By the end of the nineteenth century the Brazilian economy was predominantly dependent upon agriculture. The production of coffee in the Center-South, sugar cane in the Northeast, and natural rubber in the North were the most important activities. In foreign trade the value of coffee, sugar, and rubber exports represented about 80 percent of Brazil's foreign-exchange earnings. In fact, until the 1920s the expansion of the Brazilian economy depended almost exclusively on the agricultural sector.[5] Yet, slowly but certainly industrialization was emerging as a significant activity.

The Beginnings of Industrialization

During the colonial period Brazil's productive sector was dominated by large monocultural estates specializing in export agriculture. In the sugar-boom days commerce was a monopoly of the Portuguese. The sugar estate owners, divorced from commerce, never developed into outward-looking entrepreneurs. The continuing small internal market, due to concentration of property and income, served to maintain the stagnant colonial economic structure. One economist has contrasted the Brazilian situation with that in the North American colonies, where small agricultural properties and small farmers constituted a large part of the productive sector.[6] Aided by a more even distribution of income, a large internal market began to appear in North America, setting the stage for an early development of independent commercial and industrial activities.

When Brazil declared its independence in 1822, not only did the country lack an important indigenous commercial class but manufacturing was prohibited by the mercantilist policy of Portugal, and virtually all manufactured goods were imported. Brazilian markets for manufactured products were the special preserve of Portuguese and British manufacturers. The British had received special privileges as a result of treaty arrangements with Portugal.

The Empire, which lasted until 1889, saw the beginnings of industrialization, but manufacturing activities continued to be minor compared to agriculture. A succession of profitable opportunities in agriculture and mining for export continued to attract Brazil's economic interests. The society remained feudal and controlled largely by landowners who were able to shape policies to fit their agricultural and commercial interests. During the 1880s, however, industrial growth became significant and continued for the following decades. Cotton textile production in particular increased more than tenfold between 1885 and 1905 and almost doubled again in the following ten years. Other light industries such as clothing, shoes, and food products also developed rapidly during this early stage of industrialization.

The main force behind this early industrialization was the coffee boom based on free immigrant labor. The immigrant population employed in the coffee and coffee-related sectors provided a sizeable market for inexpensive consumer goods. Many of the immigrants brought manufacturing and business skills to Brazil. Investments in railroads, power stations, and other types of infrastructure financed by coffee planters and foreign capital to service the coffee sector gradually created a demand for locally produced spare parts.[7] This fall-out was important for stimulating industrialization, but the investor looking for action still put his money in coffee.

In the early years of the Republic a school of thought favoring industrialization emerged as a vocal but not decisive force. It claimed that Brazil had to complement its political independence by acquiring economic independence mainly through having its own manufacturing sector. The resulting popular pressure managed to secure increased tariff protection and some governmental financial assistance for new industries.[8]

During World War I manufacturing output expanded through increased utilization of the food and textile producing capacity, which had been created prior to the war. But industrial capacity did not expand, nor did the structure of the manufacturing sector change. The interruption of shipping made it difficult to import the capital goods needed to increase capacity, and Brazil had not yet developed its own capital-goods industry. The industrial structure in this early period of growth was dominated by light industries. According to the 1920 industrial census, textiles, clothing, shoes, and the food industries accounted for over 64 percent of industrial output.

Fifty Years of Economic Growth: An Overview

As is true for many countries, reliable statistical data on Brazil's historical trends are lacking. Fortunately, the Getúlio Vargas Foundation in 1968 extended the indexes of real product trends in Brazil back to the year 1920. As shown in Table 3-1, these data reveal a steady record of economic growth for at least the last 50 years. They clearly support the thesis that Brazil's recent spectacular economic record is a resumption and acceleration of a long-term trend that was temporarily disrupted in the mid-1960s. They also highlight the leading role of the ever-accelerating rate of expansion in the industrial sector. It should be noted that "industry" in Brazilian statistics includes mining, construction, and public utilities as well as manufacturing.

The economic expansion achieved over the period from 1920 to about 1947 was primarily the result of spontaneous forces and external factors as contrasted to the period after World War II when development emerged as the top national priority, and a self-propelled development drive began. The emphasis on the long-range nature of Brazil's path to development is not intended to detract from the effectiveness and importance of recent policies and development

Table 3-1
Brazil: Average Annual Real Economic Growth Rates, 1921-74
(Percent)

	Gross National Product	Sectors			
		Agriculture	Industry	Commerce	Transport and Communication
1921-30	3.7	3.4	3.3	3.4	8.1
1931-40	4.6	4.3	5.2	4.6	5.1
1941-47	5.1	3.9	6.5	4.7	8.5
1948-56	6.4	3.9	8.8	4.9	8.8
1957-61	8.3	5.8	10.7	7.8	8.7
1962-67	3.7	3.9	3.7	3.4	5.6
1968-74	10.1	5.9	11.9	11.0	11.7

Source: Brazilian Institute of Economics, Getúlio Vargas Foundation.

activities. Instead, it is intended to underline the point that, in the absence of a fortuitous discovery of rich natural resources such as oil, the development process normally requires many years of sustained and dedicated effort.

1920-47: Spontaneous Growth in
Response to External Forces

In 1920 Brazil's population was slightly above 27 million. Per-capita income was about $130 annually in terms of 1965 purchasing power.[9] Agriculture was the dominant economic activity occupying 70 percent of the labor force. Export crops, principally coffee but including cotton, tobacco, and cacao, occupied 50 percent of the area being cultivated, represented 60 percent of the value of agricultural production, and accounted for more than 80 percent of Brazil's export earnings. The small manufacturing sector was limited mainly to textiles and food products. The country was strongly dependent upon both imports and exports.

During the 1920s Brazil's national product expanded in real terms at an average rate of 3.7 percent annually (Table 3-1). The composition of output remained almost unchanged, with agriculture, industry, and commerce expanding at about the same rate. Despite the relatively slow growth in industrial production, events during the decade foreshadowed the substantial changes yet to come in an expanded role for industry and in the diversification of the manufacturing sector. The import of capital goods to increase capacity rose dramatically in anticipation of future growth in domestic markets and to replace equipment that had been intensively used during World War I. Diversification was also occurring with the appearance of new small steel plants and capital-goods enterprises, as well as the beginning of domestic cement production.

Paradoxically, the decade of the 1930s was a period of accelerated industrial expansion and rapid economic growth, in spite of the worldwide depression and economic crisis. Over the decade, the industrial sector grew at an average annual rate of 5.2 percent, almost 60 percent above the level of the 1920s. Total national product increased at the respectable growth rate of 4.6 percent annually.

Brazil's performance was especially striking because of the world coffee crisis that occurred in 1929, persisted over the decade of the 1930s, and resulted in the eventual dethronement of "King Coffee." It was Brazil's good fortune that the coffee policies adopted by the government to maintain internal coffee prices and protect the coffee growers had the unforeseen effect of causing a spurt in industrial growth.

With the drop in world coffee prices the government depreciated its currency. This meant that each United States dollar could be exchanged for a larger amount of local currency. Thus, the decline in local-currency earnings of the growers was much less than the drop in world coffee prices. At the new local prices coffee production still continued to be profitable, and production levels were maintained. With production excesses and large accumulated stocks continuing to put pressure on international prices, the government bought and eventually destroyed a large share of the country's coffee production. Even though the stocks were destroyed, the effect of the coffee policies was to maintain domestic income and demand in the same way as increased public expenditures for work relief programs helped to alleviate the depression in the United States. Government expenditures began early in the depression period and were of such a large scale that, according to one estimate, Brazil's national income at the lowest point of the crisis declined by only 25 to 30 percent compared with the United States decline of more than 50 percent.[10]

Industry was the great beneficiary of these policies. The exchange depreciation made foreign goods more expensive. Lower foreign-exchange earnings reduced Brazil's capacity to import. At the same time domestic demand remained at a reasonable level. To satisfy this demand, capital previously invested in coffee expansion went into industry and accelerated a major change in Brazil's economic structure. Not only did the traditional types of manufacturing expand, but substantial growth occurred in new fields such as metal products, chemicals, and cement. The production of cement, for example, increased from 87,000 to 745,000 tons annually between 1930 and 1940.

World War II further stimulated the development of Brazil's internal markets. Although exports were reduced by the difficulties of wartime ocean shipping, the terms of trade improved markedly, and the value of exports increased substantially. But the increased capacity to import was of little avail because of international shortages of goods to be imported. Brazil accumulated a substantial amount of foreign exchange while its domestic industries, protected from foreign competition, were able to accelerate their rate of expansion. Between 1941 and 1947 the growth rate of Brazil's real national product averaged 5.1 percent annually, led by a rate of expansion of 6.5 percent in the industrial sector.

The Dethronement of "King Coffee"

The most important economic event of the 1930s was the dethronement of "King Coffee." Early signs of regal weakness had appeared in the 1890s, but a "valorization" program initiated in 1906 staved off the downfall for more than three decades. *Valorization* was the label given to governmental programs for supporting prices by buying up surplus supply.

The exceptional conditions that made coffee planting so profitable also spelled trouble for the sector. The abundant supply of good land and labor meant that coffee production could be expanded beyond the limits of the entire world market. The planters realized this and used their political power to institute government price supports and supply restriction programs. The price supports worked better than the supply restrictions. With an almost monopoly position, Brazil was able to keep prices high with the result that, more and more, other countries entered the market as competitors. Even at home the profitability of coffee remained too high for the supply restrictions to work. Production from coffee trees, which normally take from five to seven years to mature, continued to expand with such strength that in 1929 Brazil produced about 29 million bags while exports were only 14 million, and the world coffee market collapsed. Even without the world depression that began in 1929 the consumption of coffee in the world could not keep up with the production increases stimulated by previous high prices and high profitability.

Some numbers help to illustrate the magnitude of the coffee crisis. From September 1929 to September 1931 the world price for coffee dropped from 22.5 cents to 8 cents per pound and continued at slightly below the 1931 level until 1939. The valorization program, previously the responsibility of the main coffee-producing states, was taken over in 1931 by the federal government. The government continued to support coffee prices by buying up surplus coffee stocks and in only four years, from 1930 to 1934, took 50 million bags out of circulation of which 34 million were burned. By 1944, 78 million bags, or 5.5 times total exports in 1929, had been destroyed in the valorization effort to bring supply in line with demand.

Coffee production peaked at 33 million bags in 1933 as a result of the plantings in 1927-28 but then steadily declined to less than half of that level in 1945. As a share of the value of agricultural production, coffee dropped precipitously from 48 percent over the 1925-29 period to only 16 percent in the 1939-43 years. As a source of export earnings, coffee dwindled from 72.5 percent of the total value of Brazilian exports over the years 1924-29 to only 32.5 percent over the 1940-45 period.

The fall of "King Coffee" was a momentous event because it irrevocably shaped future events in Brazil in at least four major ways. It stimulated agricultural diversification toward other export crops such as cotton and toward products for the domestic market. It reduced export earnings and the capacity to import, encouraging domestic production as a substitute for imports. It diverted investment flows previously going to the highly profitable coffee sector into industry. It unlocked the long-time stranglehold that coffee policy had on the time and energy of government officials and opened the way for industrialization and broad development issues to begin receiving government attention. In fact, it could be argued that the fall of "King Coffee" was a necessary condition for Brazil to begin an affirmative and broad drive for development.

Iron and Steel: An Early Case
of Affirmative Development

In describing Brazil's accelerating growth trends during the 1930s and 1940s, the emphasis has been both on external events, such as the Great Depression and

World War II as motivating forces, and on the absence of a broad development ideology. Yet, it should be noted that in several specific fields, particularly in the case of iron and steel, Brazil had a long-standing national consensus on the need for affirmative development action and was able to achieve its first major results during the period.

Given Brazil's vast natural resources for making iron and steel, it is not surprising that proposals for producing iron and iron products go back to colonial times. Over the centuries, in spite of many efforts by domestic and foreign entrepreneurs to establish iron and steel production, the industry persisted in a nascent state.

Government policies until the 1940s were generally passive toward industrial development, but a striking exception was the case of iron and steel.[11] Government decrees in 1918 and again in 1925 gave a wide range of special incentives to firms producing iron and steel. In 1931 Getúlio Vargas declared in a speech, "The most basic problem of our economy is that of steel. For Brazil, the age of iron will signify its economic opulence."[12] The military establishment agreed firmly with this view.

A breakthrough in Brazil's aspirations to develop an iron and steel industry finally occurred in the mid-1930s with the construction of the Belgo-Mineira charcoal-based, integrated steel plant in Minas Gerais. Even with this plant, by the end of the thirties Brazil was still a relatively small steel-producing country and heavily dependent upon imports. Vargas and the military continued their efforts to have an integrated steel plant on a substantially larger scale than Belgo-Mineira. These efforts culminated in the creation of the government enterprise, Companhia Siderúrgica Nacional, and the construction of the Volta Redonda plant beginning in 1941.

The case of iron and steel in Brazil is of special interest. First, it demonstrates the long historical antecedents that underlie some key economic sectors that have played a major role in Brazil's recent economic boom. Second, it illustrates the long-standing interest and participation of the military establishment in the development of strategic economic sectors. General Macedo Soares was a central figure in the planning, negotiation, and construction of Volta Redonda. Third, the wide range of solutions attempted by the Brazilians sharply reveals their pragmatic style for achieving development goals.

Virtually all combinations of ownership were considered, explored, and supported: including domestic private enterprise, foreign private enterprise, joint ventures between foreign and domestic enterprises, joint ventures between foreign private firms and the Brazilian government, and government enterprises. The preferred solution of the Brazilian government, despite nationalistic opposition, was a proposal by U.S. Steel to form a local company with minority Brazilian private participation. With U.S Steel's decision in 1940 to abandon its Brazilian project, a government-owned company with substantial financing from the U.S. Export-Import bank became the only feasible solution. Vargas succeeded in getting official United States support by inviting the Germans to make a competing proposal and by relating United States government support of this project to military and political considerations, especially the stationing of United States troops at strategic points in Brazil in case of war.

Affirmative Development and the
New Industrialization: 1948-56

At the end of World War II Brazil was in an exceptionally favorable position for crossing the divide from spontaneous growth to an affirmative drive for development. The economic situation was propitious. A national consensus was emerging in Brazil that the economic role of government should be expanded. The power of the national government to formulate and implement policies had been immeasurably strengthened during the Estado Novo period (1937-45) of the Getúlio Vargas dictatorship. Recent ventures into government planning had provided experience, which would help in constructing the institutional framework necessary for a drive to development. And of crucial importance, Brazil had begun to support analytical research that would enlarge and clarify understanding of its development problems and opportunities and eventually provide rational and technically sound guidance for affirmative development.

The economic situation was favorable because the wartime inability to secure capital equipment had resulted in a pent-up demand for modernization of the industrial sector. The growth of domestic demand during the war and the high utilization of capacity created promising prospects for expanding capacity as well as for modernization. The wartime increase in export earnings and the limited availability of consumer or producer goods for import resulted in large accumulated foreign-exchange reserves.

In the area of economic policy the idea that the government should act more aggressively was not new. It was eloquently urged by the protectionist forces in the economic-policy debates that followed the proclamation of the Republic in 1889. The nationalistic and affirmative development flavor of the debates is reflected in the remarks of a leading exponent of industrialization, Serzedelo Correia, who had served as minister of finance, federal deputy, and mayor of Rio de Janeiro:

It is not by increasing imports, it is not by keeping ourselves as tributaries in everything and by everything that is foreign that we shall develop our wealth, that we shall fortify our progress, that we shall increase our production; and it is certain that, without a solid and growing national activity in the economic sphere, we shall always be a poor country, without nerves and without blood.[13]

Despite their national prominence, the many early advocates of a protectionist policy to encourage industrialization were not able to prevail over the powerful vested interest in export agriculture. The government's role in economic affairs continued to be spasmodic and generally of a defensive nature. For example, in the Northeast, which since the severe drought of 1877 had been officially recognized as a national problem, federal programs to "fight the droughts" by building dams and reservoirs fluctuated greatly with their frequency and intensity.[14]

Two external events—the depression of the 1930s and the military and economic security needs of World War II—eventually overcame the inertia of the past and created a broad public consensus on the need for stronger national direction in economic affairs. In 1934 a first effort at governmental planning was attempted through the creation of the Federal Foreign Trade Council.[15] Immediately on Brazil's entry into World War II Vargas appointed a coordinator of economic mobilization with vast powers for directing the economy. Although aiding the war effort was the primary objective, the experience gained in economic intervention acted as significant preparation for the later development role of the government.

During the war period foreign cooperation was solicited for limited planning efforts. In 1943, in recognition of Brazil's strategic importance to the Allied war efforts, the United States sent a high level American Technical Mission (Cooke Mission) to assist Brazil in planning for greater economic self-sufficiency.[16] Working with 100 Brazilian counterparts, the Cooke Mission investigated measures to stimulate local production of essential goods in short supply, to develop substitutes for foreign goods unobtainable in wartime, to expand and maintain Brazil's domestic transportation system, and to establish a sound basis for industrial development. Although the Cooke Mission did not have extensive immediate results, it did have the effect of clarifying and enlarging Brazilian understanding of the development program.

An Economic Planning Commission, established in 1944 as a subcommission of the National Security Council, was active for a short period in matters of transportation, industrial expansion, and mineral resource development. By the end of the war, with the overthrow of Vargas and the adoption of a new Constitution in 1946, government responsibility in economic matters had become widely accepted. In Article 146 the new Constitution authorized government economic intervention and created for the first time a National Economic Council to work with both executive and legislative branches of government.

In parallel with the evolution of economic ideas, Brazil's political system had been moving rapidly under Vargas toward a centralization of power in the federal government. Vargas first came to power in the revolution of 1930. In 1937 elections were cancelled, and Vargas continued to rule as a dictator until he was overthrown in October 1945 by the military. But during his leadership Vargas succeeded in overcoming the inertia of centuries by moving the country's political structure from that of a loosely federated grouping of states to a highly centralized federal government with power to develop and implement national policies. The Constitution of 1946, which followed the Vargas dictatorship, perpetuated most of the provisions designed in the Vargas period to centralize government.

In the area of institutional development an important new agency was the Departamento Administrativo do Serviço Público (DASP) established in 1937. The main function of DASP was to serve as a federal budget bureau and personnel office, but during the war it also became the focus of economic planning efforts. The first public investment plans prepared in Brazil, including the SALTE plan (1946-50), had their origin in ideas of the DASP technicians.

Another major stream of institutional development that permitted the government to assume a greatly increased economic role was the creation of a number of government enterprises, particularly during World War II. Most were founded for national security considerations. The Companhia Nacional de Álcalis was founded in 1943 because of fear that shortages of soda ash would paralyze industries dependent on this raw material. The establishment in 1942 of the Companhia Vale do Rio Doce to develop the rich iron ore deposits of Minas Gerais for export was attributed in large part to nationalistic considerations.

The growing governmental initiative in economic matters was accompanied by two other supporting developments—the expansion of economic research and the training of economists. The quasi-governmental Getúlio Vargas Foundation, established in 1944, pioneered in both research and training. Its first research publication, written by an engineer turned economist, was a strong plea for the planned development of the Brazilian economy.[17] The foundation brought together some of the best talent in the country and initiated valuable work in the systematic collection and analysis of economic information. The supply of trained economists, still a critical bottleneck in Brazil, was increased by the establishment of faculties of economics in major Brazilian universities, by the on-the-job training experience of working with several foreign assistance missions, and by the initiative of a small number of Brazilians such as Roberto Campos and Celso Furtado in pursuing economic studies in foreign universities.

With the coincidence of economic opportunity and the many converging forces in support of an enlarged governmental role, Brazil moved quickly in the post-World War II period to a "new" industrialization phase shaped by an explicit growth strategy. Under the old industrialization, with little or no concerted effort by the government to promote manufacturing, the pattern of industrialization had mainly followed Brazil's static comparative advantages. In the new industrialization the key sectors to be encouraged were consumer durables, basic intermediates, and capital goods—generally industries in which it was difficult to demonstrate Brazil's comparative advantage.

The new policies began to emerge out of the balance-of-payments difficulties Brazil encountered shortly after the end of the war. The large surplus of foreign exchange accumulated during the war was quickly exhausted because of the large backlog of repressed import demand, the high rise in international prices, and a decline in export earnings from wartime levels. In response to the foreign-exchange crisis, Brazil adopted an import licensing system in 1947 intended to control both the level and composition of imports. Initially, the purpose of controls was to reduce imports. Protection of existing industries was a secondary goal, and encouragement of new industries was not an intended result.

The move toward protectionism became more deliberate about 1949 with the gradual revival of an old law prohibiting imports for which a domestic substitute existed. The so-called "Law of Similars" had been on the books in one form or other since 1911. The quantitative control of imports was replaced in 1953 with a multiple exchange-rate system that, in turn, was simplified in 1957 when heavy tariff protection was adopted. The effect of this series of protective measures was to create great incentives to establish industries that would substitute for imports.

From 1948 to 1956, with the new import-substitution policies beginning to take hold, the national product in real terms grew at an average annual rate of 6.4 percent. In the single year of 1954 the overall growth rate exceeded 10 percent. The agricultural sector continued to expand slowly, averaging only 3.9 percent a year, but industrialization attained a new high growth rate, averaging 8.8 percent annually over the eight-year period. More importantly, the expansion of manufacturing was no longer limited to the traditional industries but also included consumer durable goods and capital goods previously supplied only by imports.

Many economic measures taken by an increasingly active government helped to fuel the spurt in economic growth. Economic planning became accepted as a way of government behavior. The Dutra government (1946-51) prepared and presented to the Congress in 1948 the five-year SALTE plan for national development. The plan was little more than a listing of government expenditures in four fields—health, food supply, transport, and energy—and had spotty implementation. The Dutra government also requested United States cooperation in establishing the Joint Brazil-United States Technical Commission, which began its work in late 1948 and added significantly to the formulation of a macroeconomic and broad development type of thinking in Brazil. The United States advisors were led by John Abbink, whose Brazilian counterpart was Octavio Gouveia de Bulhões, later to become the finance minister in the Castello Branco military government of 1964.

Of much greater significance in the history of Brazilian development was the work of the Joint Brazil-United States Development Commission, called the Comissão Mista or Mixed Commission, which functioned from 1951 to 1953 under the new Vargas administration. One result of the Comissão Mista was the establishment of Brazil's National Economic Development Bank (BNDE) in 1953 to provide financing for the recommended growth and modernization program of the country's infrastructure.

Responding to nationalistic pressures in 1953, the Brazilian government created PETROBRAS to exploit the declared state monopoly of petroleum exploration. Regional development banks under the auspices of the federal and state governments were established beginning with the Bank of Northeast Brazil in 1954. A number of government enterprises in the electric power field were also launched during the early and mid 1950s, including the São Francisco Hydroelectric Company (CHESF), first authorized by Getúlio Vargas in late 1945 to develop the Paulo Afonso falls in the Northeast, and a state power company (CEMIG) in Minas Gerais.

Development Euphoria: 1957-61

With the government of Juscelino Kubitschek, beginning in January 1956, development became Brazil's top national priority. The concept of development was transformed into a political banner, and concern for achieving high growth rates within a relatively short period became the hallmark of the Kubitschek administration. The period truly became one of development euphoria. By force of his optimism and supreme confidence in the potential of Brazil and its people, Kubitschek practically eliminated the vestiges of a national inferiority complex left over from colonial days.

The day after his inauguration a National Development Council was created which prepared the Programa de Metas or Targets' Program. The council consisted of cabinet members and chief monetary authorities with the president of the National Development Bank as secretary general and the staff of the bank providing technical services. Another major step was the creation of so-called "Executive Groups" (Grupos Executivos) for specific industrial sectors such as motor vehicles. These committees brought together representatives of the several governmental agencies whose duty was to formulate sectoral plans and effectively coordinate their implementation.[18]

The Targets' Program was not a global and comprehensive development plan. It focused on so-called "growing points" industries, which would set the pace for further rapid industrialization, and on "impulse sectors." Targets were identified for both the government and the private sector. Five areas were covered: energy, transportation, food supply, basic industries, and education (especially the training of technical personnel). The infrastructure investment was mainly concerned with the elimination of bottlenecks, and in this area considerable basic planning and detailed project studies were available from the work of the Comissão Mista.

The targets for basic industries included detailed goals for output and investment in such industries as steel, aluminum, cement, cellulose, automotive, heavy machinery, and chemicals. A special project in Kubitschek's program was the construction of the new federal capital of Brasilia in the interior of the country. To implement the industrialization program the tariff laws were changed to expand and solidify the protection offered to the growing domestic industries, and attractive foreign-exchange subsidies were used to encourage new investments.

During the Kubitschek administration a substantial amount of progress was made towards fulfilling many of the targets, especially in industry and infrastructure. The most dramatic industrialization feat was the creation in less than five years of a full-fledged industry manufacturing automotive vehicles and parts. Before 1956 manufacturing activities in the automotive field were limited almost exclusively to the manufacture of parts and minor assembly operations. By 1962, in response to a planned governmental effort that offered highly attractive incentives to foreign investors,[19] ten major concerns were producing 190,000 automobiles and trucks with about 90 percent of the parts domestically manufactured.

Other important achievements, accomplished largely through attracting foreign investment and technology were the starting of a shipbuilding industry and major expansions in paper and pulp, heavy mechanical and electrical equipment, steel, and tractor production. In cement Brazil became completely self-sufficient by 1961. In infrastructure the installed capacity of electric power generation was greatly enlarged, and the 2,000 miles of paved roads existing at the beginning of the Kubitschek administration were tripled by the early sixties.

In overall terms, from 1957 through 1961, the national product in real terms grew at the new high rate of 8.3 percent annually. The industrial sector expanded at an average rate of 10.7 percent per year, and the agricultural sector with an average annual growth rate of 5.8 percent also made a major contribution. Although the rapid growth created many distortions, the period was one of drastic change in the economic structure of the country. In many respects the Kubitschek era consolidated the first phase of what has been called the Brazilian Industrial Revolution.

This success has been explained by a favorable political environment, the personality of Juscelino Kubitschek, and the fact that the president surrounded himself with an excellent staff of tecnicos, particularly economists, who were given major responsibility and support. Another factor of importance was the large flow of foreign investment that his administration attracted, averaging over US$100 million per year, or roughly 10 percent of total investment in manufacturing.

In the area of inflation Kubitschek had less success. The postwar period in Brazil was one of chronic inflation. During the five years of the Kubitschek government the rate of inflation averaged about 22 percent a year compared with an average rate of 18 percent for the previous five years. The highest rate of 38 percent came in 1959 when Kubitschek was pushing with all the force of his government to complete the new capital of Brasilia. To maintain a rapid development pace the federal government incurred a large budgetary deficit, and the monetary authorities greatly expanded the total money supply to permit loans to government enterprises and the private sector.

In spite of alleged widespread corruption and waste, the Kubitschek regime is remembered with great nostalgia by many Brazilians, especially in the lower and working classes. If a free election had been held as scheduled in the mid-1960s, many observers believe that Kubitschek would have been the winner.

A Development Hiatus: 1962-67

With the end of the Kubitschek administration the situation began to change radically. The government of Janio Quadros faced two serious economic problems inherited from the rapid development drive of the Kubitschek period. The rate of inflation reached a new high, and strong inflationary pressures persisted. The second problem was a deteriorating balance-of-payments situation because import requirements to support the new industrialization had expanded rapidly while traditional exports had stagnated. As a result of Quadros' concern for these problems, economic growth and industrialization lost their top priorities.

As governor of São Paulo Quadros was highly popular and a symbol of high moral standards in government. His campaign symbol was a broom with which he promised to sweep out corruption. As president he sought a vague legitimacy based on popular support rather than political alliances. He created a confrontation with the Congress apparently with the intention of increasing his power to deal with pressing issues and resigned after only seven months in office as a tactic to force the issue. The strategy failed, and Vice President João Goulart, after negotiations with the military, took office.

The vacillation and inconsistency of economic policies under Quadros continued through the Goulart presidency, with additional complications and turmoil in the political area. The rate of economic growth fell sharply while inflation accelerated, and the balance-of-payments situation worsened. As a study of the Economic Commission for Latin America concluded, "the whole course of events suggested that economic policy was drifting rudderless."[20]

Why did Brazil's growth rate decline in the early 1960s? One school of thought argues that stagnation was a short-run phenomenon due to the political turmoil of the Quadros-Goulart period. Another school contends that stagnation was a natural result of the policy of import-substitution industrialization and the continued concentration of income. Import-substitution industries, it was claimed, expand rapidly when they are replacing equipment that could not be imported, but then slow down to the rate of growth in domestic demand. Concentration of income is an additional factor limiting the size of the domestic market.[21]

In any event, the overall economic growth rate dropped sharply from 10.3 percent in 1961, the year in which Quadros succeeded Kubitschek, to 5.3 percent in 1962 and 1.5 percent in 1963. The rate of inflation, which jumped to 38 percent annually in 1959, continued to zoom, reaching a level during the early months of 1964, which, if geometrically projected, would have come to 144 percent for the year. With the adoption of a new law in 1962 limiting profit remittances of foreign investors, the inflow of foreign private investment declined sharply and worsened still further a persistent balance-of-payments crisis.

Political events, added to Brazil's rapidly deteriorating economic position, further aggravated the situation. Goulart supported political moves that created unprecedented turmoil and that involved challenges to the military hierarchy. By the end of March 1964, after much hesitation and discussion, the military intervened to oust Goulart, with the support of such key civilians as the governors of the major states and the middle classes.

The armed forces did not intend to remain in power, but events led them consistently along the road to total political control. Instead of taking chances on old-style politicians, they continued in power but made extensive use of civilian tecnicos.

When the first postrevolutionary president, Marshal Humberto Castello Branco, assumed office, his government faced three critical economic tasks: combating inflation, resolving the balance-of-payments situation, and restoring growth.[22] The balance-of-payments strategy emphasized export promotion, a more realistic foreign exchange policy, and renewed encouragement of foreign private investment. The decision to stimulate the expansion of exports and the adoption of incentives and administrative reforms represented a major policy shift for Brazil, and was one that took several years to begin producing results.[23] The foreign exchange policy eliminated import subsidies for petroleum, wheat, and newsprint. It also simplified the system of foreign exchange controls and made exchange rates more flexible and realistic. The principal measure to encourage foreign private investment was to repeal the prohibitive restrictions on profit remittances adopted by the Goulart government.

Controlling inflation was considered a precondition for restoring growth. The strategy adopted by the economic ministers of the new government—Roberto Campos (planning) and Otavio Bulhões (finance)—was the orthodox approach of restricting demand.[a] The principal weapons chosen were a contractive fiscal policy and forced wage restraint, with subsidiary roles for monetary policy and price controls. As a temporary measure the unorthodox technique of indexing, called monetary correction, was initiated.[b] Although indexing was to become a

---

[a]The adherents to economic orthodoxy had made three abortive attempts in the recent past to implement a similar strategy under Finance Ministers Eugenio Gudin (1954-55), Lucas Lopes (1958-59), and Clemente Mariani (1961). In each case the policies failed to secure strong and sustained presidential support. For a discussion of these episodes, see Thomas E. Skidmore, *Politics in Brazil, 1930-1964* (New York: Oxford University Press, 1967).

[b]See Julian Chacel, Mario H. Simonsen, and Arnoldo Wald, *A Correção Monetaria* (Rio de Janeiro: APEC Editora, S.A., 1970) for an excellent history and analysis of the evolution of indexing in Brazil. The authors conclude, "It is evident that monetary correction was conceived as a temporary device.... When the inflationary tendency falls to a certain critical level (perhaps between 10 and 15 percent annually), the correction of past distortions will no longer have great relevance and the real loss can perfectly well be absorbed by the economic parties" (p. 301).

permanent policy intended to neutralize the discriminatory effects of inflation, the specific goals that weighed heavily in the 1964 decision to use indexing were the government's desire to secure financing for its investment plans through the sale of government bonds and to eliminate the inflationary incentive for delaying tax payments.[24]

Other components of the government's so-called "Economic Action Program" included the establishment of a new National Housing Bank to finance a massive housing program and thereby increase employment, and a series of basic fiscal and monetary reforms, including the collection of income taxes at the source and the creation of a central bank. The announced targets of the stabilization program were to reduce inflation to 10 percent annually and raise the annual growth rate to 7 percent both by the end of 1966. Although the government argued that its stabilization policy was a "gradualist," rather than a "shock" approach, the goal of reducing inflation from an annual rate of almost 100 percent to 10 percent in two years would appear to be more accurately described as shock treatment.

As it turned out, by the end of 1966 the stabilization program was in deep trouble. Industrial production began a decline that continued through the first quarter of 1967.[25] Brazilian business firms were experiencing a record number of bankruptcies, creditor agreements, and liquidity crises aggravated by the government's stringent credit policy. Foreign enterprises with access to foreign credit were able to take over a number of Brazilian companies at bargain prices.[26] The selling out of Brazilian industry to foreigners and the fear of further denationalization, among other factors, forced the government to reverse its policy and liberalize credit to the private sector.

The orthodox stabilization policies received solid and unwavering support from President Castello Branco, but they were not uncritically accepted in tecnico circles. Professor Antonio Dias Leite, later to become minister of mines and energy under President Medici, provoked an acrimonious public debate in April 1965 on the basic validity for Brazil of the Campos-Bulhões stabilization strategy.[27] As a precursor of the policy changes subsequently to be made by Delfim Netto, Dias Leite argued that the stabilization strategy must be even more gradual, and that the progressive control of inflation would come from accelerating growth and increasing economic efficiency, particularly in the transportation public enterprises.

A series of retrospective evaluations of the stabilization period by United States scholars, who were associated with Brazil's post-1964 development drive, range from "very favorable" to "highly critical." Professor Howard Ellis, who headed an advisory group to the Minister of Planning from 1965 to 1967, judges the "corrective inflation" performance of the government as "very favorable indeed, considering its immediate antecedents and the usual quality of junta governments in Latin America."[28] The U.S. Treasury attaché in Rio de Janeiro from 1965 to 1969 concludes that the stabilization strategy was "overly optimistic and in a sense self-defeating." But he adds, "The unanswered question is whether the economy could have returned to a high growth period without the extended period of restructuring and austerity."[29] Still another economist, who worked as an adviser to the Ministry of Planning immediately after the stabilization period, states that the government during the Castello Branco period "was committed to the establishment of a functioning free market system in Brazil, perhaps even more than to the struggle against inflation," and that "the principal aim was not stabilization; it was making market capitalism work."[30]

In the actual event, although the Brazilian economy responded slowly and unevenly to the new programs, substantial benefits to the development drive flowed from them. Fiscal and monetary reforms were carried out. The federal budget was greatly reduced and put under more effective control. Relative prices were adjusted in the direction of free-market realities. The innovative concept of indexing tended to neutralize the discriminatory effects of continued inflation. By promoting exports and encouraging foreign investment, the government brought its balance of payments into surplus for most of the period, and international reserves rose. The annual rate of inflation for 1966 had dropped to 38 percent.

Nevertheless, by the end of its term in office in 1967, the Castello Branco team had achieved neither price stability nor a strong resumption of economic growth. GNP growth rates remained below 3 percent in both 1964 and 1965, rising to 5.1 percent in 1966 as a result of temporary stimulants to industrial production in 1965. The growth problem determined the next administration on a significant change in policy.

The Economic "Miracle": 1968- ?

Under the new constitution adopted by the military government, the presidency was transferred in March 1967 from Castello Branco to General Costa e Silva. The key civilian tecnico, who had managed the economy during the austerity period, Roberto Campos, was succeeded as the central figure of the economic team by Finance Minister Antonio Delfim Netto, an economics professor who was then serving as secretary of finance for the state of São Paulo. Although Delfim Netto had worked closely with the Castello Branco team, his diagnosis of the inflationary process led to a new economic strategy along the lines proposed by Dias Leite. The focus of government policies was shifted from stabilization to high economic growth.

In contrast to the orthodox anti-inflationary policies of Roberto Campos, which yielded slower-than-planned results and did not achieve the declared aim of defeating inflation altogether, Delfim Netto publicly stated that an inflation rate of 15 percent would be tolerated and began to ease credit to the hard-pressed private sector. Money supply was expanded. The policy to lag increases in the minimum wage behind the rate of inflation was changed to a policy of keeping wage increases constant with increases in the cost of living. The more flexible use of credit and tax policy begun under Costa e Silva (1967-69) and continued after his death under President Garrastazu Medici (1969-74) helped restore demand, leading to an impressive resumption of growth in 1968. Inflation did not accelerate; instead, real output did.

From 1968 through 1974 Brazil's real growth rate averaged a phenomenal 10.1 percent annually. The industrial sector expanded at an average annual rate of 11.9 percent, and agricultural output rose by 5.9 percent per year on the average. Growth rates in commerce and in the transport and communications category, 11 and 11.7 percent respectively, were slightly above the overall growth rate.

The political setting for the Brazilian boom has been an austere, authoritarian military government determined to implement the conviction, long held by the military leaders, that economic strength and "modernization" are the keys to the fulfillment of Brazil's potential. Effective political and administrative power resided in the armed forces, but they relied even more heavily than Kubitschek on civilian tecnicos such as economists, engineers, agronomists, and urban planners.

From 1964 to 1974 the two economists who were the civilian strongmen, Roberto Campos and Antonio Delfim Netto, wielded extraordinary power in orienting national policies. Under the authoritarian system, which allowed little participation by the Congress and in which state governors and key city mayors were selected by the armed forces, the civilian tecnicos did not have to deal with special interest pressures by political leaders and were able to secure quick governmental decisions and full support for their implementation.

When the focus of government turned to high economic growth, the implementation of the new policies was immeasurably aided by the automatic device of monetary correction and by the minidevaluations initiated in 1967. Monetary correction, or indexing, reduced the inequitable impact of inflation and made tolerable a relatively high rate of inflation that continued in the range of 20 percent annually. For the first time in decades it was possible to create capital markets for medium- and long-range financing. As long as investors were protected against the erosion of purchasing power, they became willing to buy government bonds and to provide long-term mortgages for housing.

The "minidevaluation" policy used frequent small exchange-rate devaluations to avoid the shock of infrequent large changes in official rates. This policy, similar to that of the "crawling peg," reduced tensions and speculation while permitting Brazilian exporters to remain competitive in international markets.

The tax reforms, imposed during the austerity period to reduce budgetary deficits, provided ever-expanding government revenues for development purposes as the economy began to grow again. The improvements achieved in the control of government expenditures, previously directed mainly toward reducing inflationary pressures, made it possible to direct government funds into more efficient development purposes during the boom period. A similar benefit resulted from the reforms in the banking system. Greater control over the amount and use of credit could be used to stimulate growth as well as to implement antiinflation goals.

Both as a growth strategy and as a means of improving Brazil's balance-of-payments situation, foreign trade policy became a keystone of the postrevolutionary governments. A drive to increase and diversify exports was considered essential for continued economic expansion. To achieve this goal state export taxes were abolished, administrative procedures for exporters were simplified, and a number of attractive tax and credit incentives to increase exports were introduced. The response of foreign and Brazilian companies to the export promotion campaign began to produce spectacular results in 1968. Exports, which had stagnated for many years, quadrupled, in value over the six-year period from 1968 to 1974.

Foreign confidence in the economic viability and political stability of Brazil steadily improved after the 1964 revolution, and an increasing flow of loans became available from foreign governments, international agencies, and foreign private financial sources. The export success, the steady growth of foreign private investment, and the availability of foreign loans permitted Brazil to increase its international reserves to new high levels. At the same time, its foreign indebtedness increased sharply.

Another feature of the boom period was greatly increased investments in infrastructure and housing. Electric power capacity continued to expand at a rapid rate, mainly through the activities of the government power companies. A major new program to expand the construction of highways was developed and implemented. The National Housing Bank (BNH) established in 1964, with a steady flow of funds from the newly established Tenure Guaranty Fund (FGTS) and the use of monetary correction to make long-term mortgages available, stimulated the construction industry to new levels.

The high growth rate in industry, averaging about 12 percent annually from 1968 to 1974, reflects the construction boom, the rapid expansion of foreign private investment, the vigorous response of the private sector, and the greatly accelerated growth of government enterprises, which have been a large and dynamic force in Brazil's growth.

Growth in the agricultural sector was also relatively high, averaging 5.9 percent annually over the 1968-74 period. This reflected governmental programs for increasing agricultural credit, establishing minimum prices for certain products, providing incentives for mechanization, greater use of fertilizers, and increasing exports.

It should be noted, however, that throughout the boom period since 1968 the initiatives of the Brazilian government fortuitously coincided with an expansionist foreign environment. In other words, such goals as expanding exports were overwhelmingly successful because of external conditions as well as governmental actions.

Against this historical economic overview it is possible to examine the motives, forces, policies, and facts of the Brazilian "miracle."

Notes

1. J.F. Normano, *Brazil: A Study of Economic Types* (Chapel Hill: University of North Carolina Press, 1935), p. 22.

2. *25 Years of the Brazilian Economy* (São Paulo: Banco Moreira Salles, S.A., 1967), p. 59. For a detailed discussion of the successive production cycles see Rui Miller Paiva, Salomão Schattan, and Claus F. Trench de Freitas, *Brazil's Agricultural Sector* (São Paulo, 1973), pp. 1-14.

3. Roberto Simonsen, *História Econômica do Brasil*, 2nd ed. (São Paulo: Cia. Editora Nacional, 1944). Cited in *25 Years of the Brazilian Economy*, p. 63, without page reference for Simonsen.

4. Rui Miller Paiva, Schattan, and Trench de Freitas, *Brazil's Agricultural Sector*, p. 12.

5. Annibal Villanova Villela and Wilson Suzigan, *Política do Governo e Crescimento da Econômia Brasileira: 1889-1945* (Rio de Janeiro: IPEA/INPES, 1973), p. 58.

6. See Celso Furtado, *The Economic Growth of Brazil: A Survey from Colonial to Modern Times* (Berkeley and Los Angeles: University of California Press, 1963).

7. Werner Baer and Annibal V. Villela, "Industrial Growth and Industrialization: Revisions in the Stages of Brazil's Economic Development," *The Journal of Developing Areas*, January 1973, pp. 218-19.

8. Werner Baer, *Industrialization and Economic Development in Brazil* (Homewood, Ill.: Richard D. Irwin, Inc., 1965), p. 14-15.

9. Mario Henrique Simonsen, *Brazil 2002* (Rio de Janeiro: APEC Editora, S.A., 1972), p. 31.

10. Celso Furtado, *Economic Growth*, p. 211.

11. See Werner Baer, *The Development of the Brazilian Steel Industry* (Nashville, Tenn.: Vanderbilt University Press, 1969).

12. Quoted in Humberto Bastos, *A Conquista Siderúrgica no Brasil* (São Paulo: Livraria Martins Editora, 1959), p. 70.

13. Quoted in *25 Years of the Brazilian Economy*, p. 331.

14. See Stefan H. Robock, *Brazil's Developing Northeast* (Washington: The Brookings Institution, 1963).

15. Octávio Ianni, *Estado e Planejamento Econômico no Brasil (1930-1970)* (Rio de Janeiro: Civilização Brasileira, 1971, p. 28.

16. Morris L. Cooke, *Brazil On the March* (New York: McGraw-Hill, 1944).

17. Américo L. Barbosa de Oliveira, *O Desenvolvimento Planificado da Economia Brasileira* (Rio de Janeiro: Fundação Getulio Vargas, June 1946).

18. "Fifteen Years of Economic Policy in Brazil," *Economic Bulletin for Latin America*, November 1964, pp. 193-94.

19. Lincoln Gordon and Englebert L. Grommers, *United States Manufacturing Investment in Brazil* (Boston: Harvard Business School, 1962).

20. "Fifteen Years," p. 198.

21. See Werner Baer and Andrea Maneschi, "Import-Substitution, Stagnation, and Structural Change: An Interpretation of the Brazilian Case," *Journal of Developing Areas*, January, 1971, pp. 177-92.

22. The basic document outlining the new government's economic policy is *Programa de Ação Econômica do Govêrno: 1964-66* (Rio de Janeiro: Ministério do Planejamento e Coordenação Econômica, November 1964). See pp. 119-44 for an elaboration of the new international economic policies.

23. See Carlos Von Doellinger, Hugo Barros de Castro Faria, Raimundo Nonato Mendonça Ramos, and Leonardo Casérla Cavalcanti, *Transformação da Estrutura das Exportações Brasileiras: 1964-70* (Rio de Janeiro, IPEA/INPES, 1973).

24. *Programa de Ação*, p. 236.

25. For a series of studies analyzing the stabilization period see Howard S. Ellis, "Corrective Inflation in Brazil, 1964-66," in *The Economy of Brazil*, edited by Howard S. Ellis (Berkeley and Los Angeles, University of California Press, 1969), pp. 177-212; Donald E. Syvrud, *Foundations of Brazilian Economic Growth* (Stanford, California: Hoover Institution Press, 1974), and Albert Fishlow, "Some Reflections on Post-1964 Brazilian Economic Policy," in *Authoritarian Brazil*, edited by Alfred Stepan (New Haven: Yale University Press, 1973), pp. 69-118. Syvrud served as U.S. Treasury attaché in Rio de Janeiro from 1965 to 1969. Ellis headed the University of California Development Assistance Program in Brazil from 1965 to 1967. Fishlow followed Ellis as head of the program to assist Brazil's Ministry of Planning.

26. Syvrud, *Foundations*, p. 92.

27. Antonio Dias Leite, *Caminhos do Desenvolvimento* (Rio de Janeiro, Zahar Editores, 1966). See pp. 171-95 for the presentation made in April 1965 to the Advisory Planning Council.

28. Ellis, "Corrective Inflation," p. 211.

29. Syvrud, *Foundations*, pp. 56-58.

30. Fishlow, "Reflections," p. 80.

Sources of Economic Growth

What motive forces and sources of economic growth underlie Brazil's development success? Following a traditional classification, the major sources of growth have been: (1) the local presence of several basic ingredients on which to build a development effort; (2) an imaginative and far-reaching role played by government through economic planning, through development policies and strategies adopted and implemented, through massive infrastructure investments, and through direct participation in business activities via state enterprises; (3) the vigorous response of both domestic and foreign private enterprise to development opportunities and incentives; and (4) external forces such as foreign loans and foreign aid.

A less traditional explanation, however, is Brazil's "secret weapon"—jeito. This frequently used word has no literal counterpart in English. A reasonably accurate translation of *jeito* would be "the ability to find *some way or other* to accomplish a purpose or to fix things." To rely on jeito is a deeply ingrained characteristic of Brazilian culture. To use jeito is to be flexible and imaginative in finding ways to achieve objectives. When used to circumvent rules and laws, jeito has been called "The Peril of Brazil."[a] But jeito also has a positive character and as such has been a dynamic and constructive force in all aspects of Brazil's development drive.

Some Basic Ingredients

One basic ingredient that nurtured Brazil's development efforts was the emergence of a national consensus after World War II that Brazil should take deliberate and affirmative action to promote development. In this respect the Brazilian experience paralleled that of most of the less developed countries of

---

[a]The pejorative meaning of jeito is illustrated by the comments of the president of a major government power company in a 1956 symposium, who observed that the institution of jeito was "the peril of Brazil. There is no law, no rule—no matter how strict—that resists the institution of *jeitinho* (diminutive form) ... and it is precisely this *jeitinho* that has been responsible for the mishandling of public funds in the past. Political spoils, nepotism, patronage, and general political interference in public enterprise have always prevailed above everything.... But I am an optimist about Brazil. I have noticed that the postwar generation—or at least the present generation—is changing considerably. They are irreproachable in the question of administration." John Cotrim, in Instituto de Engenharia, *Semana de debates sobre energia elétrica* (São Paulo: Imprensa Oficial do Estado, 1956) p. 121, as cited in Judith Tendler, *Electric Power in Brazil* (Cambridge: Harvard University Press, 1968), pp. 185-86.

the world. However, a national commitment to development is a necessary but not a sufficient condition for success, as demonstrated by the unsatisfactory results experienced in many other countries in spite of their intense dedication to development.

A second basic ingredient that supported Brazil's development drive was the physical setting described in Chapter 2. Again, rich natural resources are neither a necessary condition, as shown by the spectacular success of resource-poor Japan, nor a sufficient condition for development success, as suggested by the long-delayed economic expansion of resource-rich Indonesia.

Another supporting element has been Brazil's human resources, especially the role played by tecnicos and entrepreneurs. As a result of the critical need for trained people and of traditional social values that placed the educated in an elite category, Brazil has long given high status and positions of public responsibility to its small corps of trained people. The tecnicos, many of whom were trained under the military educational system, have played a dominant role in Brazil's development success.[1]

Brazil's human resource endowment has been surprisingly rich in entrepreneurial talents, a substantial portion of which was supplied by immigrants. An increasingly flexible social structure permitted great upward economic and social mobility for Brazilians who were not members of the oligarchy or landed aristocracy as educational and occupational opportunities expanded with economic growth.

When a national consensus for a development drive emerged Brazil had a favorable mix of several basic ingredients that could support the drive. The yeast that leavened the mix to generate economic growth was pragmatism, which follows naturally from the jeito philosophy of "getting the something done." Unlike many other countries that have been committed to some ideology such as private capitalism, free enterprise or socialism, Brazil has never for long placed itself in an ideological strait jacket. At certain times and in relation to specific events, such ideologies as nationalism, socialism, and communism have attracted popular support. Yet, adherence to ideology or doctrine has rarely gotten in the way of Brazil's development drive.

Pragmatism has permeated the development drive in virtually all its dimensions. It resulted in a nondoctrinaire approach to reliance on private versus government enterprise. It encouraged periodic reexamination of, and changes in, economic planning approaches and strategies. It characterized the evolution of policies to fight inflation and to resolve the full range of development-induced problems. Pragmatism resulted in a substantial number of failures but, more importantly, in an impressive series of imaginative innovations.

The Development Model

Out of these basic ingredients and other characteristics of the Brazilian experience came the development model, the preeminent feature of which is the government's broad responsibility for macroeconomic management of the economy and of development. Since the late 1940s, this responsibility has been implemented through economic planning, infrastructure investments, government enterprises, and through guidance and stimulation of the private sector.

Although the model has been called "capitalistic," the label is misleading. Brazil's pragmatic policy has made use of whatever capital, technological, and entrepreneurial inputs were available. Depending on the specific situation it has been receptive to foreign business firms; it has encouraged private domestic companies; it has created large government enterprises in critical production areas.

The model relies heavily on the market rather than on comprehensive and detailed economic management by government agencies. Brazilians are keenly aware of the limited capability of government institutions for detailed economic management. They also recognize that markets can be guided, and that use of the market mechanism does not necessarily mean a laissez-faire approach. Thus, the government has played a dominant role in guiding and shaping decisions in the marketplace through some controls, numerous incentives, and through fiscal and monetary management.

The central strategy of the model has been to accelerate industrialization as the leading sector, first to supply the large domestic market and later to expand exports to foreign markets. Had Brazil continued to specialize in primary exports, growth would have been penalized because of the well-known tendency (Engel's Law) of consumers to decrease the share of rising incomes spent on food and the related inelasticity of demand for raw materials. To accelerate development another sector was needed to complement the dynamic impetus given by primary exports. The industrial sector emerged as the only available alternative. As one study concludes, "Brazil's entry into an intensive phase of industrialization constitutes an inexorable imperative of its economic reality."[2]

The move toward industrialization inevitably resulted in a first-phase need to focus on internal development. New industries with little experience operating in an environment with limited infrastructure support could not be expected to compete successfully in foreign markets. As national output expanded and traditional exports stagnated the economy became more and more insulated from external forces. In 1947 exports of goods and services were about 14 percent of total gross national product. By 1960 this ratio had declined to about 6 percent. Even after the spectacular spurt in manufactured exports in the early 1970s, total exports were equal to only 8-9 percent of GNP. Germany's exports, for example, were the equivalent of 22 percent of its gross national product in 1970; for Hong Kong the figure was about 70 percent in the same year.

While the internal development emphasis did not completely free Brazil from foreign-exchange constraints, it managed to keep the development momentum going through import substitution, excessive use of foreign commercial credit, periodic foreign loans, and modest inflows of foreign capital. Although the country continued to depend on a flow of imports, reliance on foreign markets as a dynamic development force declined and remained relatively small until 1968.

The success of the industrialization effort initially forced the government to intervene in the economy to eliminate infrastructure bottlenecks and to create basic support industries. The focus on internal development permitted the government, as it increased its role, to dominate the effort with little interruption by external economic forces. It pressed most of the levers that activated the market. It controlled the supply of money and credit as well as the availability of foreign exchange. It acted directly through infrastructure investment and government enterprises. It acted indirectly through the establishment of priorities, development financing institutions, tariff policies, foreign exchange controls, and taxation.

Brazil has been able to avoid cyclical fluctuations in its development drive because of the relative freedom of its economy from external forces, because the institutional structure for macroeconomic management has been steadily improved, and because there has been an underlying consistency in the pressure and policies for development. More recently, however, external factors have become more important. As a result the Brazilian government has lost some of its pervasive control over the domestic economy, which has become more vulnerable to economic fluctuations induced by external forces.

The Dynamic Role of Government

The Vargas dictatorship era that ended with the close of World War II saw a marked increase in the authority and capacity of the national government. Concurrently, Brazilian policy makers developed a future orientation and a confidence in national purpose that could be called developmental nationalism,[3] and that evolved into the postwar drive for development. The early Vargas era thus provided the means and the motive drive for the government's dominant role in the development process. The emphasis on industrialization as a central strategy for development became widely accepted among the technocrats, the military, the private sector, the government leaders, and the politically active public, so that future governments, whether civilian or military, have had almost unified support for their broad development goals.

Government Planning

From the time of the Empire Brazilian leaders conceived and attempted to implement grand plans. More recently, during the early Vargas era, the government also undertook a number of economic planning efforts. Economic planning, which rose to world popularity among the less developed countries in the postwar years, fitted into a long Brazilian tradition. Nevertheless, there was considerable debate during the early post-World War II period centering on whether economic planning was compatible with a democratic capitalistic system.[4] The proponents of economic planning prevailed.

In Brazil the word "planning" has been used rather loosely to cover a mere declaration of principles, a development program, and a development plan. The first is only a broad statement of development goals and strategy. A *development program* goes further, assigns sectoral or regional priorities, and formulates incentives or disincentives related to the chosen priorities. A *development plan* builds on these elements by specifying a time schedule for implementation, by assigning responsibility to a chosen agent, and by allocating financial and material resources.[5] This progression of definitions roughly characterizes the evolution of governmental planning activity in Brazil after World War II.

In the early postwar years relatively crude forms of planning with heavy emphasis on project preparation were used that gradually evolved by the early 1970s into a sophisticated and comprehensive planning system. The Abbink Mission (1948) provided a macroeconomic view of development prospects and problems and presented a series of policy and program recommendations. The Comissão Mista (1950-53) took the approach of identifying bottlenecks, which resulted in giving priority to transport and power projects.

Planning activities during the Kubitschek period (1956-61) advanced to the growing-points approach aimed at identifying a large number of "impulse sectors" that should be stimulated and supported. Institution building also moved ahead with the creation of the National Development Council coincident with the growing-points approach. A modest beginning at macroeconomic planning was made through the work of a Joint Group of the National Development Bank and the Economic Commission for Latin America of the United Nations. During the Kubitschek period a major advance was also made in regional planning through the establishment of SUDENE (Superintendency for Development of the Northeast).

The next stage in the development of Brazilian planning was the Plano Trienal (Three Year Plan) prepared toward the end of 1962 by Celso Furtado, who was Brazil's first minister of planning. This plan was comprehensive in the sense that it attempted to put the sectoral plans already being developed into an overall framework. The Plano Trienal was short-lived, however, because President Goulart did not have the political strength or will to implement it.

When the revolutionary government took over in 1964 Roberto Campos became the minister of planning, and planning moved another step forward with the Economic Action Program of the Government (PAEG). In a substantive way the PAEG integrated monetary, fiscal, exchange-rate, and wage policies more closely than was done in the Plano Trienal. In the area of institutional development major advances were accomplished through reform and modernization. At the same time the position of minister of planning, which had been a Ministro Extraordinário, became a permanent ministry. To attract qualified personnel the planning ministry created two quasi-governmental "institutos" as supporting units, which were not bound by the salary scales of the regular government bureaucracy, and which could operate with greater flexibility.

The notion of comprehensiveness became firmly entrenched under Roberto Campos and continued under his successors, Hélio Beltrão and João Paulo dos Reis Velloso. The quantity and quality of the technical work continued to grow significantly, as did the institutional framework for implementation. In 1974 President Geisel created the Council of Economic Development (CDE), which he personally heads, and which gave more status to the planning activity by moving it into the office of the president.

As one of the sources of growth economic planning in Brazil made a continuing contribution through enlightening and improving the decision process at both private and governmental levels. Although planning results persistently fell short of the high technical standards for planning of economic and public administration specialists, Brazil's planning strategy recognized the technical, personnel, and institutional limits that prevailed and focused on upgrading development performance rather than on trying to prepare a perfect plan. In this way economic planning maintained a position of influence and political effectiveness throughout most of the postwar years.

In contrast, many other countries tried to begin with sophisticated and comprehensive planning when the necessary preconditions were not present. In some instances the planning activity lost its influence over the political-decision process because usable plans were not available at the time when decisions had to be made (Bolivia). In other cases the plans broke down in implementation because the institutional framework was not prepared (India).

Brazil's planning strategy involved more than a realistic recognition of prevailing limitations. Brazil also made major strides in coping with the limitations. Relatively large amounts of resources were allocated to developing more and better statistical information and to the training of personnel. To invest heavily in the advanced training of specialized personnel was consistent with Brazil's traditional educational priority for elite education. The expansion and modernization of university education, particularly in economics and administration, received higher priority than did primary and secondary education. With the help of the United Nations many special programs of training in development planning were given in Brazil. Large numbers of Brazilians were sent to foreign universities, with support from external resources provided by the United States aid program and the international agencies, and to foreign training programs provided by the World Bank and the Economic Commission for Latin America. In the field of economics, for example, the number of trained economists in Brazil at the master's level or above increased from about a dozen in 1954 to literally several thousand in 1974. As it did in a number of other fields, Brazil made massive investments in its human resources but gave priority to the preparation of technicians at the advanced level.

The great merit of Brazil's evolutionary approach to economic planning was its de facto, though not explicit, recognition that the country was not prepared in terms of technical, personnel, and institutional resources to run before it could walk. Yet, throughout the years planning activities managed to stay in the mainstream of the decision-making process while at the same time dealing with the limitations noted above.

Infrastructure Investments

A second major development role of government has been in providing infrastructure to support Brazil's development drive. Much of the economic development literature has treated infrastructure investments as a prerequisite and necessary stimulant of economic growth. A contrary view, identified with Albert O. Hirschman, sees infrastructure investments as following and being induced by shortages resulting from the expansion of "directly productive activities" such as manufacturing.[6] Brazil has been a prime example of the Hirschman view. Throughout the postwar period, Brazil's development progress has occurred in spite of persistent shortages in energy, transport, and communications services, all of which have required massive and continuing infrastructure investments. Although infrastructure investments have followed a lag rather than lead pattern, they have made a significant contribution to Brazil's development drive by virtue of the scale of investment and the support thereby given to the "directly productive activities."

The total expenditures of the public sector, excluding investments in state enterprises, increased from 1947 to 1969 about five times in real terms. As a share of the gross national product, total government expenditures expanded from 17 percent in 1947 to about 30 percent in the early 1970s.[7] This ratio has been high by international standards, and a large share of the high level of government expenditures has gone for economic and social infrastructure investments.

The capital expenditures made directly by the public sector plus those financed by public resources channelled through official intermediaries amounted over the 1969-71 period to approximately 70 percent of total fixed investment in the Brazilian economy or 12.5 percent of the gross national product.[8] The leading investment area has been economic infrastructure including highway and railway transportation, electric power, and telecommunications. Social infrastructure including housing, education, water and sewage systems, health, and social welfare accounted for another large share of total investment. The third most important category was industry, including petroleum and mining. Regional development (including Northeast industrialization) and agriculture also received significant shares of total government investment.

Transportation

Inadequate transportation facilities in Brazil have been a serious problem for centuries. Coastal shipping was the only mode of transport connecting the northern and southern parts of the country until the relatively recent construction of interior highways. Railroads were originally built in a fan-like pattern to transport agricultural exports from the hinterland to the nearest port and not to provide a national transportation system. They had few interconnections and different gauges. The large size of the country and the concentration of population along a narrow coastal strip prevented the establishment of a nationwide transport network except for aviation, which by its nature is largely confined to passenger traffic and high value cargo. The development of inland waterways was limited to the Amazon and the São Francisco rivers because most of the other rivers do not flow directly to the coast or have rapids that prevent navigation.

Over many decades the government became a reluctant owner and operator of the railways, ports, and most of the coastal shipping.[9] As government enterprises, the transportation companies were run for many years as welfare institutions primarily designed to give maximum employment at relatively high wages. Providing transportation services was a secondary consideration. Efficiency and financial soundness were even less important. As a result the railroad system consistently had a large deficit, which in 1965 amounted to 46 percent of the total federal deficit. In that year the transport sector as a whole had a deficit equivalent to 95 percent of the federal deficit.[10]

The bottleneck-identifying approach of the Mixed Commission quickly led to the establishment of a high priority for investments in railways, ports, shipping, and highways and the preparation of detailed investment projects in these fields. This priority has continued up to the present time.

Brazil's development strategy in the transport sector emphasized, until the international petroleum crisis of 1973, the expansion and improvement of the highway system for internal transportation. One of the considerations justifying this strategy was that scarce government investment resources would result in more transportation capacity through highways than through railways. In the case of highways the investment in transportation equipment was made by the private sector, whereas, in the case of railways the government would have to invest in both equipment and road facilities.

Although Brazilian highways are still inadequate for such a large country, the progress achieved can be indicated by the increase in paved highways. Brazil had less than 1,000 kilometers of paved highways after World War II. This increased to 3,133 kilometers in 1955, 26,546 kilometers in 1965, and 67,607 kilometers by 1973. In addition, the mileage of unpaved federal and state highways has about doubled since 1955 (Table 4-1).

Aside from the increase in road mileage, the transport investment has been

Table 4-1
Brazilian Road Network
(in kilometers)

Year	Federal and State Highways		
(as of Dec. 31)	Paved	Unpaved	Total
1955	3,133	74,165	77,298
1965	26,546	109,192	135,738
1973	67,607	143,909	211,516

Source: National Highway Department (Departmento Nacional de Estradas de Rodagem).

used to connect the North and South and to open up new areas in the interior. A major benefit of the project to build Brasilia in the interior came from the new roads that had to be constructed giving development access to new areas and connecting important existing centers. The Transamazon highway project initiated in 1970 that extends for more than 3,000 miles from the Atlantic Ocean to the Peruvian border had a military security as well as a development rationale. However, the success of this project as a development force has been seriously questioned.[11]

In water transportation government programs to develop river transportation and coastal navigation have not produced the hoped-for results, whereas programs to enlarge the share of ocean shipping carried by Brazilian ships—and thus conserve foreign exchange—and to implant a national shipbuilding industry have been dramatically successful. After stagnating at about the same level for many years, the tonnage of Brazil's ocean fleet increased fivefold to 3,436,000 deadweight tons (dwt) over the short period from 1967 to 1974. The share of Brazil's total international shipping carried by ships flying the Brazilian flag rose from only 10 percent in 1965 to 42 percent in 1972.

A national shipbuilding industry, started in 1958 by Japanese and Brazilian private interests, struggled along without great success until after the 1964 revolution. The industry has since revived and expanded greatly. In 1974 the shipyards delivered about 400,000 dwt of shipping as against 263,000 in 1963. The yards are presently constructing large bulk carriers up to 130,000 tons, designed to carry iron ore outbound and crude petroleum inbound, as well as even larger super tankers.

In order to attain their development goals government leaders became increasingly aware that greater administrative flexibility was required than that permitted by Brazil's regular bureaucratic system and that more continuity in long-range financing was needed than traditional budgetary methods allowed.[12] In the face of this twofold challenge, funds earmarked for special purposes and autonomous public bodies were gradually brought into being, particularly in the field of transportation.

Highway programs were placed basically in the hands of the DNER (Departamento Nacional de Estradas de Rodagem), a type of semiautonomous agency called an autarquia. In the railway sector a holding company was established in 1957, the Rede Ferroviária Federal, S.A. (RFFSA). However, the original law creating the government railway company retained in the hands of the central government control over wages of employees, rates, and fares. In water transportation, the federal government has various enterprises in the merchant shipping field, the most important being Loide Brasileiro, shipping subsidiaries of the government petroleum and iron ore mining companies, and a national coastal shipping company.

The autarquias and government companies in the transportation sector did not operate on a commercial basis, however. For many years they were typical of the fabled inefficiency of government in business. The transportation sector, the railroads in particular, operated with large deficits that became a major inflationary force in the early 1960s. By 1970, however, the operating deficits of the railway network and shipping companies had been sharply reduced. The number of railway employees fell from 154,000 in 1964 to 115,000 in 1972 while the amount of traffic carried increased sizeably.[13] In addition to administrative changes during the mid-sixties, the government engaged in extensive feasibility studies for expanding and modernizing the transportation network. By the late sixties vast investment programs were started and contributed to the boom that began in 1968.

Electric Power

In the field of electric power, for many decades up to the early 1960s, two foreign-owned companies were almost solely responsible for the generation and distribution of electric power in Brazil. A Canadian company, Brazilian Traction, Light and Power Co., now called Brascan but more familiarly known as the "Light," supplied electricity to the cities of Rio de Janeiro and São Paulo. A United States company, American and Foreign Power Company (AMFORP), supplied electricity to much of the rest of the country. AMFORP was purchased in 1965 by the Brazilian government after the expropriation of its properties in the state of Rio Grande do Sul. With the change in government AMFORP could have continued in operations, but chose not to do so, and was compensated for its properties on favorable terms. The Canadian company still continues to serve the Rio de Janeiro and São Paulo areas, but its recent expansion has concentrated on power distribution, with government companies assuming responsibility for expanding generating capacity.[14]

Within the decade of the 1960s power generation changed from a private to a government dominated sector, mainly as a result of massive government investments in new facilities rather than in the purchase of existing private companies. From 1962 to 1971 the share of Brazil's power generating capacity accounted for by government companies increased from 36 to 80 percent. At the distribution level, however, the foreign-controlled private sector in 1973 supplied about 45 percent of total electricity consumed. The electric power sector has thus become a mix of government and foreign-owned companies in a uniquely designed Brazilian pattern. The government holding company, ELETROBRAS, set up in 1961, supervises and finances federally owned companies.

Management of the government-controlled power companies has been consistently in the hands of tecnicos, many of whom received their training and experience in foreign-owned companies. In contrast to the situation in the transport sector, government power companies are almost unanimously recognized in Brazil as efficiently managed.

The fascinating feature of the Brazilian experience in the power sector is the rationale that was ultimately accepted for following the pattern of a mix between foreign and government companies. Many nationalistic voices argued for complete expropriation of the foreign companies. The tecnicos responded by emphasizing that the use of Brazil's scarce financial resources, particularly foreign exchange, to transfer the ownership of facilities that were already in Brazil would do nothing to accelerate development. On the other hand, they argued, if the same resources were used to construct new power capacity through government companies, Brazil would be able to accelerate its development drive dramatically. In Brazilian style, the pragmatic view prevailed over the ideological.

Brazil has made great progress in resolving a serious power shortage that persisted for more than two decades after World War II. From 1950 to 1973 installed capacity increased eightfold—from about 2 million to 16 million kilowatts. Yet, even with this rapid rate of expansion, power availability has at times lagged behind the explosive demand created by the unusually rapid growth of the economy.

Communications

Another infrastructure area in which government enterprises have become dominant is the field of communications. Foreign firms built and initially operated most of Brazil's communications system. During the post-World War II period they were not able to keep up with demand because the government's regulatory policies did not allow rates to keep pace with rising costs in a time of chronic inflation. The communications shortage was severe. In 1963 there were about 1.2 million telephones and an almost equal number of applicants waiting to get service, some of whom had been waiting for ten years. For those fortunate enough to have telephones, service was defective.

The situation began to improve in the mid-1960s. In 1965 the government created EMBRATEL to develop the country's interstate and international telecommunications infrastructure. At the same time the constraint on rates was removed, and new techniques for financing expansion were introduced: new telephone subscribers were required to pay a proportionate share of the investment for new lines.

In 1967 the Ministry of Communications was established to coordinate the work of EMBRATEL, the postal services, and the various telephone companies. Its first act was to acquire the principal foreign telephone company, which owned 75 percent of all the telephone installations in Brazil. In 1972 TELEBRÁS was created under the Ministry as a holding company for the major telephone firms and as the agency for coordinating and planning the national telephone system. By 1974 the number of telephones had increased to 2.8 million, 81 percent of which were accounted for by TELEBRÁS subsidiaries. In spite of this progress communication services continued to be deficient in quality and quantity.

Science and Technology

The most recent major program for building Brazil's infrastructure is a massive governmental initiative in the area of science and technology. A Basic Plan for Scientific and Technological Development (PBDCT) was approved in July 1973 with a budget of more than US$300 million annually, an amount which the government notes is more than the current world expenditures of the United Nations on technical assistance. Programs under the plan include:[15]

1. Developing new technology in nuclear energy and oceanography, and promoting such high technology industries as electronics and computers
2. Strengthening the technological absorption capacity of national enterprises, both public and private
3. Strengthening research organizations in priority sectors and expanding the supply of trained researchers
4. Consolidating the support system through the establishment of a national scientific information system
5. Integrating industry and university research.

**Government Enterprises in Key
Business Sectors**

The direct participation by federal and state governments in business operations that provide infrastructure support and that are "directly productive" has been one of the most powerful sources of growth in Brazil. As industrialization made headway, the traditional responsibilities of government were steadily augmented by the tasks of providing development financing, increasing the electric power supply, managing the transport sector, and undertaking the domestic production of certain basic inputs, notably petroleum and steel.

In most nations, particularly the industrialized countries of Western Europe, public utility industries, because of their natural monopoly nature and for ideological reasons, have long been government owned and operated. In Brazil, even in the area of public utilities, the steadily expanding direct participation of government was not the result of a carefully conceived plan or of a pervasive ideological commitment, with the possible exception of petroleum and mining. The growth of state enterprises was "much more a matter of adopting solutions imposed by the objective conditions of economic change, than the outcome of deliberately doctrinaire policy."[16] In some cases, such as the transport network, the government had to assume ownership when existing companies ceased to be profitable. In other instances producer functions were forced upon the government by the private sector's inability or unwillingness to undertake activities vital for development.

The founding in 1942 of the iron ore mining company Companhia Vale do Rio Doce (CVRD) was partly due to nationalistic opposition to the exploitation of nonreplaceable subsoil wealth by foreigners and partly to the wartime need of the United States and the United Kingdom to secure iron ore. The creation of PETROBRÁS, as a state petroleum monopoly in 1953, also had strong nationalistic overtones. However, the principal motivation was the government's concern for having domestic oil supplies in emergency situations. Many alternatives other than a state enterprise had been explored, but foreign companies had no interest in the petroleum exploration possibilities of Brazil while they had attractive alternatives in the Middle East and Venezuela.[17]

State enterprises have become dominant in a number of vital economic sectors, and their total size as a group accounts for a massive share of all business activity. As of the mid-1970s state-controlled companies were dominant in the previously mentioned infrastructure fields and in directly productive and conventional business fields such as banking, steel, petroleum, petrochemicals, and mining.

As a reflection of the capital-intensive nature of the industries in which government has entered, of the top 25 firms in Brazil ranked by assets in 1971, 17 were government companies that accounted for 82 percent of the group's total assets. Of the top 25 firms based on sales, 8 were government companies accounting for 31 percent of total sales. Of the top 25 firms in terms of employment, 7 were government companies with 51 percent of total employment by the group.[18] Among the 1,000 largest companies in Brazil as of 1973, state-controlled companies represented 50 percent of net book value and 17 percent of total sales.[19]

In spite of the pragmatic rather than doctrinaire genesis of most public enterprises, the dominant role they have come to play in the Brazilian economy has provoked periodic ideological debate and warnings from private sector spokesmen of the danger of further government encroachment in areas that should be left to private enterprise.[20] In response to the criticisms of growing "statism," the government has emphasized that its policy is to leave the "directly productive" sectors almost exclusively to private enterprise and to limit the role of government enterprises to infrastructure activities that support the private sector.[21]

It is significant, however, that the pressure for a clearer definition of the role of the state in business has occurred more as a defensive reaction by the private sector than as a general debate on affirmative development policies. The polemics reflect a growing confidence by the private sector in its ability to undertake an ever wider range of business activities and a concern that the government may expand its role, particularly in such fields as banking, without giving the private sector enough time or the necessary support to respond to emerging opportunities. Thus, in spite of the rhetoric the debate can be characterized in a real sense as a continuation of the traditional pragmatic approach, whereby choices at the action level will still be made on a case by case basis.

The participation of state-owned companies in key business sectors can be summarized as follows:

Banking

The importance of the government's role in banking derives both from the scale of its activities and from the fact that the operations of government-controlled banks have been oriented with varying degrees of effectiveness toward government development goals rather than simply toward profit maximization. The country's largest commercial bank is the Banco do Brasil in which the federal government has controlling ownership. Its deposits in 1972 were nine times as large as those of the leading private commercial bank. Direct control by the federal government extends to the Banco do Nordeste, a large regional development bank, the National Economic Development Bank (BNDE), the National Housing Bank (BNH), and a nationwide network of savings banks (Caixas Econômicas). In addition, Brazil has 32 commercial and development banks controlled by state governments.

In 1972 more than 60 percent of the loans of the entire financial system to the private sector came from government financial institutions.[22] In 1974 the annual lending operations of the BNDE reached a level of US$1.3 billion, and the Housing Bank during the same year made loans of almost US$2 billion.

Steel

In the 1950s Brazil expected that a large share of the projected increase in steel capacity would be supplied by the private sector. However, the federal government gradually became a reluctant majority owner of several new steel plants as it became apparent that the resources of private companies and local governments were too limited to finance these projects. In 1971 government-controlled companies accounted for more than half of the sales and almost three-fourths of the total assets in the industry. With the recent formation of SIDERBRAS as a holding company to manage the government's interest in the steel industry, state dominance will most likely increase even more in the future.

Iron Ore

In 1974 the government company Companhia Vale do Rio Doce (CVRD) exported US$450 million of iron ore, or more than 75 percent of Brazil's iron ore exports. Although CVRD exports are expected to continue to expand, its share of total exports will decrease. A large private firm, which is a consortium of foreign and Brazilian interests, came into operation in late 1974 as another major exporter of iron ore. CVRD has expanded its activities in the early 1970s beyond iron ore mining to include joint ventures with foreign companies in forest products, bauxite mining, aluminum production, and steel manufacturing.

Petroleum

PETROBRÁS (Petróleo Brasileiro, S.A.) is the largest enterprise in Brazil. It has a complete monopoly of petroleum exploration and a near monopoly in petroleum refining. Its marketing subsidiary, Petrobrás Distribuidora, S.A., competes within Brazil with several large international oil companies such as Esso, Shell, Atlantic, and Texaco, as well as with a private Brazilian company, Ipiranga. In 1971 PETROBRÁS accounted for 41 percent of sales and 81 percent of the asset value in petroleum exploration, refining, and marketing. PETROBRÁS founded two subsidiaries in the late 1960s, PETROQUISA and BRASPETRO. PETROQUISA is expanding rapidly in various petrochemical fields, often on a joint venture basis with private domestic and foreign firms. BRASPETRO is participating with foreign governments in petroleum exploration projects outside Brazil.

Other

The nondoctrinaire approach to government enterprise is illustrated by the Fábrica Nacional de Motores (FNM) created during World War II to provide maintenance services and also to produce engines. The firm eventually manufactured a great variety of products—tractors, trucks, cars, refrigerators—but it was always a money-losing enterprise with administrative problems. In 1968 the government sold FNM to a private foreign firm.

The dynamic role of government enterprises in the power, steel, mining, and petroleum sectors has been an especially important source of economic growth because (a) the government enterprises were created to fill an urgent development need in key sectors; and (b) they have been efficiently managed. As their goal was development and not just immediate profits, the companies were able to operate on a long-term horizon with adequate financial support and to take large and necessary risks. Over time most of the state-controlled enterprises have become highly profitable and are generally considered to be well managed. In 1974, for example, CVRD had a net profit of US$150 million on sales of US$650 million. Through their expansion into numerous joint ventures with foreign firms, the state enterprises have also become a major vehicle for attracting large foreign investments in a form that has not provoked latent nationalistic sensitivity to foreign investment in natural resource areas.

One of the most interesting questions concerning the Brazilian experience is how so many public enterprises in Brazil have been able to become efficiently managed businesses when the conventional wisdom throughout so much of the world is that government enterprises are generally inefficient and riddled with politics. The probable explanation in the case of Brazil involves the form of organization used, the success of the companies in attracting highly qualified personnel, and the willingness of political leaders to rely on professional managers and tecnicos to direct these companies because of the political consequences of failure in such large and complex ventures.

With typical pragmatism Brazil experimented with new organizational forms in creating its public enterprises. The typical model that emerged in the business sector has been the "mixed" company. The mixed company is similar to a private company and is independent of government bureaucracy. It has both private and government shareholders, but government participation is dominant. Strange as it may seem to Americans, a number of government-controlled companies—Banco do Brasil, Banco do Nordeste, PETROBRÁS, Siderúrgica Nacional (National Steel Co.), and Vale do Rio Doce—have become "blue chip" stocks for private investors on Brazilian stock exchanges.

These organizational forms have facilitated rapid decision making. They have allowed the enterprises to adopt salary scales sufficiently above traditional government salary levels to attract excellent personnel, particularly at the entrance and intermediate levels. They have permitted bonus systems that, though not strictly profit-sharing schemes, are generally related to the profitability of the enterprises. They have also operated as a mechanism to attract private capital and thereby reduce the contribution required from scarce government funds.

The ability of government enterprises to recruit excellent managers and technical staff is not simply related to salaries. In terms of alternative opportunities for professional advancement and for assuming challenging responsibilities, the state enterprises have long been attractive to young people with high potential. Until the last decade or so the private sector, consisting of small- and medium-sized companies, was dominated by family enterprises where managerial and other key positions were reserved for the owners and members of their families. In the past opportunities in foreign companies were also limited because the high posts were traditionally reserved for non-Brazilians. Since many foreign companies made their key decisions at the foreign headquarters, the responsibility and authority delegated to nationals were effectively reduced.

In contrast, the pioneering government enterprises recognized from the outset that they needed professional managers because of the scale and complexity of the ventures. There was a willingness to appoint young tecnicos in their early thirties to head major companies. Because of the pioneering nature of the industries, their size, and their importance to Brazil, employment with state enterprises provided the ultimate in professional challenge for the people who became part of these projects.[23]

Another reason for the success of Brazil's pioneer state enterprises was the use they made of personnel trained by foreign companies, their extensive investments in the training of their own personnel, and their willingness to contract for foreign technical assistance when needed. The state electric power companies appointed as the top managers many engineers who had received training and experience working for foreign-owned companies in Brazil. As the number of experienced people was small, the state companies quickly organized large-scale training programs in Brazil and in foreign countries and invested vast sums of money in them. The use of foreign experts is illustrated by the case of PETROBRÁS, which shortly after it was formed hired the chief geologist of a leading United States oil company at what then appeared to be a fabulous salary.

How were the companies able to avoid political interference and a political spoils system? In some cases, such as the National Steel Company, state enterprises did suffer from political pressures. But the government steel companies had competition from private firms. Their inability to compete with the private sector even after a long period of tolerance eventually forced a change toward professional management and greater efficiency.

The importance of the political risk of failure can be illustrated by the case of a new electric power company established in the Kubitschek years. Kubitschek invited an experienced young engineer to head the company. The engineer said he would accept only on the condition that he would have full freedom to pick all his key staff. The new company was extremely large relative to the electric power capacity of the country. Kubitschek, as a politician, knew the political risk of a failure in a project of that magnitude, particularly because he had been frequently accused of building big projects for the sake of bigness. So

Kubitschek accepted the condition, but added with a smile, "You (expletive deleted) don't leave anything for me."

Government Policies, Strategies, and Incentive Programs

The indirect contributions of the Brazilian government through a series of policies, strategies, and incentive programs have also been a major source of economic growth. They are characterized by pragmatism, flexibility, innovation, and an emphasis on using the incentive pull of "the carrot" more than the coercive push of "the stick." They have been especially important in stimulating and facilitating Brazilian and foreign private enterprises to make direct contributions to the rapid expansion of productive activities.

In the area of foreign private investment Brazil's generally flexible and self-confident policy has resulted in crucial contributions through inflows of external capital, transfers of technology, increased opportunities for filling the gap in management skills, and greatly enlarged access to foreign markets by using the export capabilities of international firms. With some discontinuities and divergencies[24] Brazil has maintained a steady course in welcoming types of foreign investment that had priority in her development strategy, and over the years has generated a high level of competence and sophistication in making use of foreign investment to achieve such goals as expanding exports. It has followed a policy of "defusing" latent antagonism to foreign ownership by encouraging joint ventures with Brazilian private and public enterprises in sensitive fields, and by achieving a mix of foreign nationalities in many fields so that foreign investment is now less likely to become a political issue in the form of anti-Americanism.

Pervading Brazil's policies toward foreign investment has been a continuing awareness that a sovereign state has substantial leverage in its dealing with foreign firms, that rapid growth of the economy has increased Brazil's bargaining power, and that in its relations with multinational enterprises Brazil must have highly competent government officials in charge of maximizing national development goals.

A second key area of policy making relates to financial institutions. Particularly since 1964 the government has provided leadership for extensive innovations in developing financial markets and institutions. One authority has characterized them as "probably the most extensive and imaginative found in the postwar world."[25] The financial market reforms are related to the anti-inflation policies discussed below and were designed to meet several specific development needs. As a policy package they were directed toward: (1) making yields on financial instruments sufficiently attractive to raise new savings and divert savings from the alternatives of real estate investment and capital flight;

(2) creating medium- and long-term debt markets to finance government, business, and housing; (3) providing access to new equity funds by corporations and to ownership of equity by the general public; (4) insuring that investment in socially desirable sectors and regions would receive financing; and (5) assuring that business was not constrained by inflation in generating funds internally for use in expansion.

The government policies adopted to develop financial institutions consisted of a comprehensive combination of measures ranging from the use of indexing, the passage and implementation of a new Capital Markets Law, and the use of incentives for investing in equity markets and for corporate reinvestment in priority regions of the country. The financial market innovations acted as a source of growth by developing an internal capacity to mobilize savings through noninflationary means. At the same time the incentives encouraged a more uneven distribution of income in Brazil because investors and business firms were the principal parties able to reap large benefits from the new government policies. A stock market boom that reached its peak in June 1971 and then collapsed resulted in a serious loss of popular confidence in equity investments. The government subsequently undertook measures to restore this confidence and had achieved some success by early 1975.

Another important policy area has been Brazil's anti-inflation strategy and the innovations associated with this effort. During the Castello Branco-Roberto Campos period (1964-67) the government relied principally on orthodox fiscal and monetary measures, but it was also responsible for two policy innovations. The first was the adoption of the indexing, or monetary correction system, intended to neutralize the inequities created by inflation and to stimulate the growth of savings.[26] A second innovation was to readjust salaries annually by the average increase in the cost of living for the previous 24 months. The wage strategy has been explained as a technique for "stabilizing by the averages and not the peaks."[27] Its effect, however, was to shift a heavy share of the cost of reducing inflation to the wage earners.

The numerous anti-inflation measures adopted after 1967 were more pioneering than those previously attempted. The most outstanding was the unorthodox strategy of reducing inflationary pressures by accelerating growth and stimulating productivity.[28] The new strategy recognized what should be, but has not been, obvious to most policy makers, namely, that there are two sides to the inflation "coin." Inflation can be considered as *either* a surplus of demand in relation to supply *or* a deficiency of supply in relation to demand. By posing the problem in this way it follows that the central focus of a price stabilization strategy should be the supply-demand balance, and that inflationary pressures can be reduced by attacking the supply as well as the demand side. In doing so the guideline should be that the measures and tools used should increase supply *at a greater rate* than demand.

In Brazil the resumption of economic growth reduced inflationary pressures because many industries had surplus capacity. As capacity utilization increased, unit production costs declined as a result of economies of scale. Also, as expansion continued, the opportunities for new products, new processes, and more efficient sized operations produced significant economies that more than offset the inflationary pressures from increased demand.

A second innovation was the policy of minidevaluation, or the "crawling peg," which permitted Brazilian exports to remain internationally competitive. A third was price controls. In 1965 a price control system was adopted that provided credit incentives for voluntary compliance with price guidelines. The system has been gradually changed to a strategy that attempts to stimulate productivity. In granting permission to raise prices, the price control agency (CIP) estimates future productivity increases and requires the industries to absorb half the projected gain. If the productivity target is achieved, the industry adds half the gain to its profits. If the target is exceeded, the industry benefits even more.

Although Brazil "backed into" import-substitution industrialization after World War II as a result of a foreign exchange crisis, it subsequently moved toward an affirmative and flexible industrialization strategy. It gave high levels of protection to industries that were initially established to supply the large domestic market. As new industries became increasingly efficient through accumulated experience and growing economies of scale, and as the shortage of foreign exchange became an increasingly difficult problem, Brazil shifted the emphasis of its industrialization policy to export expansion through competition in foreign markets.[29] By first going through an "infant industry" protection phase, its labor force gained experience, the quality of products was improved, and the management and marketing ability of local business executives was elevated to a level that has enabled Brazilian plants to compete with manufactured goods in world markets.

As a means of implementing its various strategies Brazil generally followed a policy of incentives. In the import-substitution phase of industrialization the main incentives were protection against foreign competition and the privilege of importing machinery free of import duties and without "exchange cover," that is, the capital investment could be in the form of machinery. The export promotion program offered special financing assistance and substantial tax reductions for the export of manufactured goods. Tax incentives up to 50 percent of the annual federal income tax liability were used to encourage investment in the less developed regions of the country such as the Northeast and the Amazon, and to stimulate investment in priority sectors such as forestry, fishing, and tourism. Tax incentives were also made available to investors in equity shares as part of the effort to improve capital markets.

The use of incentive programs has been extremely effective in achieving development goals. At the same time the incentive programs have contributed to income concentration because their benefits are primarily available to rich people or business firms. Foreign firms are also frequently in a better position than domestic firms to take advantage of the incentives, for example, in exports.

Contribution of the Brazilian Private Sector

It is important for a country with development aspirations to formulate and implement appropriate government policies and strategies. It is also essential that infrastructure services be available to support expansion. The final "payoff" in terms of increased output of goods and services requires still more. There must be entrepreneurship that responds to the policies, strategies, and availability of infrastructure. In Brazil such a response has come with great vigor from the indigenous private business sector and foreign enterprises. In a number of areas the government itself has assumed the entrepreneurial function.

A somewhat logical division of the entrepreneurial function has evolved over the years. Local enterprise dominates those business activities where capital requirements are relatively modest, where technology is easily available, and where managerial needs are not highly complex. State enterprises tend to function in areas where capital requirements are large, where the sector is considered to be "basic" or involves national security considerations, where technology may be reasonably advanced, and where foreign firms have shown only limited interest. Foreign enterprises are dominant in business areas where they have a quasi-monopoly advantage in the form of technology, access to capital, differentiated products built on advertising, management skills, or a global organization.

In the available research studies on Brazil's development experience, the most neglected area is the role of indigenous enterprise. Yet, there are fragments of information that suggest some of the patterns and characteristics of what must be recognized as a vigorous private enterprise response.

Development studies of many countries emphasize the weakness of local entrepreneurship and indicate that entrepreneurship potentials are inherently limited in the less developed countries. This view has often been expressed concerning Brazil. Sometimes an exception is made for the São Paulo area, where the role of immigrants and their descendents has been noted, particularly of Italians, Germans, Portuguese, and Lebanese.[30] For the rest of the country and particularly in the less developed areas such as the Northeast, local entrepreneurship has normally been characterized as weak and almost nonexistent.

The record of many years belies this long-persisting fable. Examine the field of agriculture. The overresponse of coffee producers to market incentives and profitability has already been noted. During the 1950s world markets for sisal fiber became attractive. More by serendipity and self-effort than by governmental programs in the agricultural field, producers in the Northeast responded forcefully. There are many other examples in agriculture of dramatic production increases stimulated by market forces such as the expansion of cacao production in Bahia, the sharp increase in soybean production in the South during the early 1970s, and the great expansion in sugar production, also during the 1970s.

In many of the agricultural areas the production response to market incentives has often been through more extensive use of land rather than by upgrading farming technology. Brazilian officials are generally dissatisfied with the technological lag in agricultural activities. But this does not negate the fact that Brazilian farmers throughout the country have shown strong entrepreneurial talent in expanding farm output as market incentives came into force.

In the field of commerce indigenous companies are dominant. As shown by the national accounts, the growth rates of the commerce sector have been substantial. As one specific example, a Brazilian food chain, Supermercados Pão de Açucar, S.A., ranked number 35 among Brazil's largest 1,000 companies in terms of sales in 1973.

In the field of construction Brazilian companies almost monopolize the field and have been growing at phenomenal rates. One of the companies, Camargo Correia, ranked number 23 in sales in the list of 1,000 largest companies.

Among the 1,000 largest companies in 1973, Brazilian private enterprise accounted for 46 percent of total sales for the group and surpassed the sales share of either foreign- or state-owned enterprises. In terms of net book value, as would be expected, Brazilian private enterprises ranked lower, accounting for 28 percent of the total.[31]

In the field of manufacturing domestic firms in 1971 accounted for a larger share of both sales and assets than either foreign companies or state enterprises in the following industries, as shown in Table 4-2: cement, miscellaneous metal products, electrical equipment, automotive parts and accessories, paper, beverages, plastics, in addition to the traditional industries of textiles, food processing, lumber, furniture, and printing and publishing.

Brazilian business entrepreneurs have succeeded in playing a major role in directly productive activities in spite of a number of crucial handicaps. One problem has been access to "know-how." In the capital goods industry, as one example, the necessary know-how was supplied largely from the engineering abilities of the firms' owner-managers, perhaps complemented by the experience of an immigrant or expatriate engineer. Another source of supply was the Institute of Technological Research of the São Paulo Polytechnical School. Beyond these sources, Brazilian companies imported know-how from the advanced countries by simply purchasing designs for a fee or by entering into "technical-assistance" agreements that involved licensing and royalty payments.[32]

Payments to foreigners for the transfer of technology have become a matter of concern to Brazilian policy makers because of the cost and a conviction that technology transfers are reducing the stimulus to domestic research and development.

Another difficulty faced by the private sector has been raising equity capital in the absence of efficient capital markets and with a social environment that has long favored family-owned enterprises unwilling to share ownership. In the past the problem of securing more capital was frequently solved through taking advantage of subsidies for importing machinery and through short-term loans from the Bank of Brazil. In some cases companies increased their capital through tax fraud and contraband foreign trade operations.[33]

Over the decades the conditions for successful operations by Brazilian entrepreneurs have greatly improved in terms of access to equity capital and other types of financing, and through large increases in the supply and quality of technically and managerially trained people for local industries. In addition, foreign-owned enterprises have been a breeding ground for Brazilian entrepreneurs and a means for their securing experience and confidence.

The Role of Foreign
Private Investment

Historically, foreign direct investments played an important role in the development of railroads, electric power, telephones, and other public utilities in Brazil, and a more modest but significant part in finance, air transportation, retail distribution, and mining. However, the most dynamic area of foreign investment since World War II has been in manufacturing, first for the local market and more recently for export.

The overall size of the foreign business sector is suggested by the Visão estimate that foreign private enterprises in 1973 accounted for 37 percent of the sales and 22 percent of the net book value of the 1,000 largest companies.[34] In manufacturing foreign companies are predominant in a number of important fields, including automotive assembly, shipbuilding, electrical equipment, rubber and tires, glass, household appliances, cigarettes, pharmaceuticals, and some lines of food processing (Table 4-2). But in the general run of manufacturing industry they are overshadowed by Brazilian companies.

The importance of foreign participation in the development of the manufacturing industry, however, is undoubtedly far greater than the volume of investment alone would indicate. Brazilian companies depend heavily on foreign sources for licensing of patents and industrial techniques, for technical help in designing, building, and operating manufacturing plants, and for the use of internationally known brand names with already established consumer acceptance. Many of the companies are joint ventures.

Until the 1960s the flow of foreign investment into Brazil was primarily from the United States because Japan and the principal investor countries of Europe

Table 4-2
Government, Foreign, and Domestic Firm Participation in Brazilian Manufacturing, 1971

	Percentage Share of Industry or Subindustry Assets			Percentage Share of Industry or Subindustry Sales[a]			Total Number of Firms in Survey					
							Government Firms		Foreign Firms		Domestic Firms	
	Government Firms (%)	Foreign Firms (%)	Domestic Firms (%)	Government Firms (%)	Foreign Firms (%)	Domestic Firms (%)	Number	Percent of Total (%)	Number	Percent of Total (%)	Number	Percent of Total (%)
Mining	50.9	28.2	21.0	61.6	23.1	15.3	1	1.7	21	35.0	38	63.3
Metallic minerals	59.7	27.0	13.3	71.8	23.3	4.9	1	4.0	11	44.0	13	52.0
Nonmetallic minerals	–	35.1	64.9	–	22.2	77.8	–	–	10	28.6	25	71.4
Nonmetallic mineral manufactures	–	33.3	66.7	–	40.4	59.6	–	–	28	23.9	89	76.1
Cement	–	19.7	80.3	–	33.3	66.7	–	–	7	17.1	34	82.9
Ceramics and cement products	–	36.0	64.0	–	27.0	73.0	–	–	10	17.5	47	82.5
Glass and crystal products	–	83.0	17.0	–	88.1	11.9	–	–	7	58.3	5	41.7
Other nonmetallic mineral products	–	24.7	75.3	–	28.7	71.3	–	–	4	57.1	3	42.9
Metallurgy	38.6	24.1	37.3	28.1	27.3	44.6	5	2.1	56	23.2	180	74.7
Iron and steel	64.1	19.3	16.6	52.5	29.9	17.7	5	15.2	8	24.2	20	60.6
Nonferrous metals	–	46.1	53.9	–	51.4	48.6	–	–	12	52.2	11	47.8
Miscellaneous metal products	–	25.7	74.3	–	17.9	82.1	–	–	36	19.5	149	80.5
Machinery	–	68.4	31.6	–	64.2	35.8	–	–	56	46.7	64	53.3
Industrial machinery and equipment	–	63.7	36.3	–	58.0	42.0	–	–	38	41.3	54	58.7
Office machinery and equipment	–	98.0	2.0	–	98.5[b]	1.5[b]	–	–	10	83.3	2	16.7
Tractors and earth-moving equipment	–	77.3	22.7	–	73.0	27.0	–	–	8	50.0	8	50.0
Electrical and communications equipment	–	64.9	35.1	–	68.1	31.9	–	–	33	39.3	51	60.7
Electrical equipment	–	67.8	32.2	–	48.5	51.5	–	–	15	39.5	23	60.5

Electrical appliances, accessories, communications equipment	—	63.2	36.8	—	72.1	27.9	—	—	18	39.1	28	60.9
Transportation equipment	—	57.3	42.7	—	64.8	35.2	—	—	40	38.8	63	61.2
Shipbuilding	—	50.3	49.7	—	73.3	26.7	—	—	3	23.1	10	76.9
Railway equipment	—	77.5	22.5	—	97.2	2.8	—	—	4	50.0	4	50.0
Automotive vehicles	—	61.6	38.4	—	67.8	32.2	—	—	7	77.8	2	22.2
Automotive parts and accessories	—	45.0	55.0	—	36.7	63.3	—	—	23	33.8	45	66.2
Aircraft and other equipment	—	75.9	24.1	—	82.2	17.8	—	—	3	60.0	2	40.0
Lumber and wood	—	17.3	82.7	—	18.3	81.7	—	—	8	13.3	52	86.7
Furniture	—	3.6	96.4	—	5.6	94.4	—	—	1	6.3	15	93.8
Paper	—	28.3	71.7	—	25.2	74.8	—	—	11	15.5	60	84.5
Rubber	—	67.0	33.0	—	75.0[b]	25.0[b]	—	—	4	19.0	17	81.0
Leather	—	16.6	83.4	—	20.0[b]	80.0[b]	—	—	1	4.8	20	95.2
Chemicals	52.2	30.0	17.8	26.7	54.0	19.3	3	1.7	68	38.9	104	59.4
Chemicals and petrochemicals	11.6	60.4	28.0	65.5	7.7	26.7	2	1.7	52	45.2	61	53.0
Petroleum refining and distribution	76.0	13.3	10.7	34.4	49.6	15.9	1	4.0	7	28.0	17	68.0
Natural gas	—	84.6	15.3	—	88.6	11.4	—	—	7	77.8	2	22.2
Vegetable oils	—	25.9	74.1	—	31.8	68.2	—	—	2	7.7	24	92.3
Pharmaceutical products	—	60.5	39.5	—	66.5	33.5	—	—	19	48.7	20	51.3
Perfumery	—	51.1	48.9	—	50.0[b]	50.0[b]	—	—	4	26.7	11	73.3
Plastics	—	48.7	51.3	—	48.8	51.2	—	—	13	35.1	24	64.9
Textiles	—	28.5	71.5	—	29.3	70.7	—	—	38	15.4	208	84.9
Spinning and weaving	—	29.8	70.2	—	28.2	71.8	—	—	33	15.2	184	84.8
Finished textile products	—	19.0	80.9	—	37.8	62.2	—	—	5	17.2	24	82.8
Apparel	—	32.9	67.1	—	52.5	47.5	—	—	7	11.5	54	88.5

Table 4-2 (cont.)

	Percentage Share of Industry or Subindustry Assets			Percentage Share of Industry or Subindustry Sales[a]			Total Number of Firms in Survey					
							Government Firms		Foreign Firms		Domestic Firms	
	Government Firms (%)	Foreign Firms (%)	Domestic Firms (%)	Government Firms (%)	Foreign Firms (%)	Domestic Firms (%)	Number	Percent of Total (%)	Number	Percent of Total (%)	Number	Percent of Total (%)
Food	—	14.6	85.4	—	20.1	79.9	—	—	22	7.1	289	92.9
Grain products	—	23.2	76.8	—	18.2	81.8	—	—	4	11.1	32	88.9
Meat products	—	30.7	69.3	—	42.4[b]	57.6[b]	—	—	1	2.9	34	97.1
Seafood products	—	7.9	92.1	—	28.4	71.6	—	—	2	5.7	33	94.3
Dairy products	—	7.9	92.1	—	30.0	70.2	—	—	2	20.0	8	80.0
Sugar and alcohol	—	—	100	—	—	100	—	—	—	—	123	100
Soluble coffee	—	20.7	79.3	—	5.1	94.9	—	—	2	28.6	5	71.4
Miscellaneous food products	—	37.8	62.2	—	20.1	79.9	—	—	11	16.9	54	83.1
Beverages	—	9.8	90.2	—	21.2	78.7	—	—	7	14.0	43	86.0
Tobacco	—	97.7	2.3	—	97.6	2.4	—	—	5	71.4	2	28.5
Printing and publishing	—	1.3	98.7	—	1.6	98.4	—	—	2	3.7	52	96.3
Newspapers	—	—	100	—	—	100	—	—	—	—	15	100
Printing and other publishing	—	1.9	98.1	—	2.0[c]	98.0[c]	—	—	2	5.1	37	94.9
Miscellaneous manufactures	—	39.5	60.5	—	43.4	56.6	—	—	12	27.3	32	72.7
Conglomerates	—	41.6	58.4	—	49.8	50.2	—	—	3	42.9	4	57.1
Scientific and professional instruments	—	50.5	49.5	—	52.6	47.4	—	—	7	41.2	10	58.8
Miscellaneous products	—	8.9	91.1	—	10.5	89.5	—	—	2	10.0	18	90.0

| Total Manufacturing | 18.5 | 34.4 | 47.1 | 11.3 | 45.1 | 43.6 | 8 | 0.4 | 435 | 23.0 | 1,450 | 76.6 |
| Total Manufacturing and Mining | 20.2 | 34.1 | 45.7 | 12.7 | 44.5 | 42.8 | 9 | 0.5 | 456 | 23.3 | 1,488 | 76.2 |

Source: William G. Tyler, *Manufactured Export Expansion and Industrialization in Brazil* (Tubingen, Germany: J.L.B. Mohr, 1975). Author's calculations based upon information contained in *Visão*, August 26, 1972; Banas, *Brasil Industrial 1973*, various volumes; *Conjuntura Econômica*, various issues; and *Guia Interinvest* (Rio de Janeiro: Editôra Interinvest, 1973).

[a]The number of firms included in the calculation of percentage shares of sales is smaller than that used for estimating asset shares. Sales information was not available for some firms.

[b]Sales figures for some of the more important firms were not included in the survey information. However, they were crudely estimated by the author from asset and profit data.

[c]Sales figures for the two relatively small foreign firms were estimated from asset and profit data.

were concentrating on domestic reconstruction. Since the mid-1960s, however, the inflow of foreign investment from Japan, Germany, and other European countries has accelerated. Official statistics as of Dec. 31, 1974 show a cumulative total of US$6.0 billion direct foreign investment in Brazil. These data, however, understate the level of foreign investment because they do not include large sums that have flowed into Brazil as foreign loans in place of registered direct investment owing to local tax advantages. Of the total registered investment, the share represented by United States firms has declined from about 50 percent in 1969 to 34 percent in 1974 (Table 4-3). Some additional United States investment is undoubtedly included in the amounts registered for Panama and the Netherland Antilles. Over the same period Japanese investments have increased from 3.2 to 9.9 percent of the total and the share represented by European countries such as the Netherlands, Sweden, and Luxembourg has increased sharply.

The flow of foreign investment has fluctuated over the postwar years with changes in Brazilian policies and with variations in the perceptions of Brazil's growth prospects. During the postwar years Brazil and the rest of Latin America were only of secondary interest to United States international companies because of the much greater attraction of the rapidly reviving and expanding European economies and of their emerging Common Market. The first major flow of foreign investment to Brazil in the twentieth century occurred during the Kubitschek period, in large part in response to the incentives created for the automotive industry. During the Quadros-Goulart period the principal additions were reinvestment of earnings, which had become difficult to repatriate due to restrictive policies. The inflows as reflected by registered investments began to increase shortly after the revolutionary government took over and really began to skyrocket in 1969 and thereafter (Figure 4-1).

More significant for Brazil's drive to development has been the dynamism and performance of the industrial sectors in which foreign firms have been dominant. These sectors have led the expansion of the economy. They have had high levels of productivity and stimulated additional expansion through backward and forward linkages.[35]

Although Brazilian policy has not required foreign firms to enter into joint ventures, except in certain fields such as minerals and petrochemicals, a number of the foreign companies including such firms as Volkswagen and Ford, have significant local equity participation in their companies. Brazilian officials, however, have closely supervised the expansion of multinational firms in Brazil and generally succeeded in shaping the operations of foreign firms in ways conducive to achievement of Brazil's development goals. The imposition of a "local content requirements" regulation (the progressive replacement of imports by components made in Brazil) has stimulated the growth of local supplier companies in the automotive and other industries. More recently export incentives have been especially effective in stimulating foreign companies to

Table 4-3
Brazil: Foreign Direct Investment and Reinvestment, 1969-74
(Cumulative Totals as of End of Year, U.S. Dollars)

	1969	1970	1971	1972	1973	1974	Percentage Distribution Dec. 31, 1974
				(Millions)			
Investor Country							
Total	1,710	2,347	2,912	3,404	4,579	6,027	100.0
United States	816	986	1,096	1,272	1,717	2,022	33.5
Germany	177	253	331	372	521	710	11.8
Japan	55	105	125	193	318	598	9.9
Switzerland	105	132	192	254	357	560	9.3
Canada	168	260	294	305	360	401	6.7
United Kingdom	109	208	273	281	324	401	6.7
France	35	34	130	165	205	242	4.0
Panama	49	66	80	98	132	187	3.1
Netherland Antilles	62	59	75	77*	113	132	2.2
Other	134	244	316	387	532	774	12.8
By Sector							
Total			2,912	3,404	4,579	6,027	100.0
Industry			2,384	2,802	3,526	4,515	74.9
Services			276	319	685	1,031	17.1
Public utilities			157	154	191	208	3.5
Mining			26	48	77	121	2.0
Agriculture			21	24	32	43	0.7
Other			48	57	68	109	1.8

Source: Central Bank of Brazil, *Boletim*, May 1975. Data presented refers to foreign direct investment registered by the Central Bank. Loans and "financing" are not included. These data have not been reconciled with the inflows and outflows recorded in the balance of payments accounts.

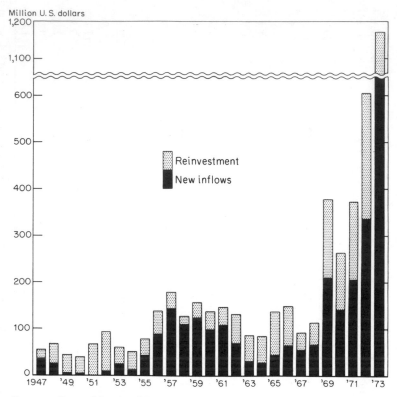

Source: Central Bank of Brazil.
Note: Data refers to foreign direct investment registered by the Central Bank. Loans and "financing" not included.

Figure 4-1. Brazil: Annual Increases in Foreign Direct Investment, 1947-73.

expand Brazilian exports of nontraditional products, particularly manufactured products. Brazilian officials are also beginning to have success through incentive measures in getting foreign firms to undertake industrial research in Brazil. Although official government policy has been favorable toward foreign private investment, there has been considerable debate about a number of issues: Are foreign firms using "appropriate technologies" to maximize employment in Brazil; are they exploiting monopoly position; and are the costs of transfers of technology excessive?

External Resources

To what extent has Brazil's development drive received support from external forces and resources other than direct investment? Until about 1967 financial flows in the forms of loans or credit from foreign private and official sources had a stop and go record and were usually not easily arranged. Foreign aid in the form of grants and technical assistance was modest, although effective in some cases, until the Alliance for Progress was initiated in 1960. Even then, aid fluctuated greatly with political factors and foreign perceptions of political crises.

Throughout most of the years since the end of World War II, Brazil has had current-account deficits in its balance of payments. Although part of the deficit was generally offset by the inflows of foreign private investment, the rest had to be financed through external debt. During much of the period Brazil found it necessary to resort to commercial credit, which frequently was in arrears, or the simple nonpayment of its deficit. To do otherwise would have meant slowing down the development drive. As one Brazilian source explains, Brazil took medium-term loans, particularly in the 1956-62 period, that it could not possibly amortize on the foreseen dates.[36] Consequently, its international creditors were placed in the position of either having to modify the terms or to face default in payment. The loans were always rescheduled, and Brazil has never defaulted on its foreign debt.

The basic problem in the external sector was the semistagnation of exports and an unwillingness to slow down the development drive. Another problem was the disapproval of the World Bank and the International Monetary Fund, until the middle 1960s, of Brazil's financial policies, particularly the tolerance of what then appeared to be a high level of inflation. From 1954 until 1965 the World Bank had Brazil on its "black list," except for two loans approved in 1958 for government electric power enterprises, "on the ground that the country was not creditworthy." A recent World Bank appraisal contains a form of apology: "As one looks back on the relations of the Bank and Brazil in the 1950s from the vantage point of 1971, . . . its (the bank's) judgment of creditworthiness seems to have been rather static and limited."[37]

The Inter-American Development Bank, after its establishment in 1960, became a much steadier source of development loans than the World Bank and the U.S. Agency for International Development. The total lending to Brazil from 1949 to 1973 was as follows:[38]

USAID	US$1.2 billion
IDB	1.4 billion
IBRD	1.7 billion
Total	US$4.3 billion

Of this amount, more than half was committed in the 1968-73 period.

On the whole the record of international and United States agencies reveals that their failure to provide adequate financial aid to Brazil in the earlier years lost them a great opportunity to serve the original development purposes for which they were established.

About 1967 Brazil's credit rating in private international financial circles, as well as with official agencies, began to improve. As a result Brazil was able to support its development efforts through larger foreign borrowings and increasing its external debt. From 1967-71 external resources through supplier credit and loans in currency averaged US$1.1 billion annually, increasing to US$4.5 and US$6.6 million in 1973 and 1974, respectively. At the same time there were repayment outflows so that the net contributions from foreign borrowing were US$2.8 and US$4.7 billion in 1973 and 1974, respectively.

The impact of external resources in terms of technical assistance is difficult to quantify. The net contribution of United States and United Nations technical assistance, despite the limited success of many projects, has been substantial. One of the most important foreign-aid activities was the financing of training for Brazilians in foreign countries and of study missions to examine the experience of other countries.

The United States gave valuable technical assistance in the economic planning field through the Abbink Mission and the Mixed Commission. The total expenditures of the United States, however, during the decade of 1950-60 on foreign assistance totalled only about US$56 million, of which about 40 percent was made available in the last three years of the period. A large share of these funds was devoted to health and sanitation projects.

Under the Alliance for Progress foreign aid to Brazil escalated greatly, first to assist development in Northeast Brazil,[39] and after the 1965 revolution, as general program and project loans, the main accomplishments of which were to permit Brazil to tidy up its foreign debt.[40]

The United Nations provided direct technical assistance in many areas including development planning for the Northeast. The United Nations Special Fund financed and supervised important project planning activities such as a major power planning study for the South-Central region. The World Bank financed and supervised comprehensive project and sectoral planning in the field of highways. The United States government assisted Brazil in its reform plans in the fields of agriculture, education, housing, taxation, health, and governmental administration by means of the largest technical cooperation program in Latin America. United States technical assistance in the field of tax administration and tax reform was a particularly successful program.

Labor Unions

The framework within which labor unions function first evolved during the Vargas Estado Novo period of the 1930s. The sindicatos or labor unions, which had been politically active for a brief period in the late 1920s, became administrative agencies to assist the governmental apparatus with social security programs. President Vargas' attitude, based on a paternalistic rationale, was that independent labor-union activity particularly in the political sphere was unnecessary because the government protected labor's legitimate needs and interests. Under the Vargas dictatorship social legislation was greatly expanded to improve the working and living conditions of the Brazilian people.[41]

The labor framework also consists of a comprehensive government-operated social security system and a system of labor courts which deal with labor issues that are left to collective bargaining between management and labor unions in some other societies like the United States. The social security system places in the hands of government the principal responsibility for providing modern social welfare services to the workers on the basis of contributions from the employers, the workers, and the government. The system of labor courts was designed to adjudicate disputes between employers and employees, and they reflect an important characteristic of Brazilian culture: the desire to avoid direct conflict by channeling problems through the offices of the administrative state.[42]

The Ministry of Labor in effect controls the labor unions. The labor unions are funded through a trade union tax collected from all workers and redistributed to the sindicatos by the Ministry. The law prohibits the use of these funds for strikes. In addition, the Labor Ministry has the right to intervene directly in the internal affairs of a labor organization by appointing a delegate or an interventor to administer it.

During the early 1960s, and particularly under the presidency of João Goulart, labor unions briefly emerged from their traditional limited role of collaborating in the administration of governmental social service programs and attempted to increase their political power. In 1962, for example, the unions called a general strike to pressure the Congress to support President Goulart's choice of a national leftist for prime minister.

With the overthrow of Goulart by the military coup, the new government quickly took steps to ensure that the labor unions would resume "their normal function as authentic representatives of the workers."[43] The autonomy that labor leaders had gained in the 1950s and 1960s was curtailed. "Undesirable" labor leaders were purged along with many other leaders of different groups. Through these and other measures labor unions have returned to the role of a quasi-government institution to assist in the administration of welfare programs.

Notes

1. For an elaboration on the role of tecnicos, see Nathaniel H. Leff, *Economic Policy-Making and Development in Brazil, 1947-1964* (New York: John Wiley & Sons, Inc., 1968), pp. 143-53.

2. *25 Years of the Brazilian Economy* (São Paulo: Banco Moreira Salles, S.A., 1967), p. 93.

3. See John D. Wirth, *The Politics of Brazilian Development 1930-1954* (Stanford: Stanford University Press, 1970), p. 217.

4. See *25 Years of the Brazilian Economy*, pp. 329-68.

5. See Roberto de Oliveira Campos, "A Retrospect Over Brazilian Development Plans," in *The Economy of Brazil*, edited by Howard S. Ellis (Berkeley: University of California Press, 1969), pp. 317-44; Robert T. Daland, "The Paradox of Planning," in *Contemporary Brazil*, edited by H. Jon Rosenbaum and William G. Tyler (New York: Praeger Publishers, 1972), pp. 29-49; and Jorge Vianna Monteiro and Luiz Roberto Azevedo Cunha, "Alguns Aspectos da Evolução do Planejamento Econômico no Brasil (1934-63)," in *Pesquisa e Planejamento Econômico*, February 1974, pp. 1-24.

6. Albert O. Hirschman, *The Strategy of Development* (New Haven: Yale University Press, 1958), Chapter 5.

7. Fernando A. Rezende da Silva, *Avaliação do Setor Público na Economia Brasileira* (Rio de Janeiro: IPEA, 1972), p. 22; and Werner Baer, "The Brazilian Boom 1968-72," *World Development*, August, 1973, p. 7.

8. Werner Baer, Isaac Kerstenetsky, and Annibal V. Villela, "The Changing Role of the State in the Brazilian Economy," *World Development*, November 1973, p. 30.

9. For some historical background, see George Wythe, *Brazil, An Expanding Economy* (New York: Twentieth Century Fund, 1949), Chapter 8.

10. Alan Abouchar, "Public Investment Allocation and Pricing Policy for Transportation," in Ellis, *The Economy of Brazil*, pp. 356-58.

11. See, for example, Alberto Tamer, *Transamazônica, Solução Para 2001* (Rio de Janeiro: APEC Editora S.A., 1971).

12. "Fifteen Years of Economic Policy in Brazil," *Economic Bulletin for Latin America*, December 1964, pp. 188-90.

13. Lafayette Prado, *Panorama Futuro dos Transportes* (Brasilia: IPEAC, 1973), p. 28.

14. For an excellent study of the power sector in Brazil, see Judith Tendler, *Electric Power in Brazil* (Cambridge: Harvard University Press, 1968).

15. Presidencia da República, PBDCT *(Plano Básico de Desenvolvimento Científico e Tecnológico) 1973-74*, June 1973.

16. "Fifteen Years of Economic Policy in Brazil," *Economic Bulletin for Latin America*, December 1964, p. 190.

17. See Wirth, *Politics*, pp. 133-216.

18. Werner Baer, Isaac Kerstenetsky, and Annibal V. Villela, "The Changing Role of the State in the Brazilian Economy," *World Development*, November 1973, p. 29.

19. *Brazil Report 1974* (São Paulo: Visão S.A. Editorial, 1974), p. 46.

20. See the speech by Professor Eugenio Gudin on the occasion of being honored as "Man of the Year" by Visão Magazine. *Jornal do Brasil*, December 13, 1974.

21. *Projecto do II Plano Nacional de Desenvolvimento (1975-1979)* (Brasilia: República Federativa do Brasil, September 1974), pp. 40-42.

22. Baer, Kerstenetsky, and Villela, "Changing Role of the State," p. 29.

23. See Tendler, *Electric Power in Brazil*, pp. 175-207, for a fascinating analysis of how pioneirismo and technological considerations helped to make the state power companies highly efficient.

24. For example, see Leff, *Economic Policy-Making*, pp. 59-76.

25. Walter L. Ness, Jr., "Financial Markets Innovation as a Development Strategy: Initial Results from the Brazilian Experience," *Economic Development and Cultural Change*, April 1974, pp. 453-72.

26. For a comprehensive description and analysis of indexing see Werner Baer and Paul Beckerman, "Indexing in Brazil," *World Development*, October-December 1974, pp. 35-47.

27. Mario Henrique Simonsen, *Brazil 2002* (Rio de Janeiro: APEC Editora, S.A., 1972), p. 81.

28. See Stefan H. Robock, "Anti-Inflation Lessons from Abroad: The Brazilian Experience," in "Inflation: Long Term Problems," *Proceedings of the Academy of Political Science*, Vol. 31, No. 4 (1975), pp. 179-87.

29. See Stefan H. Robock, "Industrialization Through Import-Substitution or Export Industries: A False Dichotomy," in *Industrial Organization and Development*, edited by J.W. Markham and G.F. Papanek (Boston: Houghton Mifflin Co., 1970), pp. 350-65.

30. Luiz Carlos Bresser Pereira, "Origens Étnicas e Sociais do Empresário Paulista," *Revista de Administração de Empresas*, June 1964, pp. 94 and 101.

31. *Brazil Report 1974*, p. 46.

32. Nathaniel H. Leff, *The Brazilian Capital Goods Industry, 1929-1964* (Cambridge: Harvard University Press, 1968), pp. 88-102.

33. Fernando H. Cardoso, *El Empresario Industrial en America Latina (Brazil),* Economic Commission for Latin America (ECN.12/642/Add.2), February 10, 1963, p. 30.

34. *Brazil Report 1974*, p. 46.

35. Álvaro A.G. Pignaton, *Capital Estrangeiro e Expansão Industrial no Brasil* (Brasilia: Universidade de Brasilia, Departamento de Economia, September 1973).

36. *25 Years of the Brazilian Economy*, p. 287.

37. Edward S. Mason and Robert E. Asher, *The World Bank Since Bretton Woods* (Washington, D.C.: The Brookings Institution, 1973), p. 662.

38. U.S. Agency for International Development, Special Tabulation (Unpublished), June 1974.

39. See Riordan Roett, *The Politics of Foreign Aid in the Brazilian Northeast* (Nashville: Vanderbilt University Press, 1972).

40. Carlos Diaz Alejandro, "Some Aspects of the Brazilian Experience with Foreign Aid," in *Trade, Balance of Payments and Growth*, edited by J.N. Bhagwati et al. (New York: American Elsevier Publishing Co., 1971), p. 447.

41. Moises Poblete Troncoso and Ben G. Burnett, *The Rise of the Latin American Labor Movement* (New Haven, Conn.: College and University Press, 1960), pp. 76-82.

42. Kenneth Paul Erickson, "Corporatism and Labor in Development," in Rosenbaum and Tyler, eds., *Contemporary Brazil*, pp. 142-43.

43. Humberto de Alencar Castello Branco, *Discursos*, 1964 (Rio de Janeiro: Departmento de Imprensa Nacional, n.d.), p. 23.

5

An Integrated Nation of Diverse Regions

Brazil's great size, its cultural and geographic diversity, and its development history have created strong persistent regional forces that must be taken into account in understanding the country.[1] All Brazilians are aware of these regional differences, and popular stereotypes delineate the personalities and behavior patterns of Brazilians from the different regions. As Anthropologist Charles Wagley describes them, the paulista from the state of São Paulo is an energetic, efficient businessman; the gaucho from Rio Grande do Sul is a crude cowboy; the carioca from the city of Rio de Janeiro is urbane, talkative, and pleasure-loving; the cearense from the northeastern state of Ceará is a keen commercial man and a wandering exile driven by drought from his homeland; the mineiro from Minas Gerais is political and highly traditional; the bahiano from the state of Bahia is eloquent and superficially brilliant. "Although these stereotypes are no truer than their counterparts in other countries, they do have some basis in fact. Regionalism has been an important factor in Brazilian politics, literature, art, and economics."[2]

For statistical purposes Brazil's 21 states,[3] 4 territories, and the Federal District are officially divided into five distinct regions that roughly follow the natural geographic and political division of the country: the North, Northeast, Southeast, South, and Central West. Regional development programs generally follow this fivefold division but also cut across state boundaries at times to follow economic patterns or physical features such as the São Francisco river basin or the Drought Polygon of the Northeast. The boundaries of these regions are shown in the map of the major regions of Brazil and selected statistics for the regions are shown in Table 5-1.

The North

The North with 42 percent of Brazil's total area covers most of the Amazon River basin. The basin also extends into neighboring countries—Venezuela, Ecuador, Colombia, Peru, and Bolivia. The vast size of this region is dramatized by the fact that only six countries of the world, including Brazil, have an area greater than this single region. In contrast, the North is the Brazilian region with the smallest population, less than 4 million, and lowest population density— 1 person per square kilometer. Much of the population is concentrated around Belém at the mouth of the Amazon River and in the interior city of Manaus.

75

Table 5-1
Brazil: Regional Economic Indicators

Region	National Area %	Population per km² (1970)	Percentage Distribution						Per Capita Income % National Average		
			Population			Total Income					
			1950	1960	1970	1949	1959	1970	1949	1959	1970
North	42.0	1.01	3.6	3.7	3.9	1.7	2.0	2.0	47	54	51
Northeast	18.2	18.23	34.6	31.6	30.2	14.1	14.0	12.2	41	44	40
Southeast	10.9	43.38	43.4	43.8	42.8	66.5	64.1	64.5	153	146	151
South	6.8	29.35	15.1	16.7	17.7	15.9	17.5	17.5	105	105	99
Central West	22.1	2.70	3.3	4.2	5.4	1.8	2.4	3.8	54	57	70
Brazil	100.0	10.94	100.0	100.0	100.0	100.0	100.0	100.0			
(Amounts in millions)	(8.5km²)	—	(51.9)	(71.0)	(93.1)	(Cr$199)	(Cr$1,697)	(Cr$165,295)			

Source: IBGE, *Anuário Estatístico do Brasil, 1973*; Fundação Getúlio Vargas, *Sistema de Contas Nacionais, Sept. 1974*, Tables 10-12.

Note: Individual regions consist of these states:

North: Acre, Amazonas and Pará; Territories of Amapá, Rondônia, Roraima.

Northeast: Maranhão, Piauí, Ceará; Rio Grande do Norte, Paraíba, Pernambuco, Alagoas, Sergipe, Bahia, Territory of Fernando de Noronha.

Southeast: Minas Gerais, Espírito Santo, Rio de Janeiro, São Paulo.

South: Paraná, Santa Catarina, Rio Grande do Sul.

Central West: Mato Grosso, Goiás, Federal District (Brasilia).

Some 100,000 Indians live scattered along river banks in the dense equatorial forests.

For centuries the North has remained virtually undeveloped and sparsely populated. During the early settlement days there were no discoveries of gold or spices to attract people to the region. Various missionary expeditions into the interior, together with vegetable extractive activities, fishing, and hunting, gradually promoted occupation of parts of the region. Development continued at a slow pace until the rubber boom that lasted from 1870 to 1914. During this period the region monopolized world rubber production. The short-lived boom collapsed as a result of competition from the more efficient rubber plantations in Ceylon, Malaya, and Sumatra, which were developed with seeds and plants smuggled from Brazil.

In later years several factors intensified the occupation of the region. Beginning in 1928 the Ford Motor Company made an effort to reestablish rubber plantations in the Amazon. Japanese settlers came to the North about 1929 to engage in agriculture. Extensive manganese deposits in Amapá began to be mined after World War II. More recently the government has been building roads and supporting special development programs for the region.

In 1946 the Constitution of Brazil provided that a certain percentage of the federal tax revenues be invested in the region and, in 1953 SPEVEA (Superintendência de Valorização Econômica da Amazônia), a special regional development organization, was created to supervise the program. In 1966 SPEVEA was replaced by SUDAM, the Superintendency for Development of the Amazon, and special tax incentives for investing in the region, previously limited to the Northeast, were extended to the Amazon North. In 1967 a "free trade zone" was established in the Manaus area to encourage industrialization. Even more dramatic has been the road-building program, which includes the Brasilia-Belém highway, the more than 5,000 kilometer Transamazônica, and others. A colonization program is also underway to assist migration from the densely populated Northeast to new areas opened up by the highways. But during the first four years of the program, the colonization effort had succeeded in resettling only 5,000 families along the Transamazon highway.

Currently, the North's economy is heavily based on extractive agriculture, forestry, livestock, and the mining of manganese and tin ore. Large new mineral discoveries of iron ore and bauxite have been made in the Amazon, and massive projects to exploit these resources are underway. In addition, as of 1973 several hundred cattle-raising projects representing an investment of some US$400 million had been approved by SUDAM for special incentives, and a series of mammoth forestry projects involving foreign investment had been initiated. The cattle projects alone cover 20 million hectares or almost twice the total area of England.

The North is clearly entering a new era of development. Yet, given its vast size, its dense tropical rain forests, the uncertain quality of much of its soils, and its distance from markets, the Amazon North is almost certain to continue for decades as one of the major development frontier areas of the world. The Amazon, as Charles Wagley notes, "is a region that catches the imagination of Brazilians and foreigners alike. It has been called 'Mysterious Amazon,' 'Green Hell,' 'Bread Basket of the World,' and other colorful epithets. It is actually none of these," he concludes, "but it is one of the most romantic of all Brazilian cultural regions."[4]

The Northeast

The Brazilian Northeast consisting of nine states is the second most populous region of Brazil after the Southeast, with about 30 percent of the country's population. The Brazilian Northeast is also the poorest area of Brazil. As the largest area of poverty in South America and known internationally for its periodic droughts, this part of the country is so often referred to by journalists and other writers as the "drought-stricken Northeast" that many people have come to accept this cliché as the official name of the region.

The Northeast was the earliest settled section of Brazil and among the first areas in the "New World" to be colonized. In 1532 sugar cane production started there. In less than a century Northeast Brazil became one of the most important sugar producing areas of the world. But with the development of the sugar industry in the Caribbean, world prices of sugar fell sharply in the last half of the seventeenth century and continued at low levels during the next century. The era of Northeast prosperity based on a sugar and slave plantation economy came to an end. At a later stage cotton agriculture became important, but the Northeast never regained its position of economic leadership in Brazil. During subsequent periods, as gold, rubber, and coffee became Brazil's principal products, the economic frontier and the center of economic gravity of the country migrated to other regions with the changes in leading commodities.

With the decline in sugar prosperity the expanding Northeast population shifted in ever greater numbers to the semiarid interior where subsistence agriculture and cattle raising became the principal economic activities. The accelerated transfer of population and economic activity from the humid coastal areas to the semiarid interior made the periodic droughts that hit the interior increasingly calamitous. Beginning almost a century ago the federal government recognized the Northeast seca, or drought, as a national problem and began the first of what has been a continuing series of federal programs for economic assistance and development.

The Northeast has many prosperous subregions, including the main petroleum fields of Bahia; yet, the region is still the lowest income area of Brazil. Per-capita income levels in the Northeast are less than half the national average and about one-third the average for the Southeast "heartland." The special federal programs for the Northeast currently operating are a regional development bank, the Bank of Northeast Brazil, that has grown over the 20 years of its existence to one of the major development banks in the country, the SUDENE regional development agency that has administered an extremely attractive tax incentive program resulting in an industrial rejuvenation of the region, and a successful regional power company, CHESF, that has supported the growth and modernization of the Northeast.[5]

Since the mid-1950s the real product of the Northeast has been expanding at an unusually high rate—almost 7 percent annually from 1954 to 1962[6]—and the regional gap between the Northeast and the rest of the country was being narrowed, until the rest of the country accelerated to a spectacular growth rate of between 9 and 10 percent beginning in 1968. By the early 1970s the Northeast was steadily getting richer, but other regions were getting richer at a faster rate. However, most of the new regional industries attracted by the special incentives and a new petrochemical complex in the Bahia area had not yet come into full production.

The principal economic activity of the region has been agriculture and cattle raising, both operating at low technological levels.[7] The major crops are sugar cane, cacao in Bahia, long-fiber cotton, manioc, beans, corn, and a variety of extractive products such as babaçu nuts for tropical oils and carnauba wax. The traditional industrial sector has been textiles and food processing, but the new wave of industrialization has diversified the manufacturing activity to include steel, chemicals, machinery, and consumer durables.

The secas have come less and less to dominate the regional thinking and governmental concern, and the development approach has increasingly shifted to one of reducing poverty through economic expansion rather than fighting the physical phenomenon of the periodic seca through building reservoirs. Although the region has been economically poor, it has long been culturally rich. Music, literature, poetry, and politics have flourished in the Northeast.

The Southeast

The Southeast is the economic heartland and the most highly developed region of Brazil. With only 11 percent of Brazil's area, the four states of the Southeast have 43 percent of Brazil's population and account for 65 percent of the national income. The nation's main industrial centers and major metropolitan areas, such as São Paulo, Rio de Janeiro, and Belo Horizonte, are located in this region, but there is great diversity among the subregions.

The economy of the region is based on industry, agriculture, mining, and services. The industrial sector includes practically all lines of production. The region contains Brazil's largest hydroelectric plants, its largest oil refineries, iron and steel plants, all Brazil's automobile and tractor factories, almost all the chemical industry, most electrical appliance and machinery manufacturing, and many types of light industries. Agriculture is highly diversified and operates at the highest technological standards for the country. In mining, iron ore is most important. The vast ore deposits in the state of Minas Gerais supply most of the ore for Brazil's exports and domestic consumption.

The region became important in the eighteenth century after gold discoveries brought a wave of settlement to Minas Gerais and made Brazil, for a time, the largest gold producer in the world. The gold boom petered out in the early nineteenth century. In the middle and late nineteenth century coffee provided the basis for a new period of prosperity centering around São Paulo. Waves of immigrants, especially Italians, Germans, Japanese, Portuguese, and Central and Eastern Europeans, participated in the agricultural boom, bringing their skills and enterprising attitudes to the states of São Paulo, Rio de Janeiro, and Espírito Santo.

The economic phenomenon of the Southeast and of all Brazil is the state of São Paulo, the nation's leading producer in both the agricultural and industrial sectors. It generates half of all federal tax revenues, employs almost 40 percent of Brazil's industrial work force, accounts for half of Brazil's industrial production, a fourth of its agricultural output, half of the country's imports, and about 40 percent of its exports. Yet, it contains less than 3 percent of the country's total area and under 20 percent of its population. The city of Greater São Paulo had a population of 7.8 million in 1970, an increase of 100 percent over the 1960-70 decade,[8] and has become the third largest city in the Western Hemisphere after New York City and Mexico City.

The coffee boom led to speculative overproduction and ended with a collapse of prices in the early decades of the twentieth century. Coffee cultivation began to decline in the 1930s, but the state remains a major producer of coffee, cotton, sugar, and a number of other important agricultural crops. The city of São Paulo developed as a commercial and industrial center for the coffee region and as the political center of Brazil's richest state. The concentration of industry around São Paulo brought considerable political influence to the Paulistas, who utilized it to foster industrial development through favorable tax treatment and protective tariffs.

The city of Rio de Janeiro based its early development on providing port facilities for shipping gold. It grew quickly into a major economic and cultural center and until 1960 was the national capital. The Rio de Janeiro urban complex with a 1970 population of almost 7 million must be considered one of the great resources of the country, second only to São Paulo in industrial activity and a leading center of commerce, finance, foreign trade, and shipping. Its striking beauty and "beauties," warm climate, and sandy beaches make it one of the world's tourist meccas.

The Southeast is in reality a series of cultural subregions.[9] The city of Rio de Janeiro has a cosmopolitan and pleasure-loving flavor. The city of São Paulo is dynamic and industrious with emphasis on progress and energetic activity. The Southeast as a whole, and the South, stand in sharp contrast to the North of Brazil in much the same way as the South of the United States contrasts with the North—with the map turned upside down. In Brazil the North has the heritage of plantations and slavery and is still semifeudal and primarily agrarian. The South has modern cities, industry, immigrants, mechanized agriculture, and a large middle class. The North is poor and has been a major source of internal migration to the prosperous South, although migration has slowed in recent years because of rapidly increasing employment opportunities in the newly industrializing Northeast.

The South

The three states of the South—Paraná, Santa Catarina, and Rio Grande do Sul—with about 7 percent of Brazil's area contain 18 percent of the country's population. This region has a subtropical climate with occasional snow in one location, the mountain town of São Joaquim in Santa Catarina. In agriculture Paraná and Rio Grande do Sul play a major national role along with São Paulo. The region is also important industrially. Although the smallest of Brazil's five main regions, the South is still larger than any West European country.

Paraná has been the fastest growing state in Brazil and has become the leader in coffee production, accounting for more than half the country's total coffee output. Rio Grande do Sul is the foremost producer of wheat, rice, onions, tobacco, and soybeans in addition to being the second most important area for livestock after Minas Gerais. Santa Catarina is the principal coal producing state and important in industry and agriculture.

Colonized first by Portuguese from the Azores and then by Europeans of various countries, the South developed a way of life more similar to that of the North American pioneers than to that of the planters of northeastern Brazil.[10] This region has never had an economic boom and bust comparable to those of the northern regions but has steadily grown in prosperity.

The first influx of European immigrants to the South occurred in the early nineteenth century when more than 20,000 Germans settled in forest lands in Rio Grande do Sul. Other German groups settled in Santa Catarina, Italian immigrants in Rio Grande do Sul, and still later, groups of Poles and Russians formed colonies in the state of Paraná. The adjustment of these European immigrants and their descendants in southern Brazil contrasts strongly with that of immigrants to other parts of Brazil. Only in the European colonies of the South has the European mixed-farming system been transplanted fully to Brazil.

Paraná, however, remained a frontier area until quite recently. As late as 1920 its population within an area approximating that of Nebraska stood at only 686,000. However, during the next 50 years Paraná's population exploded tenfold to 6,755,000, primarily through migration. This increase was all the more remarkable since it consisted largely of *rural* population growth, even through the capital city of Curitiba also expanded to more than 600,000. This spectacular rate of settlement of Brazil's richest agricultural frontier, while belated, was reminiscent of the advancing United States frontier a century earlier.[11]

The moderate climate and fertile soils are responsible for this region's paramount concern with cattle raising, and highly diversified and technologically sophisticated farming. Forestry is also important based on the exploitation of the Paraná pine, one of the region's pioneer activities and a sizeable source of income. The coal mines in Santa Catarina are Brazil's main deposits and the only ones being commercially exploited. The quality of the coal, however, is too low to be used for metallurgical purposes and must be mixed with substantial portions of imported coal. Industry is prosperous and mainly concerned with wood, paper and pulp, food processing, and leather products. Beginning about 1970 the state of Rio Grande do Sul has become a major exporter of shoes, and the state of Paraná has begun to attract many technologically advanced industries as an overflow from the burgeoning São Paulo area.

The Central West

The vast central interior, which includes the states of Mato Grosso, Goiás, and the Federal District in which Brasilia is located, is another frontier area. From 1950 to 1970 the population of the Central West tripled to slightly more than 5 million, including about 500,000 in Brasilia. But this is still a small number of people to occupy 22 percent of Brazil's area. Vast stretches of forest and pasture lands, mineral wealth yet to be explored, and prosperous cattle-raising activities in the south of Mato Grosso and Goiás make the Central West resemble the North, for both regions are sparsely populated and present attractive opportunities for future development.

The Central West has had three different colonization phases: the mineral cycle, the expansion of large cattle ranches, and the development of agriculture in forest areas with fertile soils. The mining cycle began in the eighteenth century with the discovery of gold in Mato Grosso and Goiás. With the collapse of the mining boom, many of the early settlements either died or became isolated from the rest of Brazil. The expansion of cattle raising began at the end of the eighteenth century, as the population previously supported by mining began to live from cattle raising or subsistence agriculture. The third phase of agricultural expansion was relatively recent and resulted mainly from the extension of railroads from São Paulo and Minas Gerais into the region, which made the markets of the Southeast accessible.

The settlement of the Central West, however, did not begin to be really effective until the twentieth century. The building of roads in Mato Grosso, the construction of Brasilia (1956-60), and the opening of the Belém-Brasilia highway (begun in 1968) with the colonization that it stimulated were responsible for the accelerated population movement into the region and the recent development of agriculture and livestock. Most of the region's economic activity is in agriculture. In addition to livestock raising, it has become an important producer of rice, beans, corn, manioc, and coffee. Mining is a small but growing activity.

The building of Brasilia and the accompanying investment in roads, electric power, and other types of infrastructure have undoubtedly made a significant contribution to the development of the Central West. In this respect the long standing desire of Brazil to move the economic center of the country farther into the interior is in process of being fulfilled. Whether the cost to the country of implementing this national goal was too much relative to other alternatives will long remain a controversial issue among many Brazilians.

Regional Trends

As is true for all countries, economic growth in Brazil has not been evenly distributed among all geographical regions of this large country.[12] Nevertheless, all the regions have participated in the nation's development drive, even though some have expanded at a faster rate than others. In absolute terms, the level of real per-capita income has risen steadily. In relative terms, wide disparities persist.

Reliable and comprehensive regional statistics are a problem in Brazil as in many other countries. On the basis of available regional data, it is not clear whether regional disparities have increased or decreased with the accelerated growth of recent years. As shown in Table 5-1, except for the Northeast, regional disparities appear to have narrowed over the two decades from 1949 to 1970. Per-capita income in the frontier region of the Central West clearly has grown much more rapidly than the national average, and a more modest gain has occurred in the Amazon North. The statistics for 1970, however, show a lag for the Northeast, but 1970 was a year of serious drought in the region and not a representative year for a point to point comparison. Unfortunately, regional accounts data for other recent years have not yet been revised.

Supplementary studies and data suggest three additional conclusions specifically relating to the Northeast. First, for the extended period from 1954 to 1967, when Brazil shifted from austerity to accelerated national growth, the real growth rate for the Northeast was slightly faster than for Brazil as a whole.[13] Because population was increasing more slowly in the Northeast than in Brazil, the Northeast growth rate of product per capita exceeded the average growth rate for the nation. Second, the impact of the industrialization surge in the

Northeast (and in the Amazon), stimulated by the attractive tax incentives, was only beginning to emerge in the early 1970s because of the normal time lag between planning new industry projects, securing governmental approvals, and getting into production. A third conclusion is that over the 1960-70 decade the Northeast lagged behind the rest of the country in a number of development indicators, such as literacy and average income growth in the primary producing sector.[14]

Brazilian governmental leaders, whether military or civilian, are keenly sensitive to regional considerations, and special programs to stimulate growth in the poorer regions are certain to receive continued emphasis. Of key importance for the future is the decentralization pressure that has been generated by shortages and congestion in the older areas of industrial concentration such as metropolitan São Paulo.

Notes

1. Two excellent sources for further detail on Brazil's regions are Charles Wagley, *An Introduction to Brazil* (New York: Columbia University Press, 1971), Revised Edition, pp. 23-90, and Rui Miller Paiva, Salomão Schattan, and Claus F. Trench de Freitas, *Brazil's Agricultural Sector* (São Paulo, 1973), pp. 277-284.

2. Wagley, *An Introduction to Brazil*, p. 23.

3. The states of Guanabara and Rio de Janeiro were merged on March 15, 1975 to form the new state of Rio de Janeiro.

4. Wagley, *An Introduction to Brazil*, p. 63.

5. See Stefan H. Robock, *Brazil's Developing Northeast* (Washington: The Brookings Institution, 1963); and Rubens Vaz da Costa, *O Primeiro Passo* (Rio de Janeiro: APEC Editora, 1973).

6. David Edwin Goodman and Roberto Cavalcanti de Albuquerque, *Incentivos à Industrialização e Desenvolvimento do Nordeste* (Rio de Janeiro: IPEA, 1974), p. 17.

7. George F. Patrick, *Desenvolvimento Agrícola do Nordeste* (Rio de Janeiro: IPEA, 1972).

8. Robert W. Fox, *Regional Urban Growth Trends* (Washington: Inter-American Development Bank, July 1974), p. 87.

9. Wagley, *An Introduction to Brazil*, p. 62.

10. Ibid., pp. 72-80

11. William H. Nicholls, "The Agricultural Frontier in Modern Brazilian History: The State of Paraná, 1920-65," in *Cultural Change in Brazil*, Papers from the Midwest Association of Latin American Studies, October 30 & 31, 1969 (Muncie, Indiana: Ball State University, n.d.), pp. 36-64.

12. See Vaz da Costa, *O Primeiro Passo*, pp. 195-237; Robock, *Brazil's Developing Northeast*, pp. 12-15.

13. Nilson Holanda, *O PND e o Desenvolvimento do Nordeste* (Fortaleza: Banco do Nordeste do Brasil, 1973), p. 12.

14. Rubens Vaz da Costa, *Desenvolvimento Regional: Balanço de uma Década,* Presentation at the Seminário Ação Sudene 74, Campinas, São Paulo, August 11, 1973.

6

The Economy: Trends, Structure, and Prospects

The traditional classification of developed and less developed (or developing) countries is not appropriate for describing the economic position of Brazil. As of the mid-1970s Brazil could be characterized more accurately as an economy in transition. If its development drive can be sustained, Brazil will be one of the few countries to close the "development gap" and join the select company of industrialized market economies.

Some regions of Brazil, such as the São Paulo industrial area, have reached economic levels comparable to those in many advanced economies. Rapid growth has also resulted in major structural changes and a significant degree of modernization in a number of economic sectors. Yet, for Brazil as a whole, the gap between its economic welfare levels and those in the advanced countries is still large. Brazil has wide regional variations in levels of economic welfare and many difficult economic problems still to resolve before it can join the ranks of the economically developed nations.

By 1974 Brazil's gross domestic product had reached an estimated total of US$74.3 billion (in 1972 prices). Per-capita gross domestic product (GDP) for its 104 million people averaged about US$715. In total size Brazil is the tenth largest economy of the world, surpassed only by the United States and Canada in the Western Hemisphere; by the Soviet Union, West Germany, France, the United Kingdom, and Italy in Europe; and by Japan and Mainland China in Asia. On a per-capita basis Brazil ranks only about fortieth among countries with a population of one million or more. Within South America, Brazil's per-capita income is still below those of Argentina and Venezuela and in about the same range as those of Chile, Uruguay, and Mexico.[a]

Population Trends

Population trends in Brazil have been described as a population explosion. The

[a]Note: The GDP data presented here is significantly higher than previous estimates. It is based on a revision of Brazil's national accounts published in September 1974 in *Sistema de Contas Nacionais: 1949 e 1959-1970 a 1973* (Rio de Janeiro: Fundação Getúlio Vargas, Instituto Brasileiro de Economia, September 1974). The revised data are in Cruzeiros and have been converted at an exchange rate of Cr$5.90 to US$1.00. The official explanation for the large increase in the estimates is that the 1970 census permitted the revised estimates to be much more comprehensive.

The rankings are the author's own estimates based on 1974 data for Brazil and 1972 data from the latest *World Bank Atlas* published in 1974.

annual rate of increase from 1960 to 1970 was 2.9 percent. This was a slight decline from the annual rate of 3.05 percent for the 1950-60 decade. A dramatization of the explosive nature of Brazil's population trends is that, if recent rates of increase continue, the country's population by the year 2050 will be close to 1 billion people.[1]

The population explosion has had at least five negative effects on economic growth. First is the purely arithmetic effect on the growth of per-capita income. The higher the rate of population increase, the lower the rate of increase in per-capita income. A second effect is on social infrastructure. The need to invest in housing, water supply, sewage facilities, etc. absorbs capital that otherwise might be available for directly productive activities such as manufacturing and agriculture. Third, rapid population growth has affected the age composition of the population. The 1970 census shows that 42.5 percent of the population was less than 15 years of age. Largely because of the age factor, only 31 percent of the population is in the labor force, compared with more than 40 percent in developed countries and over 50 percent in Japan. Per-capita income in Japan represents one person gainfully employed and one inactive or dependent person, whereas Brazil has 2.2 dependent persons to share the income of one person gainfully employed.

A fourth effect is the relatively large number of persons entering the labor force and for whom employment needs to be created. A related effect touches on the distribution of income. The poor, who have the largest number of children, are least able to provide advanced education for their children. With lower levels of education, the children of the poor are likely to get the lower income jobs, and a vicious income-distribution circle continues.

The last aspect is the population distribution between rural and urban areas and among regions. Urbanization has been strikingly rapid during the last 30 years. In 1940 only one-third of Brazil's population lived in urban areas. By 1970, 56 percent of the people were in urban areas. By 1980 two-thirds of the population will be urban and only one-third rural.

Brazil has also been undergoing major regional shifts in its population, mainly due to interregional migrations. From 1940 to 1970 the share of total population residing in the Northeast declined from 35 to 30 percent in spite of a relatively high birth rate. The South increased its share over the 1940-70 period from 14 to 18 percent. The Central West also had relative gains. The share of the North remained stable, between 3 and 4 percent. In the Southeast the region as a whole more or less maintained its share, but within the region the share of the state of Minas Gerais declined while that of the state of São Paulo gained.

The Changing Structure of
Economic Activity

The industrialization drive of the post-World War II period has drastically changed the structure of Brazil's economy in a pattern similar to those that evolved in other countries during their process of development.[2] In 1950 Brazil was predominantly an agricultural country with the agricultural sector accounting for 24 percent of the net domestic product compared with 22 percent for industry. By 1973, as shown in Table 6-1, industry's share of net domestic product (NDP) had expanded to 31 percent or double the contribution of agriculture. In the United States, by contrast, the comparable shares in 1973 were 33 percent for industry and only 3 percent for agriculture.

The structure of the labor force changed less dramatically. Agriculture still remains the dominant source of employment although its share declined from 60 to 44 percent over the 1950-70 period. (This contrasts sharply with the United States, where only 4 percent of total employment is in agriculture.) Industry increased its share of the labor force, but larger gains occurred in the service sector.

Manufacturing

Manufacturing accounts for 72 percent of national income generated in the industrial sector and a somewhat lesser share of total industrial employment (Table 6-2). Over the last two decades real output in manufacturing has more than tripled. Consumer hard goods, capital equipment, and chemical industries were the leaders in this rapid industrialization. Their share of value added in manufacturing increased from 15 percent in 1949 to 42.5 percent in 1971 (Table 6-3). Some absolute numbers illustrate the scale of manufacturing operations. In 1974 Brazil produced 858,000 motor vehicles (placing Brazil in eighth place in world production), 1,341,000 television sets, 2.7 million radios, slightly more than 1 million refrigerators, and 13.6 million tons of cement. In capital equipment, domestic production can supply more than 70 percent of the fixed investment needs of the country, including advanced industrial machinery and heavy electrical equipment. In the field of chemical products Brazil

Table 6-1
Brazil: Changing Structure of Net Domestic Product and Employment

Sector	Net Domestic Product (Factor Cost)				Labor Force		
	1950	1960	1970	1973	1950	1960	1970
	(Percentage Distribution)						
Agriculture	24	19	17	15	60	54	44
Industry[a]	22	27	29	31	14	13	18
Services	54	54	54	54	26	33	38
Total	100	100	100	100	100	100	100

Source: Fundação Getúlio Vargas and IBGE.
[a]Includes manufacturing, mining, construction, and public utilities other than transportation and communications.

Table 6-2
Brazil: Composition of Industrial Sector

	(Percentage Distribution)		
	Industrial Sector		
	Gross Domestic Income		Labor Force
Subsector	1970	1973	1970
Manufacturing	72.8	72.0	61.2
Public utilities	6.3	6.6	3.0
Civil construction	18.3	19.5	32.5
Minerals production	2.6	1.9	3.3
	100.0	100.0	100.0

Source: Fundação Getúlio Vargas, Instituto Brasileiro de Economia, *Sistema de Contas Nacionais* (Rio de Janeiro: Setembro de 1974) Quadro 8; IBGE, *Censo Demográfico Brasil 1970* (1973), vol. 1, pp. 76-77.

Table 6-3
Brazil: Gross Value Added in Manufacturing Industries, 1949, 1959, 1971

| | Percentage Distribution | | |
Industries	1949	1959	1971
Traditional Consumer Goods	57.4	41.3	31.1
Textiles	20.2	12.0	9.0
Clothing and footwear	4.5	3.6	2.5
Food	20.5	16.5	11.7
Other	12.2	9.2	7.9
Intermediate Goods	35.0	41.9	45.2
Nonmetallic mineral	7.3	6.6	6.1
Metallurgical	9.7	11.8	10.4
Chemicals	9.3	13.3	20.5
Other	8.7	10.2	8.2
Capital Goods & Consumer Durables	5.7	15.1	22.0
Mechanical	2.1	3.5	5.5
Electrical	1.7	4.0	6.3
Transport	1.9	7.6	10.2
Other	1.9	1.7	1.7
Total	100.0	100.0	100.0

Source: Based on IBGE, *Produção Industrial* for 1949 and 1971 data and on Fundação IBGE, *Censo Industrial: 1970* for 1959 data.

produced 154,000 tons of synthetic rubber in 1974, and its refineries processed almost 290 million barrels of crude petroleum.

The intermediate goods industries have been the second most dynamic component of Brazil's manufacturing sector. In many of these industries, recent rapid growth has caused demand to outstrip local supply, particularly in nonferrous metals and iron and steel. In petrochemicals, fertilizer, and copper, Brazil only recently began to establish domestic production capacity. Steel-ingot production reached a level of 7.5 million tons in 1974. The newly created government holding company, SIDERBRAS, expects to expand steel output to 26 million tons by 1980. If this goal is achieved, Brazil will advance from 17th to 6th largest steel-producing country in the world.

The slowest growing industries have been the traditional consumer-goods industries in the fields of textiles, clothing, footwear, and food products. Some dynamism has been achieved since the late 1960s through an expansion in exports, particularly in the shoe industry. This sector still accounts for almost one-third of the value added in manufacturing and an even larger share of employment. The textile industry has attracted some foreign investment, mostly Japanese, in the last few years and may become internationally competitive.

An important and politically sensitive characteristic of Brazil's industrialization has been a pattern of heavy regional concentration. In 1970, 58 percent of total value added was produced in the state of São Paulo, 16 percent in the new state of Rio de Janeiro, and 6 percent in the state of Minas Gerais, which is also important in mining. Only 20 percent of the total value added in manufacturing was located outside this three-state area. Furthermore, the trend until about 1970 had been increasing concentration in the state of São Paulo. The principal lagging area was the Northeast region of nine states with about one-third of Brazil's population. Over two decades from 1949 to 1970 the Northeast's share of value added in manufacturing dropped from 10 to 6 percent.

Future Prospects in Manufacturing

What are Brazil's prospects for continued rapid expansion in manufacturing? In the recent past the nation benefited from favorable external circumstances that have been changing. A sustained world economic boom was interrupted in the mid-1970s. Brazil's exports of manufactured goods, when only a small share of the demand in foreign markets, did not provoke serious protectionist reactions. But Brazil's export success changed this. In 1974, for example, the United States imposed special countervailing duties on shoe imports, claiming that they were subsidized through special tax rebates. Brazil formerly had access to foreign raw materials such as petroleum at prices that were cheap compared to subsequently escalated prices in international commodity markets. Relative stability in the world monetary system facilitated large financial flows in the form of loans and direct investments until the 1970s, when the Bretton Woods system was abandoned.

Uncertainties have also arisen over the ability of Brazil's domestic market to continue absorbing the increasing output of consumer durable goods such as automobiles and electrical appliances. Can the annual increases of 20 percent in automobile production achieved over the 1969-74 period be maintained in view of the higher cost of gasoline, chronic parking problems in urban centers, a tightening of consumer credit to combat the resurgence of strong new inflationary pressures, and the revived interest being given to public investment in railroads and other forms of mass transportation?

With many favorable external and domestic conditions in process of radical change, can Brazil maintain its industrialization momentum? Brazilians have an optimistic scenario in which the manufacturing sector will continue to expand rapidly. They have identified specific product areas in which growth prospects appear promising. They have adopted strategies that encourage state enterprises, local companies, and multinational firms to undertake the expansion opportunities that have been identified. They are also achieving considerable regional decentralization.

As an offset to a probable slowdown in the expansion of consumer durables, the promising product areas are heavy capital equipment to supply domestic needs; basic intermediate products such as steel, aluminum, copper, and fertilizer where rapid growth has caused local demand to outstrip local supplies; additional processing of agriculture, forestry, and mineral products for export; and nondurable consumer goods (such as shoes and processed foods) for domestic consumption and export.

Imports of capital equipment have increased strikingly since 1965 both in absolute value and in the share they represent of total imports. In 1973 capital-equipment imports totalled US$2.8 billion and accounted for 46 percent of Brazil's total import bill. The domestic capital-goods industry did not keep pace with the industrial boom for a number of reasons. In some cases the Brazilian market was too small to justify the establishment of an economic-size plant. The capital-goods industry also had little tariff protection. With a liberal administration of the "Law of Similars," almost any made-to-order capital equipment was, in practice, exempted from tariffs.

Another deterring factor was the inability of local industry to compete with foreign firms in offering attractive credit terms to purchasers of capital equipment. However, this obstacle is being reduced by the capital-goods financing fund FINAME. The size of the market constraint has also become less important, and a change in policy can give the capital-goods industry more tariff protection.

The expansion of industries that produce basic and intermediate products is already under way, in many cases as joint ventures of state enterprises and foreign firms. In steel production Brazil launched in 1972 a US$1.3 billion steel expansion program to double by about 1976 the output of three government-controlled steel companies. Brazil secured external financing for half the capital requirements from the World Bank, the Inter-American Development Bank, and from nine steel-equipment producing countries. More recently a completely new steel plant that will produce 3 million tons has been started at Tubarão in the state of Espírito Santo as a joint venture between Japanese and Italian enterprises and the Brazilian government. Two-thirds of the output of this plant will be exported. An even larger project is a proposed integrated steel plant to be located near the Amazon region (in Itaqui, Maranhão) that will initially produce 4 million tons and later expand to 16 million tons, or more than double Brazil's 1974 total steel production. The Nippon Steel Company has been engaged to do the planning, and two-thirds of the output of the plant, if built, will be for export, with preference for the Japanese market.

In aluminum, copper, fertilizer, and petrochemicals a series of expansion projects are also under way, while others are in advanced stages of planning and negotiation. For example, Brazil is planning a US$1 billion industrial complex to produce 60,000 tons of aluminum annually based on the recently discovered bauxite deposits in the Trombeta river area of the Amazon basin.

In giving priority to further processing of agricultural, forestry, and mineral resources, Brazil is following the same path that virtually all raw-material exporting countries and regions within countries have tried to follow. Such efforts, however, are frequently frustrated in the case of many products by the economic advantages of locating the advanced processing stages near the market. Coffee, for example, is generally roasted and packed near the market in order to provide consumers with a product that is fresh and that has been adjusted to the varying tastes in different markets. Cocoa beans are normally converted into chocolate products at market locations because the finished products are more perishable than the raw materials. Aluminum refineries are most economically located near sources of low-cost electric power rather than where the bauxite is mined. In contrast, pulp and paper can be most economically produced near the sources of raw materials because of the large weight loss that occurs in processing and the consequent savings in transportation costs. Normally, less than half the weight of pulpwood is embodied in manufactured pulp and paper.

Throughout Latin America, as well as in Brazil, there was not much advance in the area of transformation of raw materials, except for petroleum refining, during the decade of the 1960s.[3] Yet, Brazil's future prospects appear promising because of several new factors. One of these is the favorable situation of forest products. With rapidly increasing supplies from reforestation, with a growing world shortage of forest resources, and with location economies favoring the production of pulp and paper and other forest products near the sources of raw materials, Brazil's aspirations are likely to be realized and are, in fact, already on their way toward fulfillment. One example is the US$400 million Aracruz reforestation and pulp and paper mill project in the state of Espírito Santo scheduled to begin producing in early 1978 mainly for export. As another example, Cia. Vale do Rio Doce and a consortium of Japanese companies initiated in 1973 a US$1 billion project to plant eucalyptus trees in a 1 million-acre area in the state of Espírito Santo and to construct a pulp mill in Minas Gerais.

In food processing Brazil has sharply increased its exports of soluble coffee and, to a lesser extent, processed meat and orange juice. In the minerals field Brazil is already pelletizing iron ore and in the future expects to export much of its iron ore in the form of steel. One of the new factors that underlies the joint steel ventures with the Japanese is Japan's need to expand production facilities in other countries because of space shortages and environmental problems at home.

The traditional consumer industries are expected to continue their expansion to supply growing domestic and export demands. Domestically Brazil recognizes that middle-income urban classes provide the main market for consumer goods. *If* Brazil adopts effective measures for redistribution of income and *if* it succeeds in accelerating economic expansion in the agricultural sector, particularly for supplying world markets, the domestic market in rural areas and among lower income classes for many types of consumer goods could grow significantly. The hopes for continued expansion of manufactured goods for export depend on policies that are encouraging multinational companies to do more sourcing for their global systems in Brazil, and on a campaign to enlarge trade with mainland China, the Soviet Union, and other Socialist countries through bilateral trading agreements and direct exports. In the past East-West trade has been minimal.

To achieve the revised industrialization-strategy goals, Brazil relies on the enterprise of government-controlled companies, the multinationals, and local firms. The state enterprises have unusual access to capital through reinvested profits, through foreign loans guaranteed by the government, and through sharing equity and other financing needs with foreign partners. The state enterprises are not under pressure for immediate profitability in large new expansions and can be guided by long-term perspectives. They are already playing a major role in achieving future industrialization goals.

The multinationals are also implementing Brazil's goal of more manufactured exports. Two sets of special incentives have been highly effective. The export incentives, which can reduce costs from 15 to 30 percent, make Brazilian production competitive with other sourcing alternatives. Even more important to some multinationals has been a policy of allowing companies a duty-free import quota of $1 for each $3 of exports. The effect of this incentive is to give partial exemption to the automobile companies, for example, from the local content requirement that 90 percent of the finished product must be produced nationally. By earning import privileges through exporting, an automobile company can broaden its product line in Brazil by importing a range of engine sizes that could not be economically produced in Brazil on a small scale.

The Ford Motor Company invested more than US$100 million in a plant that in 1974 began producing small four-cylinder engines for export. At the same time it has been able to increase its competitive position in the local market by offering an imported V-8 engine option for its Brazilian-produced Maverick car. In order to maintain their competitive position in the Brazilian market other automobile companies are following the same pattern. In June 1974 General Motors announced that it was investing about US$150 million in a new diesel motor plant that will export to Africa and other South American countries in addition to supplying the local market.

The indigenous private sector has had difficulties in accompanying the rapid rates of growth in manufacturing, particularly in expanding equity capital. In recognition of this problem the National Development Bank created in 1974 three new subsidiaries, IBRASA, EMBRAMEC, and FIBAS, to provide financial and other assistance to the private sector. IBRASA will operate as an investment bank to strengthen the capital structure of Brazilian companies. EMBRAMEC will be specifically concerned with the implanting and expansion of capital-equipment companies, and FIBAS will finance and participate in enterprises producing basic intermediate goods. In order to avoid a further spread of state-controlled companies, the plan provides that where the government participates by buying equities, it will give first option for repurchase of these securities to owners of the companies or sell its shares at some future time in the securities markets.

A trend toward decentralization of industry appears to be taking place, but statistics are not yet available to verify this perception. The states of Paraná and Santa Catarina are receiving a substantial amount of new industry, which is an overflow from the adjacent São Paulo area where chronic conditions of industrial congestion and critical labor shortages have developed.

A special incentive program (popularly referred to as 34/18 after the section of the authorizing law) whereby a company can reduce its federal income tax liability by 50 percent through investing in approved projects located in the Northeast and the Amazon has been available since 1961 for the Northeast and since 1965 for the Amazon. The regional decentralization incentive has been supplemented by special access to long-term loans from the regional development banks, by additional incentives such as exemption from federal income taxes, tariff exemptions or reductions on imported equipment and components, and by a variety of incentives given by state and local governments.

The initial response to these incentives was slow, but the pace accelerated after the political crisis of the mid-1960s.[4] An outstanding example has been in Salvador, Bahia, where the new Aratú industrial district, which occupies an area of 168 square miles, has attracted almost 180 new industrial projects as of 1974 with a total investment of about US$560 million. More than 60 of these plants are in operation producing synthetic fibers, urea pellets, diesel engines, large buses, shoes, and textiles. In addition, Bahia also has a petrochemical complex in process of development that, as of mid-1974, had nine major plants in operation, four under construction, and eighteen projects approved. By 1980 the complex should represent an investment on the order of US$2 billion.

In the Manaus area in the center of the Amazon basin another special program has been operating to encourage industrialization. The area has been designated a free trade zone, where raw materials and components can be imported free of tariffs for further processing. From 1968 through 1974, under this program, Manaus attracted more than 100 new factories that assemble color TV sets, calculators, radios, stereo sets, watches, jewelry, and optical products, and that process raw materials such as lumber. Because of the great distance of Manaus from the major markets of the South, much of the industrial development is to manufacture products that have high value in relation to their weight so that the cost of transporting goods by air cargo can be justified.

The prospects for continued rapid expansion of the manufacturing sector appear to be promising based on the revised strategies and their implementation. A drastic slowdown in the growth of foreign economies can, of course, undermine the effort. The negative impact of external forces, however, will be limited by Brazil's heavy emphasis on producing for the expanding domestic market. But within the domestic market other industries will have to accelerate their growth rate to compensate for a probable slowdown in automobile production and a possible one in the manufacturing of inputs for housing construction.

Minerals and Petroleum

The extractive minerals and petroleum industries in 1973 accounted for 1.9 percent of domestic income generated in the industrial sector compared with 2.6 percent in 1970. As a source of employment the relative importance of this subsector was slightly greater, accounting for 3.3 percent of industrial employment in 1970 (Table 6-2). In spite of the attention given to the minerals sector, the value of mineral production in Brazil is still small. In fact, the total value of mineral production in 1973 of about US$700 million was equalled by the value of one agricultural crop—soybeans.

Of the many minerals produced by Brazil, the major sources of expansion over recent decades have been iron ore, manganese ore, petroleum, and natural gas. Coal production has been expanding, but poor quality coal has limited its importance. Other minerals being produced include chrome ore, lead, nickel, copper, bauxite, phosphate rock, dolomite, talc, gypsum, and salt.

The mining of iron ore has increased dramatically and consistently since the end of World War II (Figure 6-1) due to greater exports and the development of a national steel industry. In 1974 Brazil's iron-ore production exceeded 60 million metric tons, which ranked it as the fifth largest world producer. Iron-ore exports from current production and stocks totalled 59 million tons in the same year.

The exploitation of Brazil's manganese-ore resources has been relatively

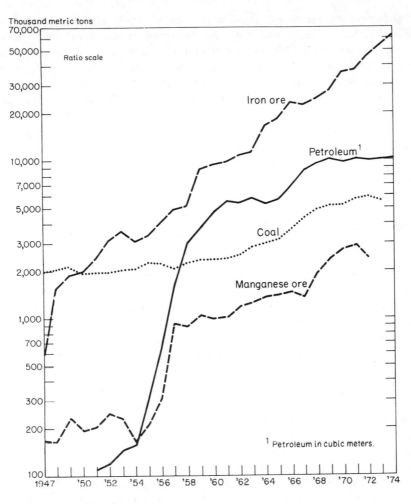

Source: *Anuário Estatístico do Brasil.*

Figure 6-1. Brazil: Mineral and Petroleum Production, 1947-74.

noncontroversial compared to the nationalistic controversies that have occurred in the case of petroleum and iron ore. A Brazilian industrial pioneer, Augusto A.T. Antunes, secured the rights to develop the manganese-ore deposits in Amapá in the Amazon region shortly after the end of World War II. He succeeded in interesting the Bethlehem Steel Company in a joint venture and securing financing from the U.S. Export-Import Bank. After large investments were made, including the construction of a 200-kilometer railroad to Porto Santana on the Amazon, the project began exporting in 1957 at an annual level of 670,000 tons that had expanded to 1.5 million tons by 1974.

Production of petroleum began in the early 1950s with the creation of PETROBRÁS as a state monopoly and increased rapidly until about 1960. Output then levelled off for several years but once again expanded sharply from 1965 to 1969 (Figure 6-1). Petroleum consumption, however, has increased much more rapidly than has domestic production. Brazil raised its production from 146,000 to 174,000 barrels a day from 1967 to 1974. In 1967 production of 146,000 barrels a day supplied 38 percent of domestic needs, but in 1974 daily production of 180,000 barrels supplied only 20 percent. Dependence on imports for 75 percent of petroleum requirements and soaring petroleum prices make the question of future prospects for expanding Brazilian petroleum production a crucial development issue.

**Future Prospects in Mining
and Petroleum**

The prospects for continued expansion of mineral production in Brazil are bright. CVRD has a joint venture with the U.S. Steel Corporation in the Amazon region to develop the newly discovered Serra dos Carajás iron-ore deposits. Output from the new mine is expected to reach 12 million tons in 1979, rising to about 45 million tons in 1985. Another Brazilian company, Minerações Brasileiras Reunidas (MBR), a joint venture of Brazilian and foreign private interests, started exporting iron ore in 1974. In its initial phase MBR will produce 12 million tons a year, and the company expects to raise production eventually to 25 million tons a year. The ongoing expansions in iron ore, manganese ore, and bauxite plus a large new project for copper that is in the planning phase clearly indicate that Brazil is still in an early stage in developing its mineral resources potential.

In petroleum Brazil's future prospects are uncertain. PETROBRÁS is investing massive sums in exploration, refining, domestic distribution facilities, and in tankers. In exploration PETROBRÁS has been concentrating on off-shore drilling and has commenced some production in the continental-shelf area. Its recent offshore discoveries, including the Garoupa field near Campos are quite promising and may stabilize or even reduce Brazil's dependence on oil imports after 1977. Brazil has also constructed a pilot plant in the South to produce petroleum from oil shale. Although the economic feasibility of converting shale to oil is still highly uncertain, some experts believe that Brazil's oil shale reserves, which rank among the largest in the world, can be economically exploited given the new high prices for crude petroleum. In addition, through its subsidiary BRASPETRO, PETROBRÁS has entered into exploration agreements with state and private oil companies in various foreign countries such as Iraq, Egypt, Algiers, the Malagasy Republic, Iran, Libya, and Colombia as a means of assuring long-term foreign sources of petroleum.

Given the urgency of the petroleum situation, public and official debate began in 1974 on allowing the international oil companies to undertake exploration in Brazil under highly restrictive contractual arrangements. The fact that Brazil's state oil enterprise has become an international oil company and is exploring in other countries greatly weakens the nationalistic justification for barring foreign companies from petroleum exploration in Brazil. The radical changes in the international petroleum picture during the early 1970s, with new high levels of petroleum prices and greatly increased bargaining power for oil producing countries due to the success of the Organization of Petroleum Exporting Countries (OPEC), suggest that Brazil could work out mutually agreeable arrangements with the private companies.

Construction

The construction area has become a dynamic sector of economic activity. It accounted for almost 20 percent of income in the industrial sector in 1973 and 33 percent of total industrial employment as of the 1970 decennial census (Table 6-2). It is apparent from the increased government expenditures for highway, port, and road construction, from the phenomenal expansion of housing construction, and from the construction needs generated by the boom in manufacturing and commerce that this area has contributed significantly to Brazil's development drive, particularly in employment. Unfortunately, virtually no overall statistics are available to describe the trends in this sector. As one quantitative measure, the decennial population census shows that the number of workers in construction increased from about 600,000 in 1960 to 1,700,000 in 1970.

The future prospects for construction will, of course, depend on the realization of expansion plans in other sectors. With the great deficits that still exist in housing, water and sewage facilities, and in transport, it is likely that construction activities in these areas will be substantial if public investment funds continue to be available.

Public Utilities

Primarily through expansion rather than expropriation of foreign-owned companies, the state and federally controlled electric-power companies now account for about 80 percent of the generating capacity and slightly more than half of the distribution. From 1950 to 1974 Brazil's installed generating capacity increased from about 2 million to 17.4 million kilowatts, about 80 percent of which is hydroelectric.

In 1977 Brazil's first nuclear power plant is scheduled to come into operation with a capacity of 600,000 kilowatts, and a second unit of 1,200,000 kilowatts at the same site (Angra dos Reis) is scheduled for completion by 1982. The plants will use enriched uranium as fuel. Although Brazil's undeveloped hydro-electric potential is huge, the construction of nuclear plants has been justified in terms of economies that would result from balancing the interconnected system in the South-Central region. The capital-intensive nuclear plants will operate at a high load factor for the base rather than peak load of the regional system. Another justification is the felt need for Brazilians to get experience in the operation of nuclear power plants. Brazil is rich in thorium, but uranium reserves are not yet well established. Extensive uranium prospecting is being carried out by the government and there is considerable optimism that future discoveries will permit Brazil to produce at least enough for its own needs.

For the future the most dramatic event in the field of electric power is the joint project between Brazil and Paraguay for construction of the Itaipu project on the Paraná river. The Itaipu project will have a capacity of 11.7 million kilowatts and is planned to come into production about 1982. It will be the largest hydroelectric project in the world. This single project will equal Brazil's total installed capacity in 1970.

The public utilities sector includes government companies supplying water and sewage services for urban areas. In 1970 about half of Brazil's urban houses were not connected to water systems, and 70 percent were not connected to sewage systems. Through its National Sanitation Plan developed in 1970 the National Housing Bank has set as goals for 1980 the provision of water supplies to 80 percent of the urban population and the construction of sewage systems to serve 50 percent of the population.[5] These goals are supported by the vast financial resources of the Bank and are being implemented through financial and technical assistance to local public enterprises.

Agriculture

The agricultural sector accounted for 17 percent of the nation's net domestic product in 1970. As a source of employment, agriculture has much greater relative importance. In 1970 the 13 million workers in agriculture constituted 44 percent of Brazil's total labor force (Table 6-1). Real output in agriculture has on the whole grown more rapidly than population and sufficiently to meet the increased demand resulting from rising income.[6] Historically, Brazil has been self-sufficient in food except for wheat, which is still imported in substantial quantities. Consistent with growth patterns in developing and developed countries, agriculture has expanded less rapidly than the industrial sector both as a contributor to GDP and as a source of employment.

The components of the agricultural sector are crops, livestock, and extractive agriculture. Livestock has been the fastest growing component, accounting in

1969 for 31 percent of total GDP generated in agriculture as compared with 22 percent in 1950 (Table 6-4). Extractive agriculture such as rubber, carnauba wax, and tropical oil-bearing seeds has lagged and accounted for only 4 percent of the agricultural sector GDP in 1969 compared with 7 percent in 1950. Crops still remained dominant, although their share of the total declined to 65 percent in 1969 compared with 71 percent in 1950.

The regional distribution of agricultural output is shown in Table 6-5. The major share of Brazil's agricultural production, measured by value, originates in the Center-South regions. Only 25 percent comes from the North and Northeast.[7]

Among the agricultural crops coffee normally ranks first in value of production and of exports. In 1974, however, both sugar and soybeans outpaced coffee as earners of foreign exchange. Other agricultural exports ranked in order of export value in 1974 were cacao, corn, castor oil, sisal, tobacco, and cotton. The principal food crops that supply the domestic market are corn, rice, manioc, beans, wheat, potatoes, bananas, and oranges.

Wheat and soybeans have expanded rapidly since the late 1960s (Table 6-6). The state of Rio Grande do Sul in the extreme South is the main producing area. The output of bananas and oranges has also increased significantly, and Brazil

Table 6-4

Brazil: Agricultural Output—Principal Components by Gross Value

	(Percentage Distribution)		
	1950	1960	1969
Crops	70.8	66.1	65.4
Livestock	21.9	28.2	30.7
Extractive	7.3	5.7	3.9
	100.0	100.0	100.0

Source: Getúlio Vargas Foundation, National Accounts Center, *National Accounts of Brazil, Volume II*, 1972. Tables 38, 39, and 40.

Table 6-5

Brazil: Regional Distribution of Agricultural Output, 1969

	(Percentage Distribution)			
	Crops	Livestock	Extractive	Total
Center-South	73	80	12	73
North-Northeast	27	20	88	27
	100	100	100	100

Source: Ministry of Agriculture.

Table 6-6
Brazil: Principal Agricultural Crops

	Value of Production 1972 (Current Cr$)	Growth Rate of Annual Physical Production 1967-72
Export Products	(Millions)	(Percent)
Coffee	3,841(1971)	0.7
Cotton	2,561	6.7
Sugar cane	2,357	2.0
Soybeans	1,316	34.8
Oranges	744	7.9
Cocoa	523	5.0
Tobacco	464	0.0
Castor seed	330	0.3
Food Crops		
Rice	3,929	2.3
Corn	3,767	3.4
Beans	2,130	1.6
Manioc	2,128	1.4
Bananas	1,033	n.a.
Wheat	574	15.7
Potatoes	543	0.7

Source: Ministry of Agriculture (EAGRI/SUPLAN).

has become a major exporter of canned orange juice. In response to favorable world market conditions and after many years of relatively slow growth, Brazil's production of sugar began to spurt in the early 1970s to the point that Brazil has become the world's largest producer of cane sugar, exceeding Cuba's production by about 40 percent. Increased cotton production and exports have also been stimulated by world market conditions. Coffee production suffered in the 1970s from frost and the effects of a new coffee rust, but the 1974-75 crop was large, and extensive new plantings should expand output in future years.

The expansion of livestock production has been led by the poultry industry as shown in Table 6-7.

Extractive agriculture, or the gathering of wild products, has not been a growth component of Brazilian agriculture. Most of the products come from the North and the Northeast: rubber and brazilnuts from the Amazon, babaçu from the palm groves in Maranhão, and carnauba wax and cashew nuts mainly from Ceará. Mate tea, however, is grown in the South.

Although world market prices have risen for many tropical oils, waxes, and nuts, the possibilities for expanding output are generally limited by the nature of

Table 6-7
Brazil: Livestock Production Trends

| | Annual Average | | Percent Increase |
	1964-65	1969-70	1969-70 Over 1964-65
	(Thousand Tons Carcass Weight)		
Beef and veal	1,467	1,650	12
Pork	587	660	12
Sheep	32	34	6
Goat	21	22	5
Poultry	17	74	335
Total	2,124	2,440	15

Source: Anuário Estatístico do Brasil.

the production process and the increasing cost of labor. The case of rubber is typical. When rubber is grown wild, the income of a rubber-tapper is limited by the fact that he is not able to collect more than 400 kilos of rubber a year. On a rubber plantation his output could increase to 8,000 kilos annually. Large-scale production of babaçu oil and processed products has not been achieved due to unsolved technical problems in harvesting, in breaking the hard shells of the nuts, and in shipping the kernels. Unlike most of the extractive products, cashew nuts can be grown commercially and some progress has been made in this direction. Nevertheless, in Brazil as in other countries there is a clear tendency in the development process for the relative importance of extractive activities to decline.

In spite of the steady growth in agricultural production, it is considered a neglected development sector. As one observer has concluded, although "Brazilian agriculture has performed remarkably well (over the 1960-70 decade), that it did so is far more attributable to the enterprise and energy of Brazilian farmers than to the sporadic and crisis-oriented agricultural policies of the government."[8]

Future Prospects in Agriculture

Three major problems exist in the agricultural sector. One has been declining coffee production. A second is the continuing low level of technology used in agriculture and the resulting low levels of productivity per hectare. The third is rural poverty, particularly in the Northeast where agriculture is characterized by small farming units and surplus labor.

Brazil has long been the largest coffee producer in the world. Consequently, the wide variations in world prices and demand for coffee have had a disturbing impact on Brazil's agricultural sector. While the International Coffee Agreement has made possible greater stability in the market, a more serious problem is the vulnerability of the crop to frost, drought and, more recently, the devastating coffee-rust disease.

In 1965-66 Brazilian coffee production reached the enormous total of almost 38 million bags, virtually half the world's total output. Since 1970 output has fluctuated from a low of 11 million bags in 1970-71, following a disastrous frost, to a high of 26.5 million bags in 1974-75. With steadily growing domestic consumption, less than half of 1973 exports of 20 million bags came from current production and the remainder from a reduction in the stockpile. The 1974 exports of 13 million bags, however, were comfortably supplied out of current production.

Brazil has used ambitious measures to reverse the declining trend in production. The government, through the Brazilian Coffee Institute (IBC), has improved production incentives by reducing the government "take," through foreign exchange controls, from coffee exports and by promoting new plantings through credit and other incentives. In 1975 because of "soft" coffee prices, the foreign exchange "take" was reduced to zero and export subsidies were being considered. Another program is aimed at shifting production away from Paraná, where the crop is most vulnerable to frost. At the same time the threat of the coffee rust disease is being countered with plans for planting more resistant varieties.

The planned increase in production will take time to achieve. If successful, production is expected to reach a level of about 32 million bags by 1980. The high prices in the early 1970s of alternative crops such as soybeans, grains, sugar, and cocoa may discourage coffee plantings which take from five to seven years to come into production. Consequently, coffee stocks promise to be abnormally thin during the next few years, even if no unusual climatic conditions occur.

The steady increase in agricultural output over recent decades has been due almost entirely to increased acreages brought into production rather than to increased productivity. While this pattern has been a matter of great concern to development officials, it is also a basis for considerable optimism. It means that the possibilities for future expansion through use of modern agricultural methods are tremendous. As only one example of low productivity in Brazil, corn production over the 1965-71 period averaged 1,290 kg/hectare compared with 4,740 for Canada, 4,100 for the United States, and 3,280 for Italy.

With the vast amount of land available in Brazil, production increases from the addition of land in cultivation rather than from increased productivity can continue for some time. Given the high cost of fertilizer, farm machinery, insecticides, etc.—in part due to protective barriers erected to encourage domestic industries and to transport costs—farmers have been following the most economic path for expanding production,[9] to the distress of many government officials for whom low productivity levels create an uncomfortable feeling of being underdeveloped.

As its latest strategy for tackling the problem of poverty in agriculture, the government in 1970 and 1972 preempted half of the tax-incentive resources previously available for industrial development in the North and Northeast to be used for new programs that emphasize labor mobility and special agricultural development programs for the Northeast.

The principal new programs are PROTERRA—the Northeast agricultural development program—and PIN—the national integration program. The former is designed to modernize Northeast agriculture and the latter to promote resettlement in promising agricultural areas of the Amazon region. PROTERRA's components include a modest land redistribution program and a large-scale credit program for the acquisition of agricultural machinery, fertilizer, and other modern agricultural inputs as well as land. PIN's components include the financing of two Amazon highways and the colonization of areas adjacent to these roads. Still another program is directed toward reorganizing the inefficient Northeast sugar industry.

More recently, in late 1973 and early 1974, the government announced additional programs to encourage agri-industries and to undertake comprehensive and integrated development of selected subareas in the Northeast and Amazon regions. Together, the new programs are intended to ease agricultural underemployment in the Northeast by removing workers from this area to new agricultural frontiers particularly in the Amazon, by increasing the productivity of farm workers remaining in the region, and by creating nonfarm job opportunities in agri-industries.

The reorientation of the government's agricultural development program for the Northeast has escalated significantly the scale of resources available for tackling the problem. However, the government colonization schemes along the new Amazon highway are proceeding at a much slower pace than originally forecast. The programs have been only loosely coordinated with the numerous agencies involved, and serious questions have been raised by development experts as to whether the various programs to modernize Northeast agriculture can be truly effective in alleviating rural poverty.[10] In 1975, however, new organizations were created in the Northeast, the North, and the Central West to coordinate agricultural programs in the respective regions.

For certain important agricultural products of the Northeast—beans, manioc, and rice—future domestic demand is not expected to increase rapidly because of the changing consumption patterns characteristic of higher income.[11] But even where the market is not a serious limitation, successful measures to increase productivity will decrease the need for rural labor. The problem then becomes one of how fast nonfarm employment can provide jobs for workers moving out of agriculture, and whether marginal farm workers, particularly those who are not young, can be trained for nonagricultural employment.

The most promising future for the agricultural sector is an expansion of exports. In a world where food shortages seem to be ever more serious, Brazil occupies the unique position of having almost infinite possibilities for expanding agricultural output through adding acreage and through increasing productivity. As one of a number of programs to encourage exports, Brazil has adopted a special "export corridors" program, which aims to increase significantly exports of coarse grains, soybeans, and meat produced in the Center-South. The program has made large amounts of investment funds available for improvement of port and railway facilities with the objective of reducing high local-transport costs so that Brazil's products can be more competitive in world markets.

World market conditions for meat exports have become highly attractive, and Brazil has favorable conditions for meat production, particularly cattle. Nevertheless, the prospects for beef becoming a major export are not bright. Domestic demand has expanded sharply due to increases in per capita income and in population. With continued rapid economic growth, it is unlikely that beef production can expand fast enough to keep up with domestic demand and still leave important exportable surpluses.

There are two traditional cattle farming areas in Brazil: Rio Grande do Sul, which borders on Uruguay and Argentina and, like the pampas further south, has mainly European breeds; and the area of São Paulo and Minas Gerais, which like most of Brazil has almost exclusively Zebu strains of cattle. The national herd is estimated at about 85 million head with 2 million in the North, 18 million in the Northeast, 28 million in the Southeast, 19 million in the South, and 18 million in the Central West, mainly Mato Grosso and Goiás.

The performance of cattle raising in Mato Grosso, Pará, Goiás, and subsequently Amazônia will probably be the most interesting feature of the sector in coming years. One large project, Agropecuária Suia Missu, on the Mato Grosso property of the Italian Liquigas group, is developing a 678,000-hectare ranch that will have an initial output of 15,000 tons of beef per year in 1975, rising to 90,000 tons in 1977. Since Amazônia with 59 percent of Brazil's area is virtually virgin territory for cattle, officials are estimating that by 1985 the Amazon will have the largest herds of cattle. SUDAM, the regional development agency for the Amazon, has already approved 315 cattle projects, including a project of Volkswagen that involves 140,000 hectares.

In 1972, for the first time, Brazil became the world's largest producer of cane sugar (6 million tons) with about one-third of domestic production going for export. High prices in world markets during 1973 and 1974 stimulated further increases in production to a level of 7.2 million tons. If Brazil can secure new sugar markets in the Soviet Union and mainland China and retain its large exports to the United States, the country's sugar production may reach 10 million tons a year by the end of the decade.

Brazil is one of the few countries in the world that can expand sugar production rapidly without additional investment and thus exploit the prospective world shortage. Twenty percent of the cane crop now goes for alternative uses, such as alcoholic beverages, and could be shifted to export if the world market permits. With world prices above 7 cents per pound, Brazilian sugar exports can be competitive.

Soybeans became the new hot item of the agricultural sector in the late 1960s and early 1970s. Production, mainly in southern Brazil, grew from 206,000 tons in 1960 to 1.5 million tons in 1970-71, 5 million in 1972-73, and an estimated harvest of 7.5 million in 1973-74. With a decline in soybean prices from the exceptionally high levels in 1973-74, however, future export earnings will probably decrease.

The large-scale switch to soya, even by cattle farmers in Rio Grande do Sul, has inevitably weakened production of less attractive crops. In Paraná, for example, some coffee plantations have been dug up in favor of soya. An interesting feature of soybean production in Brazil is its link to wheat through summer/winter rotation in the southern states.

Another important export crop has been cocoa. A 1974 World Bank study concluded that the long-term market outlook for cocoa is promising, and that increased production will not contribute to an excessive supply which would reduce world prices below the maximum price currently set in the International Cocoa Agreement. However, cocoa production is expanding rapidly in African countries, and Brazil will have to compete with the African producers.

Forestry and Fishing

With forest reserves second in area only to those of the Soviet Union and comprising half the entire reserves of Latin America, Brazil's 350 million hectares of forest lands are a potential resource that as yet has been little used.[12] The well-known problems of lack of infrastructure, hundreds of species unknown to commerce, and low volumes of commercial wood per hectare are only a few of the reasons for the slow pace of forest development.

Of Brazil's total forests, 273 million hectares are located in the Amazon Valley where, except for river margins, the forests are still largely virgin. Traditionally, the forest products industry has been based in South-Central Brazil, especially in the Paraná pine forests. Continual heavy overcutting has reduced this resource to such a low level that within the next ten years it will occupy only a minor position in the overall forest economy. Even more severe overcutting has occurred in Minas Gerais for charcoal production.

Faced with a discouraging deforesting situation, the government in 1965 extended the "34/18" tax incentive program to include reforestation investments as one of the options for deductions from income-tax liability. This action was followed in 1967 by the creation of the Brazilian Institute for Forest Development (IBDF) as an autonomous agency linked to the Ministry of

Agriculture to promote the increased and rational development of forest resources.

The tax-incentive policy dramatically reversed the long-term trend toward depletion of usable forest resources. In 1972 an estimated 600 million trees were planted compared with the estimated annual cut of 350 million, and the plantings have been increasing rapidly each year. Most of the reforestation is being done in the South-Central region where the pulp and paper industry was initially located and in the states of Espírito Santo and Minas Gerais. In 1968 less than 2 percent of the total "34/18" funds went to the forestry option; by 1972 this share had increased to 24 percent. It has been conservatively estimated that more reforestation was undertaken during the first six years of the tax-incentive program than in all of the years since the discovery of Brazil nearly five centuries ago.

There is, of course, a time lag between the planting and the harvesting of forest resources. Consequently, the forests as a source of exports were still limited in 1974 to traditional pine exports from the south valued at only US$86 million. However, Brazil is planning on becoming a major exporter of pulp and paper by 1980.

The huge reforestation and pulp manufacturing projects of Aracruz and the Japanese and CVRD in the states of Espírito Santo and Minas Gerais are yet to come into production. Also, a vast project of the American shipping tycoon, Daniel Ludwig, has recently been initiated in the state of Pará in the Amazon region. The Ludwig project comprises 1.5 million hectares, an estate the size of Holland, on which 28 million gmalina trees, a particularly suitable pulping tree from Southeast Asia, have been planted. The project expects to have 90 million trees eventually.

Investments in fishery projects were also included during the mid-1960s as an option in the federal tax-exemption program, but a significant expansion in fishery activity remains more a promise than a reality. Brazil has been an exporter of lobster and shrimp for a number of years, but the value of these exports totalled only US$26 million in 1973 compared with a high of US$46 million in 1966. Most of the fishing supplies the domestic market. The principal problem, as reported by one fishing company, is the limited amount of oceanographic research available on the location and movement patterns of fish along the coastal areas. A number of newly established fishing and fish-processing companies have encountered difficulties because of raw-material shortages.

Notes

1. Rubens Vaz da Costa, *Demographic Explosion in the World and in Brazil* (Rio de Janeiro: Banco Nacional de Habitação, 1973). Lecture given at the Brazilian War College, August 1973.

2. See Hollis B. Chenery, "Targets for Development," in *The Widening Gap*, edited by Barbara Ward, Lenore d'Anjou, and J.D. Runnalls (New York: Columbia University Press, 1971).

3. Organization of American States, *Latin America's Development and the Alliance for Progress*(Washington: 1973), p. 227.

4. See David Edwin Goodman and Roberto Cavalcanti de Albuquerque, *Incentivos à Industrialização e Desenvolvimento do Nordeste* (Rio de Janeiro: IPEA/INPES, 1974).

5. Rubens Vaz da Costa, *Urban Growth: The Foundation of Economic Development* (Rio de Janeiro: Banco Nacional de Habitação, 1973).

6. Three excellent sources on Brazil's agriculture are Rui Miller Paiva, Salomão Schattan, and Claus F. Trench de Freitas, *Brazil's Agricultural Sector* (São Paulo: 1973); William H. Nicholls, "The Brazilian Agriculture Economy: Recent Performance and Policy," in *Brazil in the Sixties*, edited by Riordan Roett (Nashville: Vanderbilt University Press, 1972), pp. 147-84; and G. Edward Schuh, *The Agricultural Development of Brazil* (New York: Praeger Publishers, 1970).

7. For detailed regional analysis see Rui Miller Paiva, Schattan, and de Freitas, *Brazil's Agricultural Sector*, pp. 277-428.

8. Nicholls, "The Brazilian Agriculture Economy," pp. 182-83.

9. See Rui Miller Paiva, Schattan, and de Freitas, *Brazil's Agricultural Sector*, pp. 18-27 on "Practical Criteria for Judging the Behavior of the Agricultural Sector."

10. See George F. Patrick, *Desenvolvimento Agrícola do Nordeste* (Rio de Janeiro: IPEA, 1972), p. 264; Rui Miller Paiva, *Elementos Básicos de uma Política em Favor da Agricultura Brasileira* (Rio de Janeiro: IPEA, 1974), p. 33.

11. *Brazil: Projeções da Demanda e da Oferta de Produtos Agrícolas 1975 e 1980* (Versão Preliminar) (Rio de Janeiro: Fundação Getúlio Vargas, Centro de Estudos Agrícolas, March 1974).

12. Rui Miller Paiva, Schattan, and de Freitas, *Brazil's Agricultural Sector*, pp. 200-205.

7 The Economy: Foreign Trade and Finance

Increasing exports are frequently mentioned in the economic development literature as a necessary dynamic factor for development. Yet, if one were to study Brazil's economic trends up to the late 1960s exclusively on the basis of exports (Figure 7-1), one would think of a semicolonial economy, lacking dynamism and possessing an extremely rigid structure. In Brazil's case, however, the more important trend to study would be the changing composition of imports rather than exports. Starting in 1957, when the country's industrial development began to accelerate, imports of machinery, vehicles and equipment, petroleum products, etc. declined as local substitute industries appeared.

The stagnation in exports was important, nevertheless, as a constraint on imports and can be explained by historical factors. For a long time during the post-World War II period both the government and the private sector showed a singular lack of interest in exports. ". . . those who favored industrialization, an increasing number in the country, tended to condemn any excessive preoccupation with exports. For them, an exporting frame of mind signified a propensity towards accepting the old colonial scheme of a growth based on foreign sales."[1] Behind this argument there existed the more concrete concern that the success of a policy to seek foreign markets, while improving the country's foreign-exchange situation, would reduce the margin of protection enjoyed by manufacturing activities. This attitude made aggressive export policy impossible and even compromised traditional exports since the government refused to adapt the export-exchange rate to the increase in domestic costs resulting from inflation.

The lack of interest by the private sector has been described as follows: "In the same years during which it revealed considerable inventiveness in promoting the country's industrialization under particularly adverse circumstances, in the export sector it maintained the traditional patterns of behavior, waiting with arms folded for foreign enterprises to come and buy products; without making any attempt to establish a chain of marketing centers overseas.[2]

Given the lack of governmental export-promotion policies and of private-sector interest in exports, the level of exports remained more or less stationary for almost two decades up to about 1967-68, except for a sharp rise in 1951-52 stimulated by the Korean conflict. Nor did the structure of exports change significantly. A few products dominated, with coffee continuing to be the principal export product. The export of manufactured goods, however, increased over the 1950s and early 1960s, but the amounts were small and not of great significance.

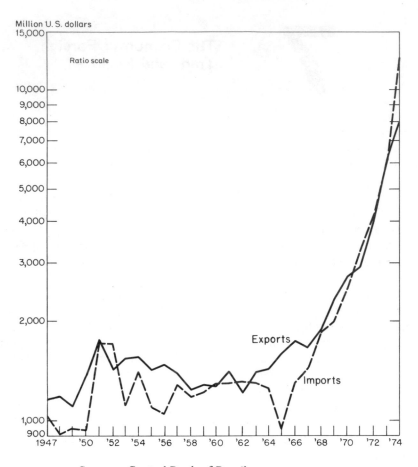

Source: Central Bank of Brazil.

Figure 7-1. Brazil: Exports and Imports 1947-74.

Pressures for an aggressive export program began to increase sharply during the early 1960s, as the capability of Brazil's newly established industries to compete in foreign markets grew. As happened in the case of Japan,[3] industries originally established to supply the domestic market developed adequate size and efficiency to evolve naturally toward export orientation. When the government introduced the flexible minidevaluation exchange-rate policy in 1968 and established attractive export incentives, both domestic and foreign industries responded with great vigor.[4] Aided further by favorable external factors, exports, which had stagnated for so many years, began to rise in 1968 and increased more than fourfold in the six-year period from 1968 to 1974 (Table 7-1).

Table 7-1
Brazil: Foreign Trade, 1964-74

(US$ Millions)

	Exports						Imports				
		Primary Products						Intermediate Goods & Raw Materials			
Year	Total Value (FOB)	Total	Coffee	Semimanu-fac-tured	Manu-fac-tured	Other	Total Value	Petro-leum	Other	Capital Goods	Consumer Goods & Others
1964	1,430	1,221	760	115	89	5	1,086	180	480	300	126
1965	1,595	1,301	707	154	130	11	941	154	338	229	220
1966	1,741	1,444	764	141	152	4	1,303	166	443	405	289
1967	1,654	1,302	705	147	196	9	1,441	154	420	515	352
1968	1,881	1,492	775	178	203	9	1,855	204	573	704	374
1969	2,311	1,796	813	211	284	20	1,993	204	609	823	357
1970	2,739	2,049	939	249	416	25	2,507	236	798	1,074	399
1971	2,904	1,988	773	241	581	94	3,245	327	1,140	1,241	537
1972	3,991	2,725	989	310	912	45	4,235	409	1,407	1,750	669
1973	6,199	4,097	1,244	476	1,465	161	6,192	711	1,923	2,599	959
1974	7,968	4,810	877	631	2,332	195	12,530	2,760	n.a.	n.a.	n.a.

Source: Central Bank of Brazil; CACEX.
n.a. = not available.

113

What was the composition of this growth? Manufactured goods were the most dynamic component increasing more than elevenfold from about US$200 million in 1968 to US$2.3 billion in 1974 (Table 7-1). Even more spectacular was the increases in exports of soybeans and soybean products from US$25 million in 1968 to almost US$900 million in 1974 and of sugar exports from US$102 million in 1968 to almost US$1.3 billion in 1974. Increases in iron-ore exports, raw beef (although exports were held back to reduce domestic prices), and semiprocessed goods such as castor oil, lumber, cocoa butter, peanut oil, and carnauba wax, also contributed to Brazil's export performance.

The range of processed and manufactured exports has been steadily expanding. It includes such products, in order of value in 1974, as transportation equipment, electrical machinery and appliances, industrial machinery, textiles, soluble coffee, footwear, office machines, processed beef, cotton yarn, steel mill products, and orange juice. About half of Brazil's manufactured exports, excluding processed agricultural products, have been going to the Latin America Free Trade Area (LAFTA). But even in the LAFTA countries Brazilian exports constitute no more than 1 percent of the total demand for manufactured imports. Most of the remainder of Brazil's manufactured exports go to the United States and the European Community (EC).

In terms of total exports the leading market for Brazil has become the EC. The share of Brazil's total exports going to the EC increased from 33 to 36 percent from 1967-68 to 1972-73 (Table 7-2). Over the same period the relative share going to the United States dropped from 33 to 21 percent. In absolute value exports to the United States increased by 75 percent, whereas those to the EC increased by 222 percent. Other expanding markets for Brazil have been Japan, other Asian countries, the Middle East, and Africa. In general, Brazil's export drive has resulted both in large increases and in a diversification of its export markets.

In the case of manufactured exports the multinational companies have played an important role. Some in the pharmaceutical and communications equipment fields have been exporting to Europe from their Brazilian plants. Others, including the automobile companies, have been exporting to their home-country markets. Volkswagen, for example, exports motors and shift gears to West Germany and motor vehicles to South and Central America, Africa, the Middle East, and even Europe.

A number of multinational companies are exporting to members of LAFTA under the program for complementarity agreements. These agreements are intended to permit the establishment of economic-size operations by allowing producers of specific products in one LAFTA country to export free of tariffs to the other countries, thereby enlarging the market. Under such agreements some of the multinational companies exporting from Brazil to other LAFTA countries are Olivetti, Mercedes Benz, Pirelli, IBM, Burroughs, Singer, and Bosch.[5]

Table 7-2
Brazil: Direction of Trade, 1967-68, 1972-73 and 1974

Importing Area	(Percentage Distribution)		
	Average 1967-68	Average 1972-73	1974
European Community (9 countries)	32.6	35.7	34.2
United States	33.2	20.7	21.5
Latin American Free Trade Area (10 countries including Andean Bloc)	9.8	9.6	11.9
Japan	3.3	5.7	5.7
Soviet Bloc (7 countries)	6.2	5.5	4.1
European Free Trade Area (5 countries)	5.3	5.2	3.7
Asia and Oceania (excluding Japan)	1.1	4.6	⎫
Spain	1.9	3.5	⎬ 18.9
Africa	1.6	2.5	⎪
Middle East	1.0	2.0	⎭
Rest of World	4.0	5.0	
	100.0	100.0	100.0

Source: *Boletim do Banco Central do Brasil*, December 1974, pp. 144-51, and March 1975, p. 193.

Imports

The trends and composition of Brazil's imports are a direct reflection of the industrialization drive. From 1948 to 1961 imports of finished products, particularly consumer durables, declined as domestic production expanded. At the same time imports of raw materials, particularly fuels and lubricants, expanded to support the industrialization momentum.[6]

Most recently imports have been predominantly of capital equipment and intermediate goods. In 1973 such capital goods as machinery, electrical materials, and transport equipment constituted 42 percent of total imports. Intermediate goods such as fertilizer, chemicals, ferrous and nonferrous metals, accounted for another 31 percent. Consumer goods, including wheat and other food imports, were next in importance with 16 percent, followed by petroleum with 11 percent.[7] In total value imports increased by 46 percent from 1972 to 1973, reflecting both increased quantities and higher prices.

Brazil's import situation moved into a new and critical phase in 1974. The value of imports more than doubled over the previous year rising from US$6.2 billion to US$12.5 billion, and Brazil's trade balance registered a deficit of

US$4.5 billion as compared with a modest surplus in 1973. About half of the increased expenditure for imports occurred in two categories: petroleum and iron and steel (Table 7-3). In the case of petroleum the major element was increased international prices. In the case of iron and steel both increased quantities and higher prices were involved, as was also true for the other categories—machinery, nonferrous metals, fertilizer and organic chemicals—that registered extraordinary increases.

The Brazilian strategy to meet the new import crisis has both short- and long range components. The short-term response has been a series of measures to curtail imports through reestablishing some customs duties, requiring Brazilian importers to pay cash for many import items, and reducing purchases abroad by the government and its agencies.[8] A longer range solution is expected from an accelerated drive to substitute local production for imported goods. The discovery of new offshore oil fields is expected to reduce petroleum import requirements. The major expansion of Brazil's steel industry that is well underway will largely relieve Brazil of the annual outlay of US$1.5 billion for iron and steel products that occurred in 1974. As Brazil expands its fertilizer and petrochemical industries and exploits its newly discovered reserves of nonferrous metals, there will be further import substitution in these categories. Still another important contribution is expected from the program to expand the local production of capital goods.

Balance of Payments and External Debt

Brazil's growth strategy of relying heavily on external capital to help finance the investment needs of economic expansion is reflected in its balance-of-payments

Table 7-3
Brazilian Imports (FOB), 1973-74

	(US $ Millions)		
Import Category	1973	1974	Increase 1973/1974
Petroleum	711	2,760	288%
Iron and steel	493	1,535	211%
Machinery & equipment	2,143	3,108	45%
Nonferrous metals	288	593	106%
Fertilizer	139	403	191%
Organic chemicals	372	635	71%
Subtotal	4,146	9,034	117%
Other	2,046	3,497	71%
Total	6,192	12,531	102%

Source: Banco Central do Brasil, *Relatório Anual 1974*, March 1975, p. 212.

and external-debt situation. In spite of an impressive performance in expanding and diversifying exports, except for 1973, Brazil persistently has had a negative trade balance (Table 7-4), which reached an unprecedented level in 1974. An additional heavy burden on the balance of payments has been in the service category, which mainly reflects (a) financial outflows in the form of interest, profit remittances, and royalty and technical assistance fees; (b) transportation costs; and (c) foreign travel. The net result has been a continuing deficit in the current account reaching a level of US$6.9 billion in 1974.

The current account deficits, until 1974, were more than offset by inflows of foreign direct investment and by foreign borrowing. Net direct foreign investment not including either reinvestments or substantial inflows in the form of intracompany loans, expanded from less than US$100 million annually in 1968 to US$1 billion in 1974. Foreign borrowing has been even more important as a balance-of-payments item. Brazil has increased its external debt from US$3.8 billion at the end of 1968 to US$17 billion at the end of 1974. It is significant

Table 7-4
Brazil's Balance of Payments, 1971-74

	(US$ Millions)			
Items	1971	1972	1973	1974
1. Trade balance FOB	−341	−244	7	−4,563
Exports	2,904	3,991	6,199	7,968
Imports	−3,245	−4,235	−6,192	−12,531
2. Services	−980	−1,250	−1,722	−2,313
Receipts	421	557	944	1,612
Payments[a]	−1,401	−1,807	−2,666	−3,925
3. Unilateral transfers	14	5	27	0
Receipts	95	104	128	137
Payments	81	99	101	137
4. Current-account balance	−1,307	−1,489	−1,688	−6,876
5. Net capital flow[a]	1,846	3,492	3,512	5,894
6. Errors and omissions	−9	436	355	−67
7. Balance (4 + 5 + 6)	530	2,439	2,179	−1,049
8. Financing operations[b]	−530	−2,439	−2,179	1,049
IMF accounts	−47	−70	−33	−8
Short-term assets	−635	−2,569	−2,798	899
Short-term liabilities	152	200	658	158
Monetary gold	−−	−−	−6	−−

Source: *Annual Report 1974, Banco Central do Brasil* (March 1975), p. 190.
[a]Excludes reinvestments.
[b]Assets: a minus means increase, a plus means decrease. Liabilities: a minus means decrease, a plus means increase.

that the capital inflows have not been used simply to balance annual international transactions. Brazil also increased its foreign-exchange reserves from a skimpy US$257 million in 1968 to an impressive US$6.6 billion in 1973. The unusually large balance-of-payments deficit in 1974, however, forced Brazil to reduce its reserves to US$5.6 billion by the end of that year.

The important feature of Brazil's balance-of-payments situation is that it has been largely guided by deliberate policies rather than by uncontrollable exogenous forces. With a growing self-confidence in its ability to manage its external financial arrangements, Brazil has not been timid about borrowing from foreign financial sources to the maximum extent considered necessary to support its development goals.

The principal financial authorities do not subscribe to the protestant ethic that it is sinful to be in debt nor do they intend to follow the advice of Shakespeare's Polonius, "Neither a borrower nor a lender be." Accepting Alexander Hamilton's view that "A national debt, if it is not excessive, is a national blessing," Brazil has concentrated on improving the structure of the external debt in terms of appropriately spaced and longer maturities and on continuously evaluating its capacity to meet external-debt obligations under different sets of unfavorable contingencies.

As of 1973 the nation's international credit had become so strong that the government was able to insist on a ten-year minimum maturity for foreign loans. And as Paulo H. Pereira Lira, the president of the Central Bank, observed in emphasizing how the impossible can become possible, "If anyone had suggested 5 years ago that this would be possible, they would have been put in a crazy house."[9]

The Brazilian debt strategy, in addition to improving the profile of its external obligations, has been to increase reserves faster than debt. In 1968 foreign reserves equalled only 9 percent of the outstanding foreign debt, compared with 50 percent at the end of 1973. But the strategy could not be implemented in 1974 when the ratio of reserves to foreign debt declined to 33 percent. As the minister of finance explained to the Congress in June 1974, "Even if Brazil did not receive a single centavo in foreign loans and foreign direct investments during a 12-month period, its foreign reserves would be more than sufficient to cover the deficit in current account and to make the amortization payments on foreign loans." And he added, "In reality, the Brazilian government does not intend to lower its foreign reserves—but it is clear that they represent a powerful insurance against a catastrophic emergency."[10]

Brazil's ability to meet its external obligations is one question, but its ability in the future to secure the quantity of external resources needed to maintain a high rate of growth is quite another. To achieve the latter goal, Brazil faces several difficult conditions. It must continue to increase its exports and to attract a high level of foreign investment. Also, it must be able to borrow large sums abroad on reasonable terms. The supply of loanable funds held by the oil producing countries has expanded manyfold. At the same time the demand for loans has also increased because a number of countries need to borrow to meet balance-of-payments deficits stemming from petroleum price increases. In September 1974, as a result of the changed situation in international financial markets, Brazil reduced the minimum repayment term required on foreign loans from ten to five years, and the tax on interest remittances from 25 to 5 percent.

Public Finance

In public finance Brazil's post-1964 accomplishments in improving tax performance through administrative reform, restructuring the tax system, controlling expenditures, developing a sophisticated system of deficit financing, and in using tax incentives in an imaginative and effective way are most impressive. As a result of a range of measures, the total tax burden levied by governments at the federal, state, and local levels (including social security taxes) increased from about 24 percent of gross domestic product (GDP) in 1965 to about 29 percent in 1968 and has remained at that level since, which means that tax revenues have kept up with the growth rate. On a comparative basis Brazil ranks near the top among the developing countries in taxes as a percentage of GDP and only slightly below the average tax ratio of the developed countries of Europe and North America.[11] A steady reduction in the cash-budget deficit of the central government from 4.2 percent of GDP in 1963 to 0.2 percent in 1972 (Table 7-5) has played a vital role in reducing the rate of inflation.

One indicator of the improvement in tax administration, which was accomplished with the aid of the U.S. Internal Revenue Service, is the number of income tax declarations filed. In 1965 tax evasion was a national pastime. Out of a population of 80 million, only about 350,000 individuals actually filed tax returns. By 1970 the number of returns filed had increased to 7 million and by 1974 to 11 million. Another indicator is that Brazil ranked first in "tax effort" among 45 developing countries studied by the International Monetary Fund. The index of tax effort relates actual tax collections to the taxable capacity of countries.[12]

On the expenditure side the central government had by 1974 eliminated its deficit while at the same time had increased substantially its revenue sharing with state and municipal governments. Excess civil-service employment was reduced through a program of severance payments. At the same time salaries of key civilian employees, especially technical personnel, and of military personnel have increased substantially in real terms. Subsidies to the airlines, shipping companies, and railroads for operating deficits have been sharply reduced. However, the railway network continues to require subsidies, which in 1974 amounted to about US$130 million.

A wide range of tax reforms was made over the 1964-67 period. The

Table 7-5
Brazil: Public Finances, Central Government, 1960-74

Year	Current Prices (Cr$ Millions)			Percent of Gross Domestic Product[a]		
	Revenues	Expenditures	Deficit	Revenues	Expenditures	Deficit
1960	220	296	76	8.0	10.8	2.8
1961	318	455	137	7.8	11.2	3.4
1962	498	779	281	7.5	11.8	4.3
1963	930	1,435	505	7.8	12.0	4.2
1964	1,889	2,637	748	8.2	11.4	3.2
1965	3,232	3,825	593	8.8	10.4	1.6
1966	5,910	6,496	586	11.0	12.1	1.1
1967	6,814	8,039	1,225	9.5	11.2	1.7
1968	10,275	11,502	1,227	10.4	11.6	1.2
1969	13,953	14,709	756	10.5	11.1	0.6
1970	19,194	19,932	738	9.3	9.6	0.3
1971	26,980	27,652	672	9.8	10.0	0.2
1972	37,738	38,254	516	10.5	10.7	0.2
1973	52,863	52,568	+295	11.1	11.0	+0.1
1974	76,810	72,928	+3,882	11.2	10.7	+0.5

Sources: *Boletim do Banco Central do Brasil*, June 1974, p. 76 for 1966-73 revenues and expenditures; *Conjuntura Econômica*, February 1975, p. 122 for 1974 data; Simonsen, *Brazil 2002*, p. 80 for 1960-65 revenues and expenditures data and for percent of GDP 1960-69.
[a]1970-74 calculation of percent of GDP based on revised GDP estimates of FCV published in September 1974.

government imposed stiff penalties on tax arrears, including a requirement that amounts due be corrected upward for inflation, and instituted withholding of taxes at the source. It transformed federal and state excise taxes from a turnover or cascade type to value-added taxes. The turnover tax was collected whenever goods moved between business firms. It encouraged the vertical integration of firms and discouraged specialization and economies of scale along horizontal lines. The shift to a value-added tax eliminated this bias.

The value-added tax on "industrialized products" produces the largest share of federal revenues, accounting for 36 percent of the total in 1974 compared with 25 percent collected from corporate and individual income taxes. The value-added tax is somewhat progressive in the sense that it exempts basic food products and has varying rates for different products—from 3 to 50 percent—of which the lowest are on consumer necessities and the highest on luxury goods such as whisky, cosmetics, jewelry, etc. Cigarettes carry a special tax of 200 percent and are the largest single commodity source of value-added taxes.

Given Brazil's extensive use of tax incentives, it may appear surprising that tax revenues have expanded so rapidly. In 1974 the government gave up the equivalent of 42 percent of the total income tax collected, or about 11 percent of total federal revenues, in the form of incentives for investment in regional and priority industry development programs. It granted the equivalent of another 9 percent of total federal revenues to approved industrial expansion projects in the form of exemption from import and value-added taxes.[13] Other tax deductions were allowed for investing in equity securities to stimulate the growth of capital markets. But even with this sizeable loss of tax income, total federal revenues were able to expand because of the rapid rate of economic growth and improved efficiency in tax administration.

In sum, the government has greatly improved its control over the fiscal system as a tool for managing the economy. It has increased revenues sufficiently to permit the government to enlarge its public investment role and to undertake social welfare programs. It has used the fiscal system as a highly effective incentive device to achieve development targets, and it has created a realization of the fact that taxes must be paid.

Banking and Capital Markets

The banking system has been crucial for the mobilization of domestic savings and for the control of the money supply. Although Brazil's banking system and capital markets are not yet fully equipped to meet the challenge, they have been steadily and significantly improved. Private sector credit has expanded enormously over the last decade, made possible in part by the turnaround of the public sector from a net claimant on banking system credit to a net supplier of monetary resources.

At the top of the financial pyramid stands the National Monetary Council, created at the end of 1964 to replace the old Monetary and Credit Authority (SUMOC). Headed by the minister of finance, the Council controls the nation's monetary policy through its supervision of the Central Bank and the Bank of Brazil. The financial system also includes private and state commercial banks, development banks, private investment banks, savings banks, the National Housing Bank (BNH), and a number of specialized agencies such as the Industrial Finance Fund (FINAME), real estate finance companies, insurance companies, and various capital-market institutions.

Commercial banks operate mainly in the field of short-term finance. During the high-inflation years of the 1950s and 1960s, commercial banks were often able to lend at effective annual interest rates of 50-60 percent and paid little attention to costs. The number of branches and personnel multiplied, and the banks became high-cost, inefficient operations. Since the late 1960s a principal goal of Brazilian monetary management has been to reduce interest rates. Efforts are also being made to reduce the cost of bank credit by encouraging mergers and the closing of uneconomical branches, although almost no bank branches have yet been closed.

The public sector dominates commercial banking. The government-controlled Bank of Brazil and commercial banks owned by the various states have grown rapidly and now account for the major share of deposits of the banking system. The Bank of Brazil acts both as a commercial and agricultural credit bank, among other roles, and as a major source of export credit. Most long-term financing also comes from official institutions, especially the National Economic Development Bank and the National Housing Bank.

Private investment banks have been playing an increased role in medium-term loans of one to two years. There are now over 40 private investment banks that specialize in industrial working capital financing, new share issue underwriting, and the management of mutual funds. They fund their operations by selling their acceptances and certificates of deposit on the open market and by borrowing abroad on behalf of local clients. Some 168 finance companies that formerly were a major source of industrial working capital presently concentrate on consumer finance, securing resources through the sale of bills of acceptance (letras de câmbio) to the public.

Government measures to promote private investment banks and to provide attractive returns to depositors through indexing savings accounts and other financial instruments clearly have been extremely successful in mobilizing private savings, although the system still needs improvement. The government has also moved to develop the market for equity capital. On the demand side it created a number of fiscal incentives for a firm to go public. On the supply side fiscal incentives for buying equity shares have been accompanied by a policy of dispersing ownership in government-controlled mixed enterprises and of distributing business profits to shareholders through stock splits and preferential subscription rights.

The incentive programs stimulated a fantastic boom in the Brazilian stock market, which began in 1966 and culminated in June 1971, when the average *real* capital gain on shares acquired a year earlier amounted to 427 percent. The number of shares traded daily on the Rio de Janeiro exchange increased from about 500,000 in 1965 to more than 11 million in 1971. The number of companies with shares traded on the Rio de Janeiro and São Paulo exchanges increased fourfold from 1968 to 1971.

But increased earnings of shares lagged behind the steep price rises, and a series of speculative excesses occurred in this immature market. The government belatedly adopted measures to discipline the market in mid-1971. A steady downturn brought the Rio de Janeiro index from a peak level of 4,908 in June 1971 to 1,641 in August 1972. Subsequently the market recovered to an index of 2,396 in February 1975, and it appears to have survived a major adjustment period that will permit it to play an important future role in the economy. New government controls have improved the system. Nevertheless, public confidence in stocks had not yet been restored by the mid-1970s. The demand for indexed government bonds and other fixed interest instruments continues strong, and real estate has again become a preferred area for speculative investments.

The idea that Brazil's security markets can be enlarged and strengthened by encouraging foreign investor participation has been discussed in Brazil for some time, and in 1975 the government took some first steps in this direction. Previously, foreigners have not been barred from purchasing Brazilian securities, but legal procedures for repatriating portfolio investment, similar to those available for foreign direct investment and foreign loans, did not exist. Brazil would like to have the increased funds and greater volume of market activity that foreign investors could bring. But it fears that an excessively large foreign component would increase the potential instability of its immature markets. Foreigners might overreact to future political and economic events in Brazil by massive withdrawals of investment funds. Consequently, Brazilian authorities are moving cautiously and trying to create safeguards that will limit inflows and repatriations.

Changes in monetary policies, reforms of existing institutions, the creation of new agencies, and other measures have massively improved the mobilization of private savings and the availability of credit to the private sector. Most importantly, monetary correction as applied to savings, coupled with the profit opportunities generated by rapid economic expansion, reduced the tendency of Brazilians to engage in capital flight. The cost of financial intermediation, however, is still high, and the domestic stock market remains in a nascent state.

Inflation

Historical studies suggest that the Brazilian economy has had a bias toward inflation since at least the beginning of the nineteenth century. According to one estimate, over the period from 1822 to 1913 prices increased at an average yearly rate of 3.4 percent.[14] From 1914 until the beginning of World War II, except for a short period during the depression of the 1930s, prices appear to have increased steadily at a higher rate—estimated at 7-8 percent annually. For more than a century Brazil experienced steady upward price trends, with some years of deflation but never a long period of falling prices.

The reasons for the historical bias toward inflation are not clear because historical quantitative data are unreliable, and historical economic research is still limited. The few available studies suggest that the inflation bias has been due to "a chronic tendency toward budgetary deficits,"[15] "limited increases in productivity," "monetary and fiscal mismanagement,"[16] periodic shortages in the supply of goods and services due to the inelasticity of agricultural production, internal transport difficulties, and the interruption of imported supplies by foreign wars and other conflicts.[17]

Brazil's inflation experience since 1939 has been better documented and analyzed. Between 1939 and 1946 prices rose 15 percent per year on the average—largely because of wartime supply difficulties and the inflationary impact of balance-of-payments surpluses. In 1947 and 1948 the increase in prices slowed, but in 1949 prices began again to rise. From then until 1958 the rate of inflation oscillated around an average of 16 percent a year, with no explosive tendency (Figure 7-2).

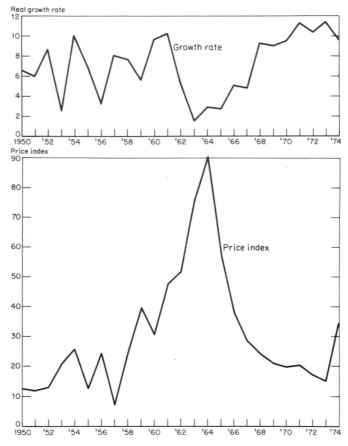

Source: Prices: *Conjuntura Econômica*, November 1972, p. 41 for 1947-61; *Conjuntura Econômica*, February 1975, for 1962-74 price data. *GNP Growth Rates*: Getulio Vargas Foundation, Center for National Accounts.

Note: The General Price Index is the weighted average of the Index of Wholesale Prices (weight 6), Cost of Living in the City of Rio de Janeiro (weight 3), Construction Cost in the city of Rio de Janeiro (weight 1).

Figure 7-2. Brazil: Price Trends and Real Growth Rates 1950-74 (Annual Rates of Increase).

Hyperinflation really began in 1959, when the general price index increased by 40 percent and then continued to accelerate for five years. During the austerity period of the new military government the annual inflation rate was reduced from the peak of 91 percent in 1964 to 28 percent in 1967. After the 1967 shift in development strategy toward rapid expansion Brazil was still able to reduce the inflation rate slowly to a level of 15 percent in 1973. The declining trend was reversed in early 1974, when the general price index soared by almost 35 percent.

The abrupt reversal in efforts to reduce inflation has been officially explained as a result of the pressure of sharp increases in international prices, particularly petroleum, and excessive monetary expansion. Although the pressure of international prices began to be strongly felt in 1973, much of the new inflationary pressure was repressed by the outgoing government in the hope of having a good official record before turning affairs over to the new administration in early 1974. With a legacy of substantial repressed inflation, the Geisel government took vigorous steps to reduce the inflation rate through a series of measures such as monetary and credit control and import restrictions on less essential goods. But within the ambiance of a worldwide, unprecedented wave of inflation, the challenge facing Brazil is formidable.

Postwar inflation in Brazil, according to the distinguished, conservative economist Eugenio Gudin was "fundamentally a by-product of the political evolution that has taken place in the past twenty or thirty years, as the old oligarchical type of government has been replaced by governments truly elected by the masses." Under popularly elected governments, according to Gudin, "The worth of a president or the governor of a state, apart from his political ability, is measured by what is called his 'capacity to accomplish' ... *no matter what the price* in terms of increased indebtedness, distortion, and disorganization of the country's economy. Seriously unbalanced budgets are a natural consequence, and the mainspring of inflation."[18] This view is supported by Mário Henrique Simonsen, who observed that, in Brazil, "There is no popular outcry against budgetary deficits" even though "the masses abhor continual price increases."[19]

Brazil's chronic inflation has also been explained as due to economic and social structural deficiencies and the inefficient operation of the system. The inflationary process maintains itself and is self-reinforcing, argues Professor Dias Leite, because Brazil is underdeveloped. "The desire to achieve progress and improve social welfare generates political conditions that induce an effort to expand consumption and investment simultaneously."[20] A low rate of savings, due to the country's poverty, "imposes in these conditions a resort to inflationary financing," and the process becomes circular with deficits in one period generating conditions for the continuation of inflation in the next period.

This "structuralist" view, offered by Professor Dias Leite during the 1965-66 debate on Brazil's stabilization strategy, coincides with the Gudin view in that it blames budgetary deficits for inflationary pressures. But the diagnosis differs in that it calls for remedial measures to change structures and increase efficiency, and it prescribes an environment of rapid growth as being necessary to achieve these anti-inflationary goals. In contrast, the Gudin view leads to the orthodox prescription of stronger fiscal and monetary discipline.

Thus, although they arrive at the conclusion by different paths, most scholars agree that the excess of federal expenditures over receipts has been the main cause of Brazilian inflation. The construction of Brasilia alone is estimated to have cost US$1 billion. Except for a major wage push in 1954, when Goulart was Minister of Labor in the Vargas administration, wage hikes over the postwar period more or less coincided with increases in the cost of living and were not a major cause of inflation.[21] Neither, until the 1973 international petroleum crisis, did the external sector act as an inflationary factor. The continuing balance-of-payments deficits, in fact, served as an escape valve for internal inflationary pressures.[22]

Federal deficit spending, financed by currency issued by the Bank of Brazil, provided the basis for a multiple expansion of the money supply and of private-sector spending.[23] Federal government expenditures rose from 8.4 percent of gross national product (GNP) in 1953 to 12.0 percent in 1963, while federal tax revenues remained fairly stable at about 8.0 percent of GNP. As a result the deficit grew from 0.4 percent of GNP in 1952 to 4.2 percent in 1963. The main causes of growing federal expenditures were government investment, swelling personnel payrolls, and accelerating subsidies to government enterprises. One reason for the deficits in the federal railway system was the inability of the enterprises, under prevailing government policies, to raise rates to meet increasing costs.

The hyperinflation of the 1962-64 period was due primarily to political instability. A brief attempt at price stabilization in 1963 was dropped for political reasons. In its efforts to obtain popular support, the government was unable to withstand the pressures of various groups. It increased the salaries of government civilian and military personnel as well as of employees in mixed enterprises. "With this, the inflation that had speeded up in the period 1958-61 became uncontrollable."[24]

To orthodox economists and businessmen, the most surprising feature of Brazilian inflation has been its coexistence, at least until 1961, with a high rate of economic growth. Between 1947 and 1961, notwithstanding the high rate of inflation, the country's real product rose at an average rate of almost 7 percent a year—one of the highest rates in the world at that time. More surprising, the growth rate rose to a new peak coincident with an acceleration of inflation during the period from 1958 through 1961 (Figure 7-2).

The recession from 1962 to 1964, when the inflation rate hit 90 percent a year, Simonsen says, "may restore some confidence in the traditional ideas" about the incompatibility of inflation and growth. But, he concludes, "it would be too simple a solution to pin the main blame for the economic recession of those years on the inflationary rate—even if we start from the sensible assumption that an 80 percent annual price increase is not a good prescription for development. Rather, it would be more reasonable to view the 1963 inflation and recession as having a common political origin."[25]

The Brazilian experience has undermined the conventional wisdom that inflation and growth are antithetical and has caused a growing number of scholars to reexamine the question. In analyzing the Brazilian experience, Alexandre Kafka concludes that growth in Brazil did not depend upon, and probably was hampered by, inflation.[26] And Simonsen cautions, "By no means should [my] observations be construed as enthusiasm for the country's inflationary experience. All that has been proved is that development may be consistent with prolonged inflation—but not that there is any positive correlation between the two phenomena."[27]

The opinion currently prevailing in Brazil is that an inflation rate of between 15 to 20 percent is "normal" for Brazil, and that any attempt to reduce the rate of inflation below this level would have undesirable trade-offs in terms of breaking the "rhythm" of development. Furthermore, with the comprehensive use of indexing, the official view is that most of the inequities of inflation have been neutralized. As Simonsen has observed, ". . . an inflation of 20 percent per year in the current Brazilian situation is less serious than an annual price increase of 5 or 6 percent in a country unprepared to live with inflation, that is, unprovided with monetary correction and a flexible exchange rate."[28]

The economic problem Brazil faced in 1975 was the need to reduce the inflation rate once again, perhaps to the 15-20 percent level. The political problem is that Brazilians at all levels—ranging from the slum dwellers to the families of high salaried business managers—were disturbed and became disaffected by the sharp rises in prices. It was easy and pleasant to adjust to the steady decline in prices up to 1973. But memories are short, and the 1974 rise was compared with price levels of the recent past rather than to the much higher inflation rates that prevailed when the military government took over in 1964.

Notes

1. *25 Years of the Brazilian Economy* (São Paulo: Banco Moreira Salles, S.A., 1967), p. 197.

2. Ibid., p. 198.

3. See William V. Rapp, "A Theory of Changing Patterns Under Economic Growth: Tested for Japan," *Yale Economic Essays* (Fall 1967), pp. 60-135.

4. See Carlos Von Doellinger, Hugo B. de Castro Faria and Leonardo Caserta Cavalcanti, *A Política Brasileira de Comércio Exterior e seus Efeitos: 1967-73* (Rio de Janeiro: IPEA, 1974).

5. Fernando Fajnzylber, *Estratégia Industrial e Empresas Internacionais* (Rio de Janeiro: IPEA, 1971), p. 184.

128

6. See "The Growth and Decline of Import Substitution in Brazil," *Economic Bulletin for Latin America*, March 1964, pp. 1-59.

7. *Annual Report 1973, Banco Central do Brasil* (March 1974), p. 222.

8. *Annual Report 1974, Banco Central do Brasil* (March 1975), pp. 213-14.

9. Personal interview, June 28, 1974.

10. Speech by Minister of Finance Mário Henrique Simonsen to the Brazilian Senate on June 26, 1974, pp. 14-15.

11. *IMF Survey*, June 3, 1974, p. 162.

12. Ibid., p. 162.

13. *Annual Report 1974, Banco Central do Brasil* (March 1975), pp. 153-54.

14. Eulalia Maria Lahmeyer Lobo et al., "Evolução dos Preços e do Padrão de Vida no Rio de Janeiro, 1820-1930—Resultados Preliminares," *Revista Brasileira de Economia*, October-December 1971.

15. Mário Henrique Simonsen, "Inflation and the Money and Capital Markets of Brazil," in *The Economy of Brazil*, edited by Howard S. Ellis (Berkeley: University of California Press, 1969), p. 134.

16. Carlos Manuel Peláez, "Long-Run Monetary Behavior and Institutions in an Underdeveloped Economy, 1869-1971," Unpublished Paper for the Sixth International Congress on Economic History, August 1974.

17. Mircea Buescu, *300 Anos de Inflação* (Rio de Janeiro: APEC, 1973), p. 225.

18. Eugenio Gudin, "The Chief Characteristics of the Postwar Economic Development of Brazil," in *The Economy of Brazil*, edited by Howard S. Ellis (Berkeley: University of California Press, 1969), pp. 13-18.

19. Mário Henrique Simonsen, "Brazilian Inflation: Postwar Experience and Outcome of 1964 Reforms" in *Economic Development Issues—Latin America* (New York: Committee for Economic Development, 1967), p. 272.

20. Antonio Dias Leite, *Caminhos do Desenvolvimento* (Rio de Janeiro: Zahar Editores, 1966), p. 93.

21. Gudin, "Chief Characteristics of the Postwar Economic Development of Brazil," p. 17. See also Albert Fishlow, "Some Reflections on Post-1964 Brazilian Economic Policy" in *Authoritarian Brazil* edited by Alfred Stepan (New Haven: Yale University Press, 1973), pp. 84-97. Donald E. Syvrud, *Foundations of Brazilian Economic Growth* (Stanford, California: Hoover Institution Press, 1974), p. 152 argues that public sector wage increases, particularly in transportation government enterprises, "played a major causal role in Brazilian inflation."

22. Simonsen, "Brazilian Inflation," pp. 276-77.

23. Syvrud, *Foundations*, p. 19.

24. *25 Years of the Brazilian Economy*, p. 256.

25. Simonsen, "Brazilian Inflation," p. 309-10.

26. Alexandre Kafka, "The Brazilian Stabilization Program, 1964-66," *The Journal of Political Economy*, August 1967, pp. 596-631.

27. Simonsen, "Brazilian Inflation," p. 315.

28. Mário Henrique Simonsen, *Brazil 2002* (Rio de Janeiro: APEC Editora, S.A., 1972), p. 91.

The Fruits of Economic Growth—Good or Bad?

How has rapid growth improved the economic and social welfare of individual Brazilians and their families? As all nations have come to appreciate, economic growth must not be an end in itself. Instead, it must be a means of improving the quality of life of a nation's people.

To evaluate economic and social welfare trends is not an easy task. There is the problem of dealing with many intangibles, and there are widely varying views of the appropriate standards to be used for such evaluations. One test is whether the economic and social welfare of an individual is currently better than it was for the same individual in the recent or more distant past. Another examines the *rates of improvement* among different social classes or income groups, and a third assesses the current status of individuals and their families against some hypothetical minimum welfare standard. The first approach assumes that the absolute gains of individuals and families are the most relevant. The second approach assumes that absolute gains are less important than the fact that some groups gained at a faster rate than others. The third approach evaluates the welfare levels of individuals and families against an implied minimum standard, rather than on what gains have been made. It is not surprising, therefore, that the same welfare trends in Brazil have been judged "good" by some evaluators and "bad" by others.

The principal areas for evaluating the economic and social welfare impact on the Brazilian people are employment, wages, social security, distribution of income, education, housing, urban development, and health. Although the data for such welfare trends are less comprehensive than the statistical measures of production and often controversial, they do provide considerable information on the fruits of economic growth and their distribution.

Employment

To what extent has economic growth in Brazil created new job opportunities? This is a key issue because Brazil's high rate of population increase has meant large numbers of new entrants to the labor force seeking employment. The annual labor force increment in 1970 was on the order of 780,000 workers. In addition, many new job opportunities in nonagricultural employment are needed for farm workers being made redundant by technological innovations to improve agricultural productivity. Still another element in the employment picture is

131

Brazil's desire to reduce the significant amount of underemployment that has existed in the past. Unemployment has always been far less important than underemployment in Brazil. With a limited unemployment compensation program available, workers cannot afford to be unemployed. Unskilled workers in particular take part-time or marginal jobs rather than declare themselves unemployed.

As is true for many countries, Brazilian employment statistics are weak for past periods. Although they have improved markedly, there is still a long time lag in securing current data. Nevertheless, the employment picture is available from the decennial census for each period up to 1970 and for 1972 from the most recent National Household Sample Survey (PNAD).

Over the 1950-60 and 1960-70 decades total employment in Brazil increased by an average annual rate of 2.8 and 2.7 percent, respectively (Table 8-1). The rate of increase over both periods was less than the rate of increase in population. These data, however, provide no information on changes within the long intercensal period. This is especially important for the 1960-70 period when Brazil went through hyperinflation, stabilization, and later resumption of growth. The National Household Sample Surveys show an average annual increase of 2.4 percent from 1968 to 1970 and 5.4 percent from 1970 to 1972.

For the early 1970s the broad picture of employment trends in Brazil pieced together from numerous sources indicates that the employment gains have finally begun to be substantial. The trends can be summarized as follows:

Total Employment. Productive employment opportunities have been increasing more rapidly than the total labor force.

Underemployment. Underemployment has decreased significantly. The National Household Sample Surveys show that the number of workers employed 40 hours or more per week increased to 79 percent in 1972 from 74 percent in 1968 (Table 8-2).

Unemployment. The picture is mixed. The Household Surveys show unemployment rates of 3.8 percent for 1968, 2.4 percent for 1970, and 3.1 percent for 1972. This compares with a rate of 7 percent in other Latin American countries.[1] Other more recent evidence indicates critical labor shortages in numerous skilled and unskilled occupational groups and in geographical areas such as São Paulo and Brasilia for all groups.

Types of Activities. Agricultural employment has provided relatively few new jobs—only a 0.7 percent annual increase over the 1960-70 decade—whereas industry and commerce have been the dynamic employment areas (Table 8-1). For unskilled workers construction jobs have been the most important source of new employment.

Table 8-1
Brazil: Sectoral Distribution of Labor Force, 1950-1970

Sector	Percent Distribution			Average Annual Rate of Increase		1960-70 Increment	
	1950	1960	1970	1950-60	1960-70	Number 000	Percent Distribution
Agriculture	59.9	53.7	44.2	1.7	0.7	908	13.2
Industry	13.7	13.1	17.8	2.4	5.9	2,301	33.4
(Manufacturing)	(7.5)[a]	(n.a.)	(7.9)	—	—		
(Mining & construction)	(n.a.)	(n.a.)	(9.9)	—	—		
Commerce	5.6	6.7	8.9	4.7	5.6	1,104	16.0
Services	9.8	12.1	11.0	5.0	1.8	529	7.7
Transport & communications	4.1	4.8	4.3	4.5	1.5	170	2.4
Social services	2.5	3.1	4.8	4.9	7.3	715	10.4
Public administration	3.0	2.9	3.9	2.6	5.7	493	7.1
Other	1.4	3.6	5.1	13.1	6.2	674	9.8
Total	100.0	100.0	100.0	2.8	2.7	—	100.0
(Number of Workers-000)	17,117	22,651	29,545	5,534	6,894	6,894	

Source: IBGE, Decennial Censuses.

n.a. = not available.

[a]1949.

Table 8-2
Brazil: Employment Trends 1968, 1970, 1972

Hours Worked per Week	Percent Distribution		
	1968	1970	1972
Temporarily absent	6.3	5.3	3.2
To 14 hours	1.5	0.7	0.8
15 to 34 hours	14.1	12.5	16.9
35 to 39 hours	3.7	2.6	
40 to 49 hours	46.4	53.4	49.6
50 or more hours	27.9	25.5	29.5
Unknown	0.1	--	--
Total	100.0	100.0	100.0
Total Workers (000)	28,222	29,570	32,779

Source: IBGE, National Household Sample Surveys.

Technology and Employment. Employment in manufacturing has expanded at a much lower rate than has manufacturing output. This pattern, which is characteristic of industrialization in virtually all countries, has stimulated considerable debate in Brazil as to whether the technologies being transferred to Brazil are too capital intensive and not sufficiently labor intensive. This issue is discussed further in Chapter 10.

Although it is hazardous to draw conclusions from personal observations, a traveler in Brazil during 1974 could see many specific indications of labor shortages ranging from "Help Wanted" signs outside factories in the northeastern Aratu industrial district of Salvador and in the São Paulo area to confirmed reports in Brasilia that construction companies were offering color television viewing in on-site shacks to attract unskilled workers.

Wages

Another key economic and social welfare measure is wages. To what degree, if any, have the wages of Brazilian workers increased in terms of real income? Although the limitations of Brazilian wage data make it difficult to offer a comprehensive and well-supported answer to this crucial question, for the late 1960s and early 1970s there is persuasive evidence that many, if not most, workers have had substantial gains in real wages.

The recent favorable wage trends are documented by special wage surveys initiated in the late 1960s, based on actual payments by employers, and by the broad data on total payrolls for all urban nongovernment workers available since 1968 and based on payments by employers to the Tenure Guaranty Fund (FGTS), discussed below in the section on social security.

If the question as to wage trends were answered simply on the basis of trends in the legal minimum wage, one would have to conclude that workers' wages have not kept up with inflation. And because the legal minimum wage data has been referred to so extensively, they warrant special attention. The tendency to rely on these data is understandable because they are easily accessible, cover all regions, are available as a historical series as far back as 1940, and because other satisfactory data have been scarce until the last few years. The legal minimum wage, however, is only a lower limit set by the government that has not been rigorously enforced. Even more important, it is not a direct measure of the actual wages received by a specific worker nor the wages being paid for a specific skill category.

When originally established in 1940, the minimum wage was intended to ensure the worker the minimum necessities of nutrition, clothing, and housing. Over time and particularly in the early 1950s the minimum wage became more of a standard basic wage for industry rather than a floor. More recently, with the lag in real purchasing power of the minimum wage, it returned to its original significance as a subsistence minimum. But even as a subsistence minimum the level is low. In May 1975 the legal minimum for the city of Rio de Janeiro was only about US$68 a month, and the lowest legal minimum for the country was about US$48.

From 1964, when the military government took over in Brazil, until 1970 the real value of the minimum wage declined by some 25 percent. The data for the city of Rio de Janeiro shown in Figure 8-1 is representative of the national trend. From 1970 to 1973 the real minimum wage recovered somewhat and then fell back again in 1974 because of the inflationary spurt in that year.

The loss in purchasing power of the legal minimum wage during the stabilization period of the military government has received a great deal of attention. What has been frequently overlooked is that the real value of the minimum wage has steadily eroded since 1957 (see Figure 8-1), including the 1961-64 years of the Goulart presidency.

The post-1964 loss in purchasing power of the legal minimum wage resulted from deliberate stabilization policies of the new government, as a result of which the workers had to bear a major share of the anti-inflation burden. The policy makers believed that wage adjustments would have to be moderated, or lagged, in order to reverse the runaway inflation situation that the new government inherited. They also believed that they could reduce inflation more rapidly than proved possible. Thus, the nominal wage adjustments granted during the austerity period and the beginning of the period of resumed growth led to a continued and significant decline in the real value of the legal minimum wage. The government policies changed after 1968, when minimum wage increases became proportional with prevailing inflation rates plus a small increase to reflect increased productivity.

The decline in the purchasing power of the legal minimum wage and its later partial recovery are not in dispute. A more important issue, however, is the

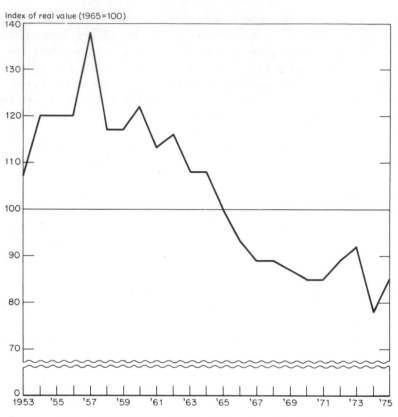

Index of real value (1965=100)

Source: *Anuário Estatístico*, IBGE; *Conjuntura Económica*, November 1972; and *Boletim do Banco Central*, February 1975.

Figure 8-1. Trends in the Real Value of the Legal Minimum Wage for the City of Rio de Janeiro: 1953-75.

degree to which the trend in legal minimum wages is a measure of the actual wage for individual workers. For example, a special study of the average earnings of industrial workers for the period from 1959 to 1964 concluded that the actual earnings of workers had increased in spite of reductions in the real minimum wage over these years.[2] The study also notes that the flow of cash receipts to the workers, in addition to real wages, increased through two new fringe benefits legally prescribed in 1962 and 1963. Employers were required to pay a year-end bonus, called the "thirteenth month salary," and a family allowance to workers with children below the age of 15.

Another shortcoming of the legal minimum wage data is the matter of coverage. The 1970 census showed that at least 60 percent of the agricultural workers and 20 percent of the urban workers were earning less than the lowest legal minimum wage prevailing in Brazil in that year.[3] Of the remaining workers a substantial share was earning more than the basic minimum wage.

To the extent that workers who previously received less than the minimum wage are now receiving the minimum wage or above, and that workers who previously received the minimum wage are now receiving more than the minimum wage, the economic and social welfare of workers, as measured by wages, has increased even though the real income of the legal minimum wage has declined. As of the mid-1970s partial but impressive evidence indicates that both these phenomena have occurred, and that the significance of the legal minimum wage as a measure of the real wages of specific individual workers has declined greatly. With the surge in employment the market has increasingly taken over. In many areas it has become difficult or impossible to hire even unskilled workers at the prevailing minimum wage.

The broadest evidence of real wage gains arises from the Tenure Guaranty Fund payroll data, which covers all urban nongovernment workers. From 1968 to 1974, according to these data, payrolls for the urban private sector increased from Cr$46 billion to Cr$135 billion in constant 1974 cruzeiros.[a] Thus, payrolls increased *in real terms* by 193 percent over the six-year period or by an average of 32 percent annually. The payroll data reflect increases in number of workers as well as higher income per worker. Although the data cannot be adjusted for changes in the number of workers, a most liberal allowance for this element would still leave a large share of the 32 percent annual increase, presumably indicating substantial wage gains for urban nongovernment workers.

The general impression of increasing real wages in Brazil is strongly supported by the recent special wage surveys for manufacturing, construction, and some farm areas. In manufacturing over the period from January 1969 to August 1974, the index of average wages increased by 48 percent per year and of monthly earnings by 70 percent annually.[4] These gains can be compared to annual rises in the cost of living of 20 percent over the same period. The index for earnings in manufacturing reflects increases in the hours worked as well as in wage rates.

In construction the index of hourly wages available for the five major cities rose between January 1969 and January 1975 from a base of 100 to between 333 (Rio de Janeiro) and 444 (São Paulo) for unskilled workers, 287 (Rio de Janeiro) and 382 (Recife) for painters, 269 (Rio de Janeiro) and 389 (Belo Horizonte) for carpenters, and even higher levels for fitters and master builders.[5]

In agriculture earnings appear to have improved dramatically over the 1969 level reported in the 1970 decennial census. Average cash earnings for regular farm hands increased over the four-year period from 1969 to 1973 by amounts ranging from about 25 percent a year in the northeastern state of Pernambuco to more than 40 percent annually in the state of São Paulo.[6] Again, these gains should be compared to the cost of living rise of about 20 percent annually over the same period.

[a]For Tenure Guarantee Fund collection, which are 8 percent of payrolls, see *Conjuntura Econômica,* February 1975, p. 172. The adjustment from current to 1974 cruzeiros was made on the basis of the General Price Index as reported in the same issue of *Conjuntura Econômica,* p. 225.

Another set of statistics that has been used as an indicator of worker economic and social welfare is the ratio of wages to value added in manufacturing. Although the ratio has fluctuated somewhat, the trend over the last decade appears to be a decline in wage payments as a component in manufacturing value added. This measure, however, is most meaningful as an indicator of change in the capital-labor mix toward more capital intensive industries in Brazil's rapid industrialization and modernization drive.

As would be expected, wage trends have varied by skill levels. The greatest shortages have been in many skilled and semiskilled categories, and have resulted in above-average gains by workers in these groups. One of the severest manpower shortages has been in the field of plant managers and business executives. A study of salaries paid by the National Steel Company (CSN), over the period 1966-72, showed that the salaries of managers increased annually by 8.1 percent in real terms as compared with 2.3 percent for the workers.[7] Still other evidence indicates that Brazilian business executives are earning higher salaries than their counterparts in either the United States or Europe. A new but common experience for foreigners working in the Brazilian subsidiaries of their companies is to find the local marketing manager or comptroller earning a higher salary than the foreign manager.[8]

What conclusions can be drawn from such a mix of data? For the austerity and stabilization period from 1964 through 1969, it appears that real wages in Brazil declined sharply, as reflected in the trend of the legal minimum wage. But as the momentum of development accelerated, market forces increasingly took over as the determinant of real wage levels. The surveys of actual wages and earnings all show gains in real wages since about 1969, including those for unskilled workers in the construction industry. Generally supporting evidence of recent gains in real wages comes from the FGTS data on payrolls.

At the same time it must be noted that wage trends vary greatly among regions, between urban and rural areas, and by skill categories. The minimum wage, still at a low subsistence level, is the prevailing wage in much of the service sector and in the less rapidly developing regions.

Social Security

Over the years Brazil has created an extensive welfare system more comprehensive than that of many developed countries. The services are often substandard, but the real benefits are nonetheless significant in a country with low wage levels and extensive underemployment. The system operates on a compulsory basis under state management, and, as one political analyst has observed, the "system is so comprehensive in coverage and satisfactorily adequate in benefits that it undercuts what might otherwise be a source of urban discontent."[9]

The principal program is that of the Social Security Institute (INPS), which provides medical services and administers pensions and survivor benefits to workers and their dependents comprising about 40 percent of Brazil's population. A large number of agencies of lesser importance administer programs for military pensions, for employees of state governments, and for rural workers.[10] Until recently the major groups not effectively covered were the farm and domestic workers, but through new programs for farm workers (1971) and for domestic servants (1973), virtually all Brazilian workers are now covered by social welfare programs of varying degrees of effectiveness.

Brazil's social security programs are financed through payroll taxes, which had risen by the early 1970s through the addition of new benefits to a total of 44 percent on top of Brazilian payrolls. The principal benefits are medical services, pensions and survivor benefits, a family bonus for each employee's child under 14 years of age, the "13th month wage" as a compulsory bonus equal to one month's wage, accident insurance, and vocational training.

Of the various social security programs, the issue of job security has been of foremost importance in Brazil. Prior to 1966 the Brazilian worker was guaranteed his job by law after working ten years for the same employer. Under the system workers discharged without cause after one year of service received one month's pay for each year of work. After ten years this amount was doubled and the definition of "just cause" became sufficiently stringent to make it virtually impossible to discharge workers.

In practice, however, job security was illusory. Before the ten years was completed the employer would normally dismiss the worker on the grounds that the worker would lose interest in his job and become less productive if he no longer could be separated from his job. As a consequence the employee lived in a permanent situation of mistrust, and the relationship between employer and employee was often charged with suspicion and hostility.

In 1966 the Tenure Guaranty Fund (Fundo de Garantia do Tempo de Serviço—FGTS) was created as an alternative to the system of severance pay for termination of employment. Under the new program the employer pays a payroll tax of 8 percent to the Tenure Guaranty Fund, which accrues to the account of each worker. The fund is held by the National Housing Bank. The workers can withdraw the deposits in their accounts if they lose their job, if they wish to start their own business, if they want to buy a home (after five years of participation in the fund), if they need to cover extraordinary medical expenses, and on retirement. In the case of death their survivors can withdraw the deposits. The deposits are subject to monetary correction and bear interest at the rate of 3 percent.

The ingenious feature of the program is that it combines improved worker welfare with sources of financing for growth. The "float" formed by these funds, which totals the equivalent of several billion United States dollars, has been used by the National Housing Bank to finance its massive housing program. Participation in the fund was made optional for the workers, but most of them have chosen the new type of job security in preference to the old. The FGTS, a Brazilian invention, has already been adopted by Mexico, Argentina, and El Salvador.

Another pioneering social security program, called the Program for Social Integration (PIS), was established in 1970. This program implements a long-standing but inoperative provision of Brazilian constitutions calling for "integration of the worker in the life and development of the enterprise" through profit-sharing.[11] Since 1971 employers have been required to pay a share of their income tax liability into the Social Integration Fund. These payments become worker-owned deposits, allocated by a formula that gives equal weight to the worker's salary and years of service, that are subject to monetary correction, and that earn interest at the rate of 3 percent annually. Because the employer deducts his PIS payments from his tax liability, the PIS program is in effect a transfer of tax revenues to the worker rather than an additional employer tax.

A counterpart fund for government workers, called PASEP (Programa de Formação do Patrimônio do Servidor Público) was also established in 1970 with employer contributions based on government receipts. As of the end of 1973 an estimated 7,200,000 workers were participating in PIS and another 3,000,000 in PASEP.[12] Withdrawals of principal from these deposits are restricted in much the same way as are those from the Tenure Guaranty Fund. But workers are free to withdraw interest earnings and distributed profits without restriction. The "float" from these funds is used mainly by the National Economic Development Bank to finance industrial investment.

Historically, Brazil's social security system expanded by the creation of new "institutes" or funds for all the workers in a specific type of economic activity such as banking or commerce. Since 1964 the government has tried to rationalize the network of funds into a single system under the INPS. The monumental task assigned to INPS, however, has resulted in serious problems of efficiency in providing medical care and other services. In an attempt to improve this situation, the government in 1974 established a new Ministry of Social Welfare in order to separate this responsibility from the previous Ministry of Labor and Social Welfare.

The seriousness of the situation was reflected by the following editorial comment of the *Jornal de Brasilia* (July 2, 1974) in welcoming the new ministry:

Everybody recognizes that the INPS is an institution out of phase with the times, surprised by the development of the country and incapable of responding to the social responsibilities that development generates. It is not only the sight of chaotic waiting lines that stretch from the doors of the institution, an eloquent testimony of its incapacity to serve, but the lack of a vision for the major problems of medical assistance and global welfare, that does not aim only at a part of the population, those economically active, but that recognizes social security as a right common to all citizens.

In addition to the quality of service problems Brazil is facing and the uncertainties as to whether effective social welfare coverage can be provided to the formerly excluded groups, another significant issue relates to the method of financing the social security system. Through reliance on payroll taxes the nonwage labor costs that have to be paid by employers have become sufficiently high to have a restraining effect on the expansion of employment. The steady rise in nonwage labor costs creates a preference for capital-intensive rather than labor-intensive technology when a choice is available, and a bias in favor of overtime work as against adding new workers. For example, the family bonus payments would increase if new workers are added. In the case of some welfare programs alternative ways of funding are available that would be neutral as far as labor absorption is concerned. For example, some of the payroll taxes might be replaced by higher corporate income taxes.

Other criticisms of the social security system are that resources are too heavily allocated to individual medical assistance in preference to preventive public health programs, and that imbalances exist in the provision of services among regions and among groups of workers.[13] But in spite of the numerous shortcomings of social welfare services in Brazil, the system is reasonably impressive given Brazil's stage of development and steadily being expanded. It is noteworthy that even within Brazil's authoritarian political system, welfare services and agencies have continued to be a subject for criticism and evaluation by the press and by numerous studies of official planning agencies.

Income Distribution

One of the most controversial features of Brazil's development pattern has been the changes that have occurred in the distribution of income. Reliable data for historical comparisons of income distribution are among the most difficult to secure for most countries and even more precarious for the less developed countries. Nevertheless, estimates have been made for Brazil comparing the distribution of money income to individuals for the census years of 1960 and 1970[14] that, in spite of many statistical limitations, have become generally accepted as a reasonable representation of what has happened.

The data show that the richest 10 percent of the population increased their share of total money income from 40 to 48 percent in 1970. In other words, as total national income increased, the income of individuals in the top decile increased at an even faster rate. In all of the other deciles the *relative* share of total money income received was less in 1970 than 1960 (Table 8-3).

But while the rich were getting richer, the poor were also getting richer—even though at a slower rate. Income recipients in all deciles had absolute gains in money income adjusted for price increases. The highest rates of gain were in the top and bottom categories. The lowest rates of gain occurred in the middle income levels. Urban incomes grew more rapidly than rural earnings. Those with university education gained at a faster rate than the less educated.

Table 8-3
Size Distribution of Brazilian Income, 1960 and 1970

		% Share of Total Income			Average Monthly Income		
					(1970 CR$)		Average
Deciles		1960	1970	%	1960	1970	Annual %
1st	(Lowest)	1.17	1.11	−5.13	25	32	2.5
2nd		2.32	2.05	−11.64	48	58	1.9
3rd		3.42	2.97	−13.16	71	84	1.7
4th		4.65	3.88	−16.55	96	110	1.4
5th		6.15	4.90	−20.32	127	139	0.9
6th		7.66	5.91	−22.75	158	168	0.6
7th		9.41	7.37	−21.68	195	210	0.7
8th		10.85	9.57	−11.80	225	272	1.9
9th		14.69	14.45	−1.64	305	411	3.1
10th	(Highest)	39.66	47.79	+20.50	815	1,360	5.2
Highest	5%	27.69	34.86	+25.90	1,131	1,984	5.8
Highest	1%	12.11	14.57	+20.32	2,389	4,147	5.7
Lowest	40%	11.57	10.00	−13.57	60	71	1.7
Middle	20%	13.81	10.81	−21.73	142	153	0.7
Highest	40%	74.62	79.19	+6.13	385	563	3.9
Total		100.00	100.00		206	282	3.2

Source: Carlos Geraldo Langoni, *Distribuição da Renda e Desenvolvimento Econômico do Brasil* (Rio de Janeiro: Editora Expressão e Cultura, 1973), p. 64.

The data have a number of serious limitations[15] that, if they could be corrected, would undoubtedly show a lesser degree of income concentration. Nevertheless, the broad pattern would still be one of significant income concentration. Some of the data and conceptual limitations are:

1. *End-point comparisons.* The available data are only for the two end-point years of 1960 and 1970 and cannot provide enlightenment on trends between 1960 and 1964 when the military government took over, from 1964 to 1968 during the stabilization period, and from 1970 to the present. Only two of the recent years of high growth rates are included in the period up to 1970.
2. *Individual versus family incomes.* Only the 1970 census has data on family incomes. Consequently, the historical comparisons with the 1960 situation has to be in terms of individual incomes. With Brazil's upsurge in employment since the late 1960s the number of workers per family has increased, with resulting gains in family income much greater than those in individual incomes. In comparing levels of well-being, the trend in family incomes would be more relevant than individual incomes, except where children may be deprived of schooling by "dropping out" to work.

3. *Money income versus economic welfare.* The studies measure only the change in money income over the period whereas measures of social and economic welfare improvement should also include changes in the availability of such services as education, subsidized housing, social security, recreation facilities, and health—all fields in which Brazil has sharply increased its government expenditures in recent years.

4. *Good or bad compared to what?* When compared to other Latin American countries for which data are available, the Brazilian pattern of income distribution is mixed. Using the lowest 20 percent for comparison, Brazil appears to have a less equitable distribution than its neighbors. On the other hand, an intercountry comparison of the shares received by the richest 5 percent shows that income was more concentrated in Argentina, Mexico, and Peru as of 1960, the latest date for which comparative information is available, and for Bolivia as of 1970.[16]

The criticisms of Brazil's income distribution pattern have been of two types. One has been on egalitarian and social justice grounds—generally expressed in terms of the rich are getting richer and the poor are getting poorer. The criticism then proceeds to argue that income distribution patterns are generating an explosive potential of popular discontent that will result in widespread disaffection and an erosion of popular support for the government and its development efforts.

The second type of criticism has focused on economic issues. The argument has been made that Brazil's development model has relied upon income concentration to set in motion and maintain the demand for consumer durables as a causal force for economic prosperity. But, the argument continues, the high income market has become saturated, and unless the size of the market is enlarged through a better distribution of income, economic growth in Brazil will soon begin to stagnate.[17]

One response to the egalitarian criticisms has been that the facts are being erroneously represented. It is true that the rich are getting richer, but the poor are also getting richer, even though the rich are gaining at a faster rate. Furthermore, the income distribution studies do not shed any light on the economic status of specific individuals. The deciles do not necessarily include the same individual in both 1960 and 1970. Over the period an individual in the lowest decile may in fact have moved to a higher income decile or vice versa.

The degree of popular discontent that exists in Brazil because of differing rates of gain and changes in the distribution of income has been difficult, if not impossible, to verify empirically. An inextricable mixture of human rights, political and economic issues, and personalities were involved in the surprising 1974 election success of the opposition party. Income distribution was widely debated but probably less of an economic concern to individual voters than the sharp resurgence of inflation. Casual empiricism and the weight of logic support the view that Brazilian individuals and families are primarily concerned with whether they are making absolute progress as compared to their own previous situation. In a relative sense they compare this past progress to that of their neighbors and co-workers rather than to that of the super rich.

Even more important as a source of content or discontent are the future perspectives of the individual Brazilian and his family for continuing to improve their welfare status. To the extent that this reasoning is valid, income distribution patterns have been more of an issue in the minds of international agencies, foreign observers, some Brazilian scholars, opposition politicians, and government officials than a widespread matter of personal concern among the Brazilian rank and file.

The counterargument to the economic criticism of income distribution patterns has been that it does not apply to Brazil for at least two reasons. First, the government sector is extremely large and, if correctly manipulated, can keep growth going. Second, there is the size of Brazil's population. Even if 20 percent of the population received 60 percent of the country's income, this represents 20 million people, which is a large market.[18]

The effect of changes in the distribution of income on Brazil's pattern of growth has been analyzed through a series of simulation experiments, which suggest that "plausible variations in income distribution had surprisingly little effect on the pattern of growth."[19] This conclusion has been explained by the failure of demand to change substantially when income is transferred from one class to another and by the importance of the intermediate and capital goods industries, whose growth rate does not vary significantly with different patterns of final demand. To the extent that these experimental results are valid, the stability of growth rates undercuts the economic criticism. But it also indicates that the Brazilian government could follow a policy of highly progressive income redistribution without jeopardizing its growth goal or unduly penalizing important industries such as automobiles or consumer durables.

The income distribution controversy has raised the issue to a high priority status in official policy-making circles. The government has unequivocally accepted a more equitable distribution of income as an important development goal, but it differs with its critics as to the timing and means for achieving this end. To quote an official spokesman for the government, "The orientation of the Government is rigorously and clearly defined: to bring about a redistribution of income in order to guarantee that the results of growth are disseminated and that the economic-social viability of accelerated growth is self sustained; to avoid premature and excessive redistribution that would retard the same growth and, in consequence, make inviable or innocuous the policy of income redistribution itself."[20]

Premature or excessive income redistribution, the government argues, would only mean a sharing of poverty. The government officials fear that the growth momentum will be slowed by channeling a greatly increased share of resources to those who would consume rather than save and invest. The emphasis until the 1974 elections was on maintaining the growth momentum with a modest amount of distribution now but with a greater degree of redistribution at a later stage. As Minister Velloso has argued, if Brazil can achieve its goal of doubling per capita income over the decade of the 1970s, the welfare level of persons in the lower income levels can double even if there has been no improvement in the distribution of income. Since the election, however, the government has modified its position and increased its emphasis on direct rather than indirect measures to improve income distribution.

In further support of its welfare strategy the government has released some dramatic results from the annual hold Sample Surveys showing the recent increases in ownership of major consumer durables.[21] In the two-year period from 1970 to 1972 the number of households, including rural areas, reported the following gains:

Households with

Gas or electric stoves	from 43% to 63%
Radios	from 59% to 85%
Refrigerators	from 26% to 33%
Television Sets	from 24% to 34%
Automobiles	from 9% to 12%

For urban areas the comparable data are: refrigerators, from 42% to 45%; television sets, from 40% to 50%; automobiles, from 14% to 17%.

From a welfare point of view the issue of income concentration is less important than the problem of absolute poverty. In 1970 fully one third of all income earners in Brazil received incomes below the minimum wage for the lowest income region, about US$25 per month. The major welfare challenge that confronts the government is to generate the resources and to devise the methods needed to reduce absolute poverty. To meet this challenge the principal strategy of the government has been to maintain rapid growth rates, to invest more in the education and training of people, and to undertake special development programs for the poor regions of the Northeast and the Amazon.

The critics of the government's strategy claim that these measures are not enough. One proposal is that minimum wages should be increased by a more accurate adjustment that reflects actual productivity gains. Another recommendation is that property rights need to be reallocated in many agricultural areas to deal with the hard core problem of rural poverty. In general the critics emphasize that there is not necessarily a dichotomy between growth and income distribution, and that many opportunities are being neglected to influence the pattern of growth in ways that will achieve both growth and more equitable income distribution.[22]

Education

One of Brazil's greatest opportunities for indirect income redistribution and for raising economic and social levels is in the area of education. For several decades

Brazil has been steadily moving from an elitist educational system for the privileged few to a broad domestic educational system for the masses. Yet, in spite of the advances made, Brazil's educational situation is strikingly deficient.[23]

The Brazilian heritage of colonialism, slavery, and latifundia was not conducive to providing an educational system for the mass of the people. The mercantile policy of Portugal was perhaps even more strict than that of other European powers: it denied the Brazilian colony the printing press and any form of university education. Throughout the colonial period, what primary and secondary education did exist was mainly in the hands of the Church.

Brazil began its modern educational life only in 1946 with the end of the Vargas dictatorship and the reestablishment of democracy. The task of redressing the shortcomings of the past has been monumental, and progress has been slow. Dr. Anisio S. Teixeira, one of Brazil's great educators, pictured the situation as follows:[24]

The education which we have been organizing until now in this country was never directed to the people. It was education for *our* class. We permitted it to the people as a tolerance. Although stratified in a society of classes, we have always had the sense of humor to maintain our classes open. And, thanks to a selective education, we removed from the popular classes those demonstrating capability to participate with us in the banquet of Brazilian life. We did not close the door . . . but we selected those who might enter. . . .

Until the last decade or so the Brazilian educational system was directed toward the upper classes. It was theoretical and encyclopedic in orientation with little emphasis on empirical and pragmatic problems, as was characteristic of the European systems from which it evolved. With recent reforms the availability of education at all levels has expanded dramatically, and the orientation of the curriculum particularly at university levels has shifted drastically from programs intended to prepare students of the upper classes to enjoy more fully the "good life" to professional training in such fields as engineering, agronomy, economics, and business administration.

In 1970 almost one-third of Brazil's population 10 years and older were illiterate. Of Brazil's labor force, only 2.5 percent had university level training, 5.2 percent upper secondary school training, and 8.0 percent lower secondary school training. Some 29.8 percent of the labor force was illiterate. Moreover, there were great variations among the industrial sectors and the regions in educational attainments.

In Latin America Brazil's rate of illiteracy is surpassed by only six countries: Bolivia, El Salvador, Guatemala, Haiti, Honduras, and Nicaragua. The share of the school-age population enrolled in Brazilian schools is low, particularly at the secondary level, even when compared to other poor countries. And the share of the nation's resources invested in education has been traditionally low though increasing.

With a long past to overcome Brazil has been making significant progress. Public expenditures on education at all governmental levels increased from 2.3 percent of Brazil's gross domestic product in 1960 to 3.2 percent in 1970. From 1960 to 1973 the number of students enrolled in primary and secondary schools increased by 230 percent and the number of university students by over tenfold. In absolute numbers, as of 1974 Brazil had about 20 million students enrolled in primary and secondary schools and slightly more than 1 million in its universities. The primary school enrollments, however, were only 65 percent of the total population between the ages of 5 and 14, and the secondary enrollments were only 15 percent of the 15 to 19 years of age population group. Furthermore, the enrollment data give an overly favorable impression of the educational situation because the dropout rate is still high.

Also, the national data obscure sharp regional differences. In the Northeast, for example, the educational attainments of the labor force are about half the national average. Within the same region, the educational situation in urban areas is infinitely superior to that in rural areas.

With primary education becoming increasingly available to children throughout the country, Brazil's hard core illiteracy problem is now confined to adults who did not have access to schools during their early years. As a special effort to reduce illiteracy and provide some continuing education for adolescents and adults, the MOBRAL (Brazilian Movement for Literacy) program was created in 1967 under President Costa e Silva.[25] MOBRAL operates as an independent Brazilian-type "foundation" outside the traditional educational bureaucracy. It provides extra employment and income for school teachers, but their compensation is result-oriented in the sense that their remuneration is based on the number of students who complete the five-month course. The program is available outside normal working hours and at locations convenient to the participants.

The MOBRAL program had its normal share of organizing difficulties but by 1970 began to operate on a major scale. Between 1970 and 1973 a total of 12 million persons had been enrolled in the literacy programs, and about half of those enrolled completed the course. With current enrollments of several million participants the MOBRAL program has become one of the largest adult literacy programs in the world. But, as one of the major Brazilian papers has noted, Brazil still had 13.5 million illiterates in 1973, and this number forms a contingent that is larger than the entire population of the majority of the countries in the world.

Quality as well as access to education has been a critical problem in Brazil. As the ad hoc group of the Inter-American Economic and Social Council concluded in a 1975 review of the Brazilian educational situation,[26]

... the major problems seen at the primary education level, which are the problems most responsible for the relative failure of efforts in the educational process, have still not been solved. As has been emphasized repeatedly, problems at this level are represented by high dropout and repeat rates, thereby bringing about a slowness in the flow of students, not very efficient use of resources and frustration of students. In addition, it is well known that this situation is closely related to ill-suited examination systems, insufficient textbooks and school materials, and inadequate preparation and remuneration of teachers (especially those working the rural areas).

Various educational reform programs have been adopted from time to time in an effort to improve the quality of education. The latest major reform law adopted in 1971 moves grades five through eight back from the secondary into the primary cycle so that students will have access to an initial eight years of schooling without having to overcome the obstacle of the old, extremely difficult ginásio entrance examination. The reforms have also modified the curricula and promotion procedure with emphasis on vocational training in both the primary and secondary cycles so that dropouts at the primary level will be equipped with skills for productive employment. Other major reforms have been directed toward higher education.[27]

The implementation of the latest effort to reform primary and secondary education will depend primarily on state and municipal governments for administration and funding. Although the federal government assists through a revenue-sharing program that gives more heavily to the poor regions than to the rich, it is likely that the program will be less effective in the poorer states.

Without doubt one of the most important fruits of growth in Brazil has been greatly improved access to education and training. In large part the momentum for this progress has come from the emphasis of economists and others on providing the necessary valuable human resources needed to support the drive for development. Changing an educational system is not an easy task in any country, and Brazil will have to struggle for some time to come in order to achieve satisfactory levels of quality in its educational system and to reduce the sharp regional divergencies.

The Geisel government has linked Brazil's educational problem to the issue of income distribution. It has given heavy emphasis to the relationship of low incomes to low levels of educational attainment and it supports a strategy of improving the distribution of income by raising the education levels of the low income groups. In contrast, the critics of Brazil's income distribution patterns focus attention on the need to improve minimum wage levels in addition to improving education and training.

The need for continued improvement in education is only too apparent. Illiteracy and the lack of education account for a major share of the lag in agricultural areas in adopting new technology and in achieving higher rates of productivity. The educational deficiencies of potential industrial workers have required employers to make large expenditures on basic worker training. The shortage of managers and engineers has made Brazil highly dependent upon foreign enterprise for transfers of technology. Until recently the virtual absence of a research and development capability in both the private and public sectors has added to the dependence of the Brazilian economy on foreign transfers of scientific and production know-how.

Housing and Urban Development

The field of housing has been another area of critical need and of opportunity in which Brazil has made striking progress. Through imaginative and novel techniques Brazil has sharply reduced its massive housing deficit, expanded greatly the availability of water and sewage facilities, and contributed to a redistribution of income by subsidizing to some degree the programs for lower income groups. The housing program has also been a major source of new employment, both directly and indirectly. It has favored traditional labor-intensive construction techniques as against prefabricated methods and has stimulated the expansion of labor intensive industries.

Brazil's housing shortage dates back to the early 1940s when rents were frozen by law. The situation deteriorated steadily in the postwar period as the process of urbanization accelerated. As ever larger numbers of rural workers moved to the cities, housing construction lagged farther and farther behind the growing need of the urban population. The resulting shantytowns, called favelas, that sprung up on the hillsides in Rio de Janeiro and other cities became densely populated areas where residents lived in makeshift housing with an almost total lack of water and sewage facilities.

The government policy of freezing rents while allowing other prices to rise made existing rental property a poor investment and discouraged the further construction of rental housing. For persons who wished to purchase homes, the situation was equally grim because long-term mortgages were not obtainable in a situation where inflation was continuing at an annual rate of 15 to 25 percent and higher. As a consequence, by the early 1960s the building industry had come to a virtual standstill, and critical social tensions were emerging in those urban areas where subhuman housing conditions prevailed.

To meet this crisis situation in both housing and employment, the National Housing Bank (BNH) and the National Housing Plan (PNH) were established in 1964. The foundation stone for the plan and the operations of the bank was the principle of monetary correction. With this device it became feasible for the program to be self-sustaining because the funds loaned for mortgages would preserve their real value and earn an adequate return. The alternative of expanding housing through direct government expenditures would have vitiated the program to restrain and reduce runaway inflation. Since its establishment the National Housing Bank has become the core of a financial system for urban development that works with real values protected by indexing. It has promoted home ownership, in preference to rental housing, and it supports urban planning and the expansion of urban water and sewage disposal facilities.

Another key feature of the housing and urban development program is its source of funds. The resources of the BNH come mainly from the 8 percent tax on all payrolls that is paid into the Tenure Guaranty Fund (FGTS), which by the end of 1974 had collected Cr$32 billion or about US$4.5 billion. Thus, the expansion of social security for workers has been linked to the expansion of social welfare programs. In addition, through a system of savings and loan associations, voluntary savings are collected by the sale of housing bonds and by accepting savings deposits, both of which are indexed and guaranteed by the BNH. This combination of financial sources has made huge sums available for housing and urban development. By 1974 about 1.2 million new dwelling units had been financed under the BNH program.

The BNH operates through financial intermediaries rather than directly in the financing, selling, buying, and building of dwellings. It has channelled the larger part of its funds as long-term financing for "popular-market" housing, defined as families whose incomes ranges from one to three times the minimum wage, through housing corporations (COHABS) created by states and municipalities. It supplies a lower middle-income market, defined as families with incomes between three and six times minimum wages, through large projects undertaken by housing cooperatives formed by unions and labor associations. Borrowers for higher cost housing normally have to pay prevailing interest rates, but the lower income groups served through the COHABS and cooperatives are given subsidized rates of interest ranging down to 1 percent per annum.

The construction of new housing has required an expansion in water supply and sewage disposal facilities that the state and municipal governments have not been financially able to provide. To meet this problem in 1970 the BNH created a National Sanitation Plan (PLANASA), which has many original features and involves financial sharing by the housing bank in the financing of water and sewage facilities. As of mid-1973 loan commitments had been made that together with state and municipal financing will make good quality water available to 25 million people. The sewerage program, however, had been initiated in only seven states because the plan requires that the water supply systems reach a certain point of development before loan requests for sewerage projects are entertained.[28]

The governmental targets for 1979 are to finance an additional 1.5 million housing units, to increase the urban population served by water systems from 65 percent in 1974 to 79 percent, and the share of the urban population connected to sewage disposal systems from 29 to 44 percent.

In spite of Brazil's dramatic gains in improving the availability of housing and urban facilities, the country still faces major challenges in trying to meet the needs of rapid urbanization. During the present decade the urban population will grow by some 27 million people, calling for at least 6 million new houses over and above those needed to replace inadequate dwellings and to eradicate urban favelas.[29] This need is more than double the present goals of the government.

It is also true that the housing programs have been least successful in reaching the lowest income groups. In recognition of this fact the government established in 1973 an additional plan of low-income housing (PLANHAP) with a target of constructing 2 million dwellings in 10 years at an average cost of about US$2,500. The probable success of this and previous programs in serving the low-income group has been placed in doubt by the large numbers of home purchasers who have become delinquent in their payments.[b]

Still another problem has been the pattern followed in resettling the former slum dwellers. The many favelas that have been eliminated have been replaced by new housing generally located in the outskirts of the cities. As a result the distance to work "often is so great that the ex-*favelado* must spend as much as a third of the minimum wage on transportation, and his wife forfeits her service occupation because the high cost of transportation relative to her smaller earnings makes continued work economically unrewarding."[30]

Brazil still has a substantial housing deficit as a residue of years of practically no residential construction. It has an even larger backlog in other urban facilities and rapidly expanding new urbanization needs to fulfill. Most of Brazil's cities are still in an early stage of preparing urban development plans to meet the needs of parking, mass transportation, recreation facilities, and pollution control. A spectacular exception is the city of Curitiba with a population of about 1 million, which may provide a valuable stimulus and body of experience that will help other Brazilian cities to meet the challenge of urbanization.[31]

Health and Nutrition

The health situation in Brazil has been improving as measured by various national averages, but extreme regional variations exist with the Northeast still lagging as the nation's most serious health problem. Two of the most common measures of progress are changes in life expectancy and in infant mortality rates. Life expectancy in Brazil increased over the period from 1960-65 to 1965-70 from 56 to 59 years for men and from 60.6 to 63.8 years for women.[32] In this respect the Brazilian situation is comparable to the average for the Latin American countries but significantly worse than in Mexico.

Infant mortality rates in Brazil are high, particularly in the Northeast, and are exceeded in Latin America only by Bolivia, Haiti, and Honduras. As of 1973 the national average was 105 deaths per 1,000 live births, compared with an estimated 112 for 1964. In 1973 the lowest rates of 70 and 76 were in the North and Southeast, respectively. The highest rate of 180 per thousand was in the Northeast. As a reflection of the problems of urbanization, the infant mortality rate in São Paulo went up from 63 to 89 per thousand from 1960 to 1970.

---

[b]" . . . nearly 40 percent of the beneficiaries of those institutions (PLANHAP and BNH) financing home loans are behind in their payments," according to Fernando Henrique Cardoso. *Financial Times*, November 13, 1973.

Other indicators such as population per physician, population per hospital bed, and nutrition also reflect deficiencies in Brazil's health situation. In spite of the fact that general health conditions have improved considerably over the past three decades, much remains to be done. Communicable diseases—notably infectious diarrhea, influenza, pneumonia, tuberculosis, measles, and tetanus— still account for about 40 percent of deaths in the country. In addition, thousands are incapacitated each year by such maladies as schistosomiasis, Chagas disease, plague, and trachoma.[33]

The nutrition situation has improved in Brazil in terms of both calories and proteins.[34] The caloric intake in 1970 was slightly higher in Brazil than the average for Latin America, and the protein intake was at a slightly lower level than the average. In Northeast Brazil, however, the poorest one-third of the population suffers a caloric deficiency of more than 50 percent, and malnutrition largely accounts for the high preschool mortality rates in the region.

The availability of health services has been increasing as measured by federal expenditures for health,[35] the number of doctors per total population (1 per 2,000 population in 1970), by the availability of hospital beds, and by the share of the population receiving medical coverage under the social security programs. According to government statistics, 82 percent of the population is "permanently attended" by medical assistance.[36]

The inadequacy of public health programs and sanitation activities rather than private medical attention has been the major health problem in Brazil. Communicable diseases have been responsible for a large share of the deaths in Brazil, and the problem of communicable diseases has been aggravated by the rapid rate of urbanization together with the lag in public health education and the construction of urban potable water and sewerage facilities. The programs initiated in the early 1970s to improve urban sanitation facilities may be among the most important steps Brazil is taking in the health field.

Under Brazil's social security program, the resources going to the Institutes for medical services, which finance the large bulk of medical expenditures, have been increasing much more rapidly than the resources available for public health. Thus, there has been a progressive relative concentration in expenditures for curative as opposed to preventive medicine.[37] Through the social security system, individuals and regions receive medical services in relation to their coverage under the system rather than on the basis of need.

Brazil, along with the rest of the countries of the world, has begun to recognize that the more relevant goal of development is the improvement of the quality of life for a nation's people, and that increasing the national output of goods and services should be a means of achieving the development goal rather than a goal in itself. Nevertheless, until the mid-1970s, the emphasis of Brazil's drive for development has been primarily focused on expanding output and increasing the size of the economic "pie" rather than on a more equitable distribution among the people of gains in economic and social welfare.

153

Notes

1. Organization of American States, *Latin America's Development and the Alliance for Progress* (Washington, 1973), p. 207.

2. Peter Gregory, "Evolution of Industrial Wages and Wage Policy in Brazil, 1959-67." Mimeographed. (Washington: Agency for International Development, September 1968).

3. Fundação IBGE, *Censo Demográfico—Brasil, VIII Recenseamento Geral— 1970, Série Nacional, Vol. 1* (Rio de Janeiro, June 1973), p. 93.

4. *Boletim do Banco Central do Brasil*, April 1975, pp. 106-9.

5. Ibid., April 1975, pp. 110-11.

6. Ibid., September 1974, p. 69.

7. Edmar Lisboa Bacha, "Hierarquia e Remuneração Gerencial," Mimeographed Discussion Paper. University of Brasilia, Department of Economics, September 1973, p. 23.

8. Eileen Mackenzie, "The Brazilian Phenomenon: Executive Salaries Among the World's Highest," *Brazilian Business*, April 1974, pp. 14-16.

9. Thomas E. Skidmore, "Politics and Economic Policy Making in Authoritarian Brazil, 1937-71," in *Authoritarian Brazil*, edited by Alfred Stepan (New Haven: Yale University Press, 1973), p. 35.

10. See Fernando A. Rezende da Silva and Dennis Mahar, *Saude e Previdência Social* (Rio de Janeiro: IPEA, 1974).

11. See Article 158-V of the 1967 Constitution. The same article also provides for worker participation in management "in exceptional cases."

12. *Almanaque Abril 1975* (São Paulo: Abril S.A., 1975), pp.386-87.

13. Rezende da Silva and Mahar, *Saude e Previdência Social*, p. 183.

14. See Carlos Geraldo Langoni, *Distribuição da Renda e Desenvolvimento Econômico do Brasil* (Rio de Janeiro: Editora Expressão e Cultura, 1973); Albert Fishlow, "Brazilian Size Distribution of Income," *The American Economic Review*, May 1972.

15. Mário Henrique Simonsen, *Brasill 2002* (Rio de Janeiro: APEC, 1972), pp. 48-50.

16. Langoni, *Distribuição da Renda e Desenvolvimento Econômico do Brasil*, pp. 200-201; Simonsen, *Brasil 2002*, pp. 55-57.

17. See Celso Furtado, *Análise do "Modelo" Brasileiro* (Rio de Janeiro: Civilização Brasileira, 1972); Maria da Conceição Tavares, *Da Substituição de Importações ao Capitalismo Financeiro* (Rio de Janeiro: Zahar Editores, 1972); Paul I. Singer, *O "Milagre Brasileiro": Causas e Consequências* (São Paulo: Cadernos EBRAP, 1972).

18. Werner Baer, "The Brazilian Boom, 1968-72," *World Development*, August 1973, p. 12.

19. Samuel A. Morley and Gordon W. Smith, "The Effect of Changes in the Distribution of Income on Labor, Foreign Investment and Growth in Brazil," in Stepan, *Authoritarian Brazil*, p. 139.

154

20. João Paulo dos Reis Velloso, Minister of Planning and General Coordination, *Jornal do Brasil*, March 31, 1972.

21. *Projeto do II Plano Nacional de Desenvolvimento (1975-1979)* (Brasilia: República Federativa do Brasil, September 1974), p. 64.

22. For example, see Albert Fishlow, *Brazilian Income Size Distribution—Another Look*, 1973 (mimeo).

23. See Richard and Francis Weisskoff, "The Political Economy of the Educational System," in *Contemporary Brazil: Issues in Economic and Political Development*, edited by Jon Rosenbaum and William G. Tyler (New York: Praeger Publishers, 1972), pp. 371-98.

24. Address to the National Federation of Industries in São Paulo, June 15, 1956 as cited in August F. Faust, *Brazil: Education in an Expanding Economy* (Washington: U.S. Department of Health, Education and Welfare, 1959), p. 8.

25. See Simonsen, *Brasil 2002*, pp. 145-49.

26. Organization of American States, Inter-American Economic and Social Council, *The Economic and Social Development of Brazil: Characteristics, Policies and Prospects* (Washington: April 22, 1975), OEA/Ser. H/XIV, p. 25.

27. See Douglas Hume Graham, "The Growth, Change, and Reform of Higher Education in Brazil," in *Brazil in the Sixties*, edited by Riordan Roett (Nashville: Vanderbilt University Press, 1972), pp. 275-324.

28. Rubens Vaz da Costa, *PLANASA: A Dynamic Plan for a Dynamic Problem* (Rio de Janeiro: BNH, 1973).

29. Rubens Vaz da Costa, *Demographic Growth and Environmental Pollution* (Rio de Janeiro: BNH, 1973), p. 38.

30. Lawrence F. Salmen, "Urbanization and Development," in Rosenbaum and Tyler, *Contemporary Brazil*, p. 429.

31. See *Curitiba: An Experiment in City Planning* (Curitiba, 1973); *Integrated Transport System in Curitiba and Metropolitan Area* (Curitiba, October 1972).

32. *Economic Bulletin for Latin America*, Vol. XVIII, No. 1 and 2, 1973, p. 104.

33. Inter-American Development Bank, *Economic and Social Progress in Latin America, Annual Report, 1973* (Washington, 1974), p. 156.

34. CEPAL/FAO study as reported in *Notas* of the Economic Commission for Latin America, No. 171, September 16, 1974.

35. Fernando A. Rezende da Silva, *Avaliação do Setor Público na Economia Brasileira* (Rio de Janeiro: IPEA, 1972), p. 59.

36. *II Plano Nacional de Desenvolvimento (1975-1979)*, September 1974, p. 93.

37. Rezende da Silva and Mahar, *Saude e Previdência Social*, p. 34.

Politics, Parties, and
Politicians

In economic and social development Brazil has a clear perception of the broad future goals that it hopes to achieve. Brazilian views may differ as to specific components of the development model, such as the relative emphasis on agricultural versus industrial development or the timing and pattern for broadening the distribution of the fruits of economic growth, but the broad goals have widespread popular support. In political development, however, even after a decade of rule by a military authoritarian government, the nature of the political system toward which Brazil is moving is largely undefined. There are widely divergent views and considerable popular uneasiness over what kind of political system should evolve.

The political situation in Brazil is not one where two or more well-defined political models, supported by different organized groups, are competing for political power. Instead, it is a situation where neither the military group in power nor the opposition have clearly articulated political models toward which they desire to move. There is general agreement that Brazil's future political system must be a special Brazilian creation to fit unique conditions. What this system will be or should be is still unknown.

Some open political debate has begun in Brazil, such as the Seminar on Strategies for Political "Decompression" held in 1973 by members of the national congress[1] and in the congressional elections of November 1974. After the elections and despite a stunning defeat for the government's political party, the Geisel government permitted and encouraged an even greater degree of open political debate under its proclaimed policy of gradual political liberalization, labelled distensão or relaxation.

Yet, public debate on the political system has been cautiously self-restrained. The major issues that concern many Brazilians are whether and to what degree political power should be in the hands of military or civilian leaders, direct versus indirect elections, civil liberties, and safeguards for individual freedom. In order to understand the political tensions that exist, it is necessary to go back to the origin of the present government and the evolutionary role of the military in Brazilian politics.

The Historical Role of the Military in Politics

Since 1889, when the Republic was established, the military have intervened on several occasions in the political arena to effect political change. Until 1964 the

155

military after intervening always retreated to the supportive role of "always subordinate, always ready,"[2] in the tradition of their patron, the Duke of Caxias.

Military men as individuals rather than as representatives of the military establishment have a long tradition of political involvement. General Eurico Dutra, former minister of war, was elected president in 1945 after the overthrow of the Vargas dictatorship and, as a civilian, had the distinction of serving out his elected term. A number of military leaders were unsuccessful as major presidential candidates during the "democratic era" from 1945 to 1964. Other military leaders were elected governors, in such states as Pernambuco and Bahia.

Military officers also have a long record of serving as civilian tecnicos with government agencies, public enterprises, and in some instances with private companies. The outstanding case was General Macedo Soares who built the Volta Redonda steel works and later served as president of Mercedes-Benz do Brasil, vice president of the Federated Industries of São Paulo, president of the National Confederation of Industries, and governor of the State of Rio de Janeiro. A number of military officers, particularly engineers, have served with public enterprises such as PETROBRÁS and in key nonmilitary government positions.

In a country where the opportunities for higher education are limited, as was true for Brazil in the past, it is common for ambitious individuals to seek a technical education through the military system. Some Brazilians became military officers because of their desire for advanced education rather than their interest in a military career. This phenomenon and the general shortage of technically trained people would in large part explain the extensive movement of military officers into nonmilitary pursuits.

The change in the role of the military as an establishment was heavily influenced by events following World War II. In the early part of the twentieth century a number of junior officers spent time in command positions with the Imperial German Army and on their return to Brazil tried to implant German military patterns and philosophies in the military corps. Germany's defeat in World War I undermined this trend, and the Brazilians turned to France for their military doctrine and training assistance. Prior to World War II Brazilian officers were ardently wooed by both Germany and the United States, but events gradually led Brazil into World War II on the side of the Allies and into close political, military, and economic ties with the United States.[3]

World War II was the first major war for the Brazilian military since 1870. The Brazilian Expeditionary Force (FEB) fought in Italy with distinction. With the Allied victory and the discrediting of French military doctrine, the new army was modeled after that of the United States, except that generals headed the Brazilian military whereas civilians headed the United States military establishment.

In the rapidly industrializing Brazil of the postwar period the military sought a new rationale for their peacetime existence and found it in the "Cold War" doctrine of national security developed in the United States and emphasized in United States military schools. In 1949 the officers who had served in the FEB established the Superior War College (Escola Superior de Guerra—ESG) in unpretentious quarters in Rio de Janeiro. Politicians at first looked upon the school with suspicion and referred to it scornfully as the Brazilian "Sorbonne." The chairman of the ESG's Department of Studies was Humberto de Alencar Castello Branco, a lieutenant colonel on the general staff of FEB and the first president of the 1964 revolutionary government.

As one leading scholar has observed, "Rarely if ever has one educational institution, in less than two decades of existence, had so profound an impact on the course of a nation's development."[4] On the twentieth anniversary of the school a magazine described the ESG as "The School that Changed Brazil." The expressed purpose of the ESG is to involve the military in a more vigilant way in national life and to encourage the civilian and military elite to work together in developing the country. Thus, Brasilitarismo seeks national security through planned economic development. The central theme at the ESG has been that development and security issues are inseparable.[5]

The ESG exists to indoctrinate the civilian sector as well as to educate the military. About half the participants in the ESG programs have been specially selected civilians, and invitations to civilians to participate in these programs, some lasting as long as one year, have great prestige. The invited participants are aware of the importance of ESG credentials for opening doors to higher positions in the political, business, and military structures that ESG graduates have been building.

The curriculum of the ESG stresses internal problems and takes a broad social science approach to their solution. In a recent year, for example, the courses dealt with creation of a development model for Brazil's use of science and technology, regional planning, communications expansion and its impact on national security, national student organizations and student problems, civilian defense, coordination of research plans for strengthening the power of the armed forces, and overall military policy. On the international level the courses gave special emphasis to ways of strengthening Latin America in the face of East-West ideological rivalry, the growing economic disparity between the developed and the less developed nations, and the division of the world into nuclear and nonnuclear powers.[6]

Since its founding the ESG has graduated some 2,000 officers and civilians with the number almost equally divided between the two groups. Thus, the output of two decades is less than the number of students graduated by Harvard University in one year. The role of the ESG would not have been so vital had it not been for the weakness of the universities and the scarcity of highly trained people in Brazil. Through extension courses, which its active alumni association sponsors, and the influence of ESG graduates on training in military schools and universities, the ESG has been the largest social science institution in Latin America and a dominating influence on those disciplines in Brazil. It has also become the source of officers of general rank. In the post-World War II period the ranking generals have tended to be FEB veterans with ESG connections. Thus, the ESG has been providing the generals, indoctrinating the civilian technocrats, and influencing the policies that both are to implement.

In October 1945 the military intervened to end the Vargas dictatorship and to turn the country back to a democratic form of government. When General Dutra was elected president in December 1945 the military were content to stay in the barracks. Vargas returned to power in 1951 as the elected president, but in 1954 the military again became involved because of their concern about "corruption." In that year, as a result of the pressures exerted by the military, Vargas committed suicide. In the considerable political turmoil that followed (in one period of three days Brazil had three different presidents), the military was again involved but not in a unified way. The navy and the army could not agree on goals and desirable political leaders. The scheduled presidential elections were held in 1955, and the crisis ended with the election of Juscelino Kubitschek as president.

The military's next political venture took place in 1961, when Quadros unexpectedly resigned as president and Vice President Goulart was scheduled to assume the presidency. For various reasons, including the fact that Goulart was visiting mainland China at the time Quadros resigned, the military were greatly concerned about his leftist tendencies. Goulart returned from his trip to China and was kept waiting in Uruguay until he agreed to become president under a parliamentary form of government in which a prime minister exercised much of the presidential power.

The economic, political, and military crisis of 1964 was by far the most serious crisis of the post-World War II period. The military intervention of that year had the support of key civilians, governors of the major states, and the middle class. The armed forces did not intend to remain in power for long, but the conflict between the objectives of their revolution and the opposition to these goals led them consistently along the road to total political control. With 15 years of ideological and economic development preparation, the military felt reasonably confident in assuming a new role of protecting the fatherland from internal as well as external enemies. In an extension of the philosophy of the ESG, the revolutionary government became an alliance of military officers and technocrats.

Pre-1964 Political Patterns

In Brazil political parties have been for long periods a mechanism for controlling popular participation in politics and for representing special interests. As one Brazilian writer has concluded, "The origins of present mechanisms of political control are found in the earlier organization of Brazilian society, which was based on a power structure dominated by an agrarian elite."[7] During the early stage of party development in Brazil—that is, beginning with independence in 1822 and ending with the collapse of the monarchy in 1889—franchise restriction was one of the control mechanisms. Only "active citizens" with a constitutionally defined minimum income were permitted to vote.

The second stage of party development—that beginning with the proclamation of the republic and ending with the fall of Getúlio Vargas in 1945—was characterized by the absence of strong national parties and some changes in the mechanism of control. The agrarian elite continued to dominate the political scene. The legal-institutional framework brought about by the 1946 redemocratization, however, provided for direct elections and free party competition, with literacy becoming the only condition for political participation. But with 60 percent of the population over nine years of age classified as illiterate in the 1940 census, a majority of Brazil's adult population was effectively disenfranchised.

Among the most distinctive features of Brazilian political life after 1946 were the multiplicity of political parties of recent origin, their lack of ideological content or meaningful differences in program, and the highly personal nature of their leadership. At the time of the 1964 coup 14 parties were legally registered, but only 3 were organized on a national basis. In virtually every party, national or regional, the personal element predominated over questions of program and policy. Consequently, a party's strength or weakness at the polls was usually a reflection of the popularity of the individual candidate rather than of the party platform.[8]

Thus, without previous experience of any sort with an open and competitive party system, Brazil suddenly emerged in 1946 with both a mass multiparty system and an increase in popular participation. The number of people voting in the presidential election rose from 6 million in 1945 to almost 13 million in 1960. Over the same period the share of the total population voting increased from 13 to 18 percent, which in both years represented more than 80 percent of the registered voters. However, the share of the total population voting was still low relative to other Latin American countries at an equivalent level of social and economic development[9] and to the 38 percent of total United States population voting in the 1960 United States presidential election.

The Brazilian political experience over the 1946-64 period has been studied in great depth by many political scientists. A common characterization of the system in the jargon of the political scientists is praetorian, that is, a political system manifesting low levels of institutionalization and high levels of participation. In these systems social groups act directly in the political process. Regime authority is weakened, and the military is given frequent opportunities to intervene in politics.[10]

These scholars almost unanimously conclude that political development over the period did not succeed in meeting Brazil's needs. Neither strong political parties nor effective governmental institutions emerged to meet the growing socioeconomic demands of an urbanizing country. With the slowing down of economic growth in the early 1960s it became increasingly difficult for the regime to respond to new social and economic demands, and the government slid into a state of chronic instability. The political immobility and the threat of violence that characterized post-1960 politics led to a series of confrontations that activated the armed forces on March 31, 1964 and resulted in the present authoritarian regime.[11] As Philippe C. Schmitter concludes, "The coup of 1964 put an end, at least temporarily, to (the) disintegration and paralysis of the *sistema.*"[12]

In evaluating political developments in Brazil it is important to recognize the true features of the system that was displaced in 1964. The multiparty, popular election system had not developed strong party organizations. Political involvement was still significantly restricted by a literacy requirement for voting. Control of the system by agrarian and urban elites was still strong, and considerable political corruption prevailed. It was not a system of healthy political parties based on issues and widespread popular participation in the electoral process.

The Post-1964 Evolution of Military Political Control

Having taken the initiative to intervene in 1964, the military were confronted with the inevitable choice of returning power to the civilian elite or retaining it for an indefinite period. Although there was initial uncertainty, a consensus emerged among the military during the first year that the changes they believed necessary would take considerable time, and that the immediate return of power to the civilians would probably result in political breakdown once again. For these and other supporting reasons the military opted in late 1964 for the establishment of a military regime.

In Brazilian tradition it is important that the actions of the governing group be cloaked with legality and constitutionalism. Accordingly, a new constitution was written in 1967 to replace the 1946 instrument, but the military departed from previous practice through the use of Institutional Acts, which did not cancel the constitution but superseded and restricted the scope of that document. Seventeen Institutional Acts and 77 Complementary Acts were issued between 1964 and the end of 1969.[13]

The military government faced intensive, though probably not widely based, opposition during its early years and considerable dissension within its own ranks. Under the first Institutional Act the president had the power to revoke legislative mandates and to suspend political rights. During the first months of the new regime, three former presidents—Kubitschek, Quadros, and Goulart—6 governors, more than 40 members of Congress, and some 300 individuals active in political life had their rights suspended. In addition, a large number of university faculty members and an estimated 9,000 government employees were fired under a special dispensation from the existing legislation guaranteeing employment.[14]

The lowest point in the revolutionary government occurred in 1969 when President Artur Costa e Silva became ill and could not perform the duties of his office. In choosing a successor considerable infighting erupted among the military between those pushing the "repressive" demands of the linha dura or hard line and those advocating the "democratic" ideas of the linha branca or soft line. General Emilio Garrastazú Medici, who emerged as the new president, has been described as "a bland compromise figure chosen simply to maintain a minimum of military unity."[15] Medici was almost unknown to the Brazilian public, though he had been head of the National Information Service, which is concerned with intelligence and security and was associated with the harsh or repressive group in the military.

The most important achievement of President Medici was to unite the armed forces, eliminating their public differences and providing internal governmental channels for airing their disagreements. His success in harmonizing conflicting interests within the armed forces, which mirror to some extent the divergent interests within Brazilian society, helped build a wide popular consensus in favor of the government. After his first year in office Medici steadily gained in popularity with the point of transition occurring in June 1970 when Brazil won the world soccer championship. Some of the details surrounding this event deserve attention because they explain important characteristics of the Brazilian character.

Futebol, or what Americans would call soccer, is the most extensively played sport in the world, despite its neglect in the United States. Futebol is the most popular virtue or vice, depending on one's point of view, in Brazil. As a passion, it ranks higher with Brazilians than carnaval or politics, and the most famous and revered person in Brazil for more than a decade has been Pelé, internationally recognized as the world's greatest soccer player.

In 1958 Brazil first won the Jules Rimet trophy or World Cup, which is the emblem of international soccer supremacy. In the next world competition in 1962 Brazil again won the World Cup. In 1966 Brazil competed again but did not reach the finals. With Brazil in a difficult economic phase of its austerity period, this blow to national pride was so intense and widely felt that the event could be characterized as a near political crisis. Whether true or not, the story is told that the coach was not allowed to return to Brazil.

President Medici had long been an avid futebol fan and, in the preparatory phases for the 1970 championship matches to be held in Mexico City, he was interviewed by a newspaper reporter on the prospects for Brazil. In a casual way he expressed some specific views on the desirability of selecting certain players for the national team. Not too surprisingly these suggestions were implemented, and the players endorsed by the president ultimately performed with great distinction.

The Brazilian team progressed through the championship matches to the finals against Italy. Again the president was interviewed, and he forecast that Brazil would win by a score of 4 to 1. Subsequent events confirmed this forecast of both the victor and the score, and the victory aroused Brazil into national celebrations exceeding the enthusiasm of carnaval.

The victory was of special importance because, by winning for the third time, Brazil gained permanent possession of the prized Jules Rimet trophy. Shortly after the victory President Medici attended a soccer game in Rio de Janeiro at the Maracanã Stadium, which holds about 200,000 spectators. As he entered to take his seat the entire mass of people present stood and applauded him. The event had obvious implications for his role as political leader and for popular support of the military regime.

The Current Political Structure

The present political system that has evolved over the 1964-74 decade has two political parties, ARENA (Aliança Renovadora Nacional) and MDB (Movimento Democrático Brasileiro). ARENA is the government party whereas MDB is an opposition party established to give legitimacy to the government. The president, who holds office for a nonrenewable term of five years, is selected by the High Command of the Armed Forces and "elected" indirectly by the vote of the Electoral College, which is composed of members of the national congress and delegates from each state appointed by the majority party in the state legislature. The vice president and the governors of the states are also elected indirectly. The federal and state legislators are elected directly, but all candidates for public positions are screened by the military government. The mayors of the key cities are appointed by the governors, subject to the approval of the state legislatures. The responsibility and authority of the legislators are limited, and there has been little room for federal senators or deputies to initiate or influence policies. In large part the national congress performs a ritualistic function. Effectively, Brazil has a one-party system with a symbolic opposition that has been allowed to operate within narrow limits.

However, in November 1974 elections were held for one-third of the Senators and all members of the Chamber of Deputies and State Assemblies. The opposition MDB made significant gains in the Congress winning 16 out of 22 federal Senate seats at stake and 160 of the 364 seats in the Chamber of Deputies. Its candidates campaigned on human rights, censorship, income distribution, inflation, and foreign investment in Brazil. When the Congress assembled in 1975 the MDB began to use its new muscle and freedom. It succeeded in establishing a Parliamentary Commission of Inquiry on the Activities of Multinational Companies in Brazil, and it announced that it would summon the minister of justice to explain the fate of missing political prisoners. This and other pressures on the political prisoners issue caused the minister of justice to schedule a nationwide television report on the matter, which still did not satisfy opposition leaders.

Effective political power remains in the hands of the military. But, consistent with previous tradition in matters of economic policy, power has been delegated even more completely than in previous periods to the tecnicos. In a real sense Brazil became a technocratic government under military guardianship. In 1974 the role of the tecnicos was somewhat reduced by the Geisel administration. As former head of Petrobrás, General Geisel had both tecnico and military credentials.

The tecnicos do not, however, work in a vacuum. The decisions they make are based on an economic model concurred in by the military, which determines such questions as major priorities for investment and the role of foreign private investment. It is significant, nonetheless, that military personnel are not directly involved in a number of vital economic sectors. For example, the banking, electric power, and financial sectors are completely civilian managed. Apparently, the military prefer to stay out of the areas in which they are not experienced and where the results of management are shown in measurable terms, such as profit and loss or an electric power failure.

The record of the military in economic development is not unmarred. Military officers have assumed the leadership of regional development agencies like SUDENE in the Northeast and resource development agencies such as the commission for the São Francisco Valley. In both areas, their record of accomplishment has not been distinguished.

The road travelled by the revolutionary government over its first decade has been erratic at times. The economic performance since 1968 has unquestionably strengthened Brazil's military revolution. The country has been riding a wave of national confidence based on economic success, considerable social improvement, and extensive fulfillment of national aspirations. After a decade of rule the revolutionary government is strong and confident that it holds all the cards in any determination of its future. The political system will most certainly not return to the past. As one scholar notes, "The revolution is now an established part of national history; and the political future, whatever it is, will be a product of the revolution."[16]

Terrorism, Torture, and "Taboos"

Using "threat to national security" as both a criterion and a rationale for disallowing political opposition, the military regime has moved against any resistance with resolution and firmness. One response was for the opposition to go underground. An early source of opposition was the National Student Union (UNE), which had supported President Goulart before the coup. In October 1964 the Congress voted to abolish the UNE and replace it with a new organization controlled by the government. Tensions between the student groups and the government steadily increased and culminated in an armed confrontation in April 1968 in which a student was killed.

After the regime's display of violence and force in disbanding the student demonstrations, politically motivated terrorist activities began. The nation was subjected to a wave of bank robberies, several kidnappings including that of the United States ambassador, and a few assassinations. The government's reaction was to employ more violent means of repression, which in turn were met by increased activity from nascent urban guerrilla groups. The escalation continued when numerous police and military organizations retaliated with arbitrary seizures, mass arrests, torture, and murder—activities which were well publicized in European and North American news media. The guerrilla groups were no match for the better organized and better equipped military and police forces, which systematically penetrated and destroyed most resistance organizations by the early 1970s. Guerrilla activities have not been a uniquely Brazilian phenomenon; the Middle East, Ireland, Uruguay, Argentina, and even the United States have had similar and more recent experiences of the type.

The use of torture has not been uncommon in Brazil, but both the victims and the extent of torture changed dramatically during the military regime.[17] With the exception of the Vargas Estado Novo years, torture for political purposes had not been employed in recent times. While previously the victims generally were the criminal poor, the military regime brutalized the politically active sons and daughters of the middle and upper classes. Although the degree of political repression has decreased from the early period of the revolutionary government, Brazilian church officials and the Brazilian Bar Association were protesting during 1974 that a number of political prisoners had disappeared and that abuses by the security forces were continuing. "It is not that there is an increase in political repression," a São Paulo lawyer commented, "But now we have hopes that the government will do something about it and that's why we're pushing the issue."[18]

Torture and assassinations have also been carried out by unofficial paramilitary groups of off-duty policemen, such as the notorious Death Squads, whose members take it upon themselves to rid society of "hard-core" criminals and sexual deviants as well as suspected political activists. The Geisel government has denounced the Death Squads, which are composed almost entirely of state civil police and not of members of the army. Efforts have been made to prosecute those engaged in these illegal activities.[19]

The "taboos" refer to the continued existence of censorship in Brazil. As of 1975 several of the major newspapers and periodicals had censors stationed in their offices to review all the material to be published. Other news media are censored through phoned instructions. The most important effect is to make the press more cautious. Even though a specific subject or treatment of it has not been forbidden, the editors are frequently unwilling to take a chance on publishing many types of news. The world-renowned newspaper, *O Estado de São Paulo*, has made a career of defying government regulations no matter what their orientation. As a centenary gift in 1974 the government quietly removed its censors from the newspaper's offices.

In view of the unfavorable domestic and worldwide reactions to Brazil's use of torture, violence, and censorship, the question arises as to why the government has tolerated such practices, especially since the regime has been concerned about its public relations image and has developed an extensive and solid base of public support.

There are several reasons why it has been difficult to end these practices. First, both torture and vigilantism are hard to control administratively. Military and police organizations are numerous and decentralized, making the restraint of zealous members of these groups difficult. Second, the military consists of a number of different groups with widely varying and opposing views on the internal security threat and the danger of resistance groups. In order to achieve a united military front, the military leaders had to make concessions to the extremist military groups by giving them resources to pursue their internal security campaigns. Perceived security threats then became self-fulfilling, because the security groups had to discover subversives in order to justify the initial support and to continue receiving funds. Third, in some cases the rumors and assorted horror stories, even though exaggerated or untrue, had the effect of discouraging forces that might want to engage in resistance to the regime. In this way the government has forced a great deal of depoliticization in Brazil.

A key question for the future is whether President Geisel will be able to impose effective control over repressive activities of military and police groups, or whether concessions are still necessary to maintain a united military front. The security system of the military-intelligence services and the police, created during the decade of military government, has become almost a state within a state. Another question is whether the government will continue the Geisel initiative of opening up the political system for wider participation and a greater degree of debate and dissension. If repression is eliminated or greatly reduced and greater democratic participation is permitted, the features of the military-technocratic regime that have evoked the most bitter domestic and foreign criticism would be eliminated.

Some Speculations About the Future

The elections of November 1974 marked the abrupt beginning of a sensitive new political phase for Brazil. In an experiment designed to end a decade of authoritarian government and in the belief that Brazil can move peacefully on a step-by-step basis toward democracy, President Geisel risked open elections in which the government party suffered a surprising defeat. Immediately after the elections, some Brazilians feared that the "hard-liners" in the military establishment might attempt to annul the election results. But Geisel was successful in retaining the support of the military and was able in his January message to the nation to congratulate the opposition party on its victories and on its "measured and self-disciplined" campaign.

The open elections for federal and state legislators and the process of distensão, or political liberalization, that has continued since the elections with what has been described as homeopathic gradualism does not mean democratic rule has been restored in Brazil. But the process of moving in that direction has begun. If the liberalization process is not interrupted by some crisis incident, a contingency that both parties to the process seem anxious to avoid, and the direct election of state governors takes place as scheduled in 1978, President Geisel's faith in Brazil's ability to move peacefully toward democracy will be substantially vindicated.

With authoritarian rather than democratic governments in power throughout much of Latin America and the rest of the world, why is Brazil attempting to move against the tide—particularly when the conviction has been growing in many parts of the world that rapid development can only be achieved through a strong and even repressive government?

The principal motivation apparently comes from a deep philosophical commitment by many, but not all, Brazilians to a broader political participation in the political system than has been possible over the last decade. The military men who have emerged as presidents in recent years have shared this commitment. When he became president in 1969 Medici promised to move to a more democratic government but did not, or was not able, to keep these promises. President Geisel made similar promises when he assumed office in 1974.

In one of his first pronouncements President Geisel reaffirmed his conviction that the "revolutionary movement of 1964" would support the two goals of "development and security" and that he would carry out "sincere efforts for gradual but secure democratic improvement *(aperfeiçoamento democrático)* intensifying honest and mutually respectful dialogue and stimulating participation by the responsible elites and the people in general, for the creation of a healthy climate of basic consensus and the completion of the institutionalization of the principles of the 1964 Revolution."[20]

Those in power are fully convinced that the political structure of the past decade has proven successful in what is really significant, namely, guaranteeing national development. The leaders also believe that they have done an excellent job and as one outside observer suggests, this is far more determinative of the present and future capacity to maintain power than what outsiders may think of the Brazilian government.[21] But economic and political success has seriously weakened the initial justification for a repressive authoritarian government. The chaos that reigned in 1964 has changed to order. The old political leaders held in such low esteem by the military have been purged, or passed over by time. On the economic front, by choice of the military, civilian tecnicos have been mainly responsible for developing and administering the policies that have produced such spectacular results and consequently have earned a lion's share of the credit.

The question Brazil faces is not whether a strong government is required to implement economic policy. Obviously, to a large degree it is—regardless of whether a government is civilian or military. The real question is to what extent political participation and civil liberties must be sacrificed.[22] Brazil's leadership views the revolution not only as a movement to develop the country economically but also to establish viable political institutions. The political goal will not be easy to achieve because the Brazilians have not yet been able to design a model that they feel will fit their situation, and because changes will have to be experimental and gradual. Furthermore, the future strength of the regime is, of course, dependent on the performance of the economy. The government will not be expected to continue achieving the unusually high growth rates of the 1968-74 period. But, a precipitous slowdown of the economy could seriously erode the regime's nonmilitary support and popular tolerance for "homeopathic gradualism" in political change.

Whatever the evolution of political institutions, for the foreseeable future the "quality" of political leadership will be controlled by the military powers. One of the clear objectives of the post-1964 governments has been to erase from public participation and attention the traditional political class, which was often parochial and self-serving in the rural areas and populist in the cities. The regime has tried to substitute the technocrat-public administrator, preoccupied with national development. As a result of this policy the prerevolutionary political leaders have largely been eliminated, and a new crop of leaders with political experience and a popular following has only recently had a chance to emerge.

Thus, the Geisel political liberalization program can abort for a number of reasons. The hazards of an economic reversal or sharp slowdown and the absence of experienced political leaders have already been noted. It is also essential for Geisel to preserve the tradition of unity within the armed forces by maintaining a balance between those favoring further liberalization and those suspicious or opposed to such developments. Even more critical is the president's ability to control the quasi-independent security system within which opposition is most likely to arise. If the military government chooses to open the gates to democratic and civilian participation, it may let loose forces such as antimilitarism and populism that are anathema to the armed forces and which their intervention was designed to eliminate. Such a situation may be hard to accept.

The views and forecasts of the future fate of political development in Brazil have run the gamut. At one extreme is exiled former congressman Marcio

Moreira Alves who foresees increased terrorism and armed struggle as the only alternative to Brazil's "terrorist state."[23] A more moderate view is that "The military regime in Brazil, as in other Latin American countries, is neither a throwback to the past interventions of ambitious military leaders in the nineteenth century nor simply an escalation of arbitrary, dictatorial government—although the incidents of official repression indicate that the latter is not absent. The military government represents in a very real sense a logical extension of major trends and characteristics of Brazilian politics. . . . The military regime constitutes merely a new form through which elitism has been maintained."[24]

Still another interpretation of the political regime that has emerged is the "associated-dependent development" model that "stresses the dynamic process by which new forms of national political power and new international economic forces have interacted" to influence Brazil's political system.[25] This view argues that a basic change in the main axis of the power system has occurred with the result that "groups expressing the interest and modes of organization of international capitalism"—meaning multinational enterprises and foreign investment—have gained disproportionate influence. As a consequence the future evolution of the Brazilian political system, it is argued, will be heavily shaped by foreign enterprises and Brazilians associated with foreign corporations. This view is an application of the "dependência" concept that has become popular among many Latin American scholars,[26] although they have not as yet defined the future political pattern that is likely to emerge in Brazil.

An important point to consider in attempting to foresee the future is that the present regime represents a military generation already in decline as retirement takes its steady toll. As Ronald M. Schneider suggests, the army "College of Cardinals" will have a distinctly different complexion within only a few years, and this may result in a significant policy reorientation.[27]

In sum, much of the extensive analysis by political scientists of the problems Brazil faces in trying to institutionalize an authoritarian regime suggests that slight variations of the present military authoritarian pattern may persist for some time without becoming institutionalized.[28] In other words, the government will do what military governments are expected to do: remain in power as long as it can. Another more optimistic view is that President Geisel has a reasonable chance of succeeding with distensão. As one experienced observer of Brazil has concluded, this will not be easy, "but at least the first fresh political breeze" in a decade is blowing over this vast country.[29]

Notes

1. Instituto de Pesquisas, Estudos e Assessoria do Congresso, *Estratégias de Descompressão Política*, Brasilia, 20 de setembro de 1973.

2. The words are Deodora's. See Nelson Werneck Sodré, *História Militar do Brasil* (Rio de Janeiro, 1965), p. 147.

3. Frank D. McCann, "The Military and Change in Brazil," in *Cultural Change in Brazil, Papers from the Midwest Association for Latin American Studies, October 30 and 31, 1969*, edited by Merrill Rippy (Muncie, Indiana: Ball State University, no date), pp. 1-12.

4. Ronald M. Schneider, *The Political System of Brazil* (New York: Columbia University Press, 1971), p. 244.

5. Alfred Stepan, "The New Professionalism of Internal Warfare and Military Role Expansion," in *Authoritarian Brazil*, edited by Alfred Stepan (New Haven: Yale University Press, 1973), p. 58.

6. McCann, "The Military," pp. 8-9.

7. Paulo Roberto Motta, "Elite Control and Participation in the Party System," in *Contemporary Brazil*, edited by H. Jon Rosenbaum and William G. Tyler (New York: Praeger Publishers, 1972), p. 213.

8. Ronald M. Schneider, *Political System*, p. 35.

9. Philippe C. Schmitter, *Interest Conflict and Political Change in Brazil* (Stanford, California: Stanford University Press, 1971), p. 381.

10. Riordan Roett, "A Praetorian Army in Politics: The Changing Role of the Brazilian Military," in *Brazil in the Sixties*, edited by Riordan Roett (Nashville, Tennessee: Vanderbilt University Press, 1972), p. 4.

11. Two excellent sources on Brazil's political situation before the 1964 revolution are Thomas E. Skidmore, *Politics in Brazil, 1930-1964* (New York: Oxford University Press, 1967), and John W.F. Dulles, *Unrest in Brazil: Political-Military Crises 1955-1964* (Austin: University of Texas Press, 1970).

12. Schmitter, *Interest Conflict and Political Change*, p. 386.

13. Roett, "Praetorian Army," p. 28.

14. Ibid., p. 30.

15. Alfred Stepan, *Military in Politics: Changing Patterns in Brazil* (Princeton: Princeton University, 1971), p. 265.

16. Thomas G. Sanders, *The Brazilian Model* (TGS-7 '73), Fieldstaff Reports, East Coast South-America Series, Vol. XVII, No. 8, August 1973.

17. See Amnesty International, *Report on Torture* (London: Gerald Duckworth & Co., 1973), pp. 185-88.

18. *New York Times*, July 9, 1974, p. 9. © 1974 by the New York Times Company. Reprinted by permission.

19. Edwin McDowell, "The Murderous Policemen of Brazil," *Wall Street Journal*, November 1, 1974.

20. Speech of March 19, 1974 to the first meeting of cabinet ministers (author's translation).

21. Thomas G. Sanders, *The Brazilian Model*, p. 8.

22. Roett, "Praetorian Army," p. 21.

23. Marcio Moreira Alves, "Urban Guerrillas and the Terrorist State," in Rosenbaum and Tyler, *Contemporary Brazil*, p. 61.

24. Douglas A. Chalmers, "Political Groups and Authority in Brazil," in Roett, ed., *Brazil in the Sixties*, p. 75.

25. Fernando Henrique Cardoso, "Associated-Dependent Development: Theoretical and Practical Implications" in Stepan, ed., *Authoritarian Brazil*, pp. 142-43.

26. See Osvaldo Sunkel, "Big Business and 'Dependência': A Latin American View," *Foreign Affairs*, April 1972, pp. 517-31; Raimar Richers, "Dependência: Fatalidade ou Falácia do Desenvolvimento?" *Revista de Administração de Empresas*, Vol. 13, No. 1, March 1973, pp. 41-55.

27. Schneider, *Political System*, p. 362.

28. Juan J. Linz, "The Future of an Authoritarian Situation or the Institutionalization of an Authoritarian Regime: The Case of Brazil," in Stepan, ed., *Authoritarian Brazil*, p. 254.

29. Tad Szulc, "Letter from Brasilia," *The New Yorker*, March 10, 1975, p. 87.

# 10 Challenges for the Future

"Brazil can, with justification, aspire to development and grandeur." This proclamation introduces Brazil's Second National Development Plan (1975-79), released in late 1974. The last decade, the plan asserts, has shown that the nation is capable of realizing policies of a great country, "with a sense of its own importance and an awareness of its responsibility—the habitual price of greatness."[1]

Such euphoria and self-confidence is not surprising for a nation that succeeded in expanding its national output in only seven years by as much as was achieved over all the previous centuries of existence. Within this spirit of optimism the Second Plan establishes ambitious economic and social targets for the end of the decade. Income per capita, for example, is projected to exceed US$1,100 (in 1973 prices). Gross domestic product is expected to reach US$138 billion, making Brazil the eighth largest market in the world in terms of the total size of the economy. Similarly ambitious development goals have been defined for the fields of infrastructure, education, health, and social welfare. These targets are to be met through annual average growth rates of 7 percent for agriculture, 12 percent for the industrial sector, and more than 20 percent for exports.

In articulating its development aspirations the Geisel government was aware of many internal and external challenges it would have to meet in fulfilling its announced goals. In particular, the surge of international oil prices had already occurred, and the Second Plan presents a strategy for attempting to adjust to this new situation. However, the widespread economic recession in foreign countries that became a reality in late 1974 was not clearly apparent at the time the Second Plan was prepared and does not appear to be taken into account adequately. In realizing its ambitious goals, Brazil will have to adjust to a wider range of new uncertainties in the international environment than anticipated, in addition to resolving a plethora of domestic, economic, political, and social challenges, many of which are the result of past successes. And Brazil will have to defy the conventional wisdom that such high growth rates cannot be sustained for long periods without at least a temporary pause. Also, a significant slackening of development momentum would aggravate many social and political problems.

New External Challenges

Brazil's most difficult challenge undoubtedly arises out of the world economic slowdown that began in late 1974. Because Brazil has succeeded in becoming more closely integrated into the world economy, its future prospects are more dependent upon and more vulnerable to changes in the world economic situation. Furthermore, unlike many of the domestic challenges that confront the nation, the external factors are largely outside Brazil's control.

The cloud of uncertainty cast over the world economic situation by increases in world petroleum prices and related events affects several crucial development goals. Can Brazil continue to expand its exports at a rapid rate despite a significant economic slowdown in most foreign countries? Can large inflows of foreign private investment be sustained? Can Brazil continue to secure large amounts of foreign loans on reasonable terms when the demand and supply situation in international financial markets has changed markedly?

Brazil's export goal is to expand from a level of US$6.2 billion in 1973 to US$24 billion in 1980 in constant prices. The projected increase of almost 400 percent in 7 years assumes that manufactured and semimanufactured exports can be increased from a level of about US$2 billion in 1973 to almost US$15 billion in 1980, and that exports of primary products will expand from US$4.1 billion to slightly more than US$9 billion over the same period.

These aspirations will be influenced by both domestic supply and foreign demand uncertainties. In the case of primary products such as agricultural commodities the future outlook for an expanding foreign demand is promising, but the high levels of world market prices prevailing in the early 1970s are almost certain to soften considerably. In some product areas such as meat Brazil may also experience problems of increasing the supply for export because of sharply increased domestic demand and a desire to keep domestic prices low. Regarding exports of minerals and forest products, foreign demand is likely to weaken with the slowdown of foreign industrial expansion.

The projected expansion of manufactured and semimanufactured exports will be a difficult goal to achieve. Foreign demand is almost certain to be constrained by a slowdown in the economic growth trends in foreign countries. Furthermore, the projected expansion, if achieved, is likely to change Brazil's position from that of a small participant in many foreign markets to that of a major supplier in a number of countries, thus making Brazilian exports more vulnerable to rising protectionist sentiment in nations concerned about maintaining domestic employment and improving their balance-of-payments position.

The Brazilian strategy is to rely heavily on multinational enterprises operating in Brazil to expand their exports as suppliers to overseas units of their systems. Among other benefits, this strategy is expected to reduce the risk of protectionist barriers. In particular, the automobile industry is being relied upon to expand its exports. But will Volkswagen (VW) be able to increase its exports of components and vehicles when the VW plant in Germany is not operating at full capacity, and there is great pressure in Germany by the government and labor unions to keep local employment levels high? Or how long can Ford continue to export small car engines to the United States when United States automobile sales have fallen drastically?

Brazil has other dimensions to its export expansion strategy, such as increasing its trade with the Soviet Union, mainland China, and other communist countries as well as with its Latin American neighbors. Nevertheless, the mammoth size of the export expansion goals for manufactured goods in a period of world economic recession presents Brazil with one of its most serious challenges for the future.

Brazil's prospects for maintaining large inflows of foreign private direct investment depend on both future domestic and international growth trends, as well as the outcome of new domestic political pressures to make Brazil's policy toward multinationals more restrictive. On the economic side, such questions arise as to whether, and at what pace, Japanese investors will proceed with the plan for building a large steel mill near the Amazon to supply their home market at a time when the Japanese economy has slowed down because of the impact of higher petroleum prices and domestic inflation. Similar questions can be raised about possible lags in foreign investments for developing exports of iron ore, bauxite, aluminum, and forest products. To the extent that internal growth rates decelerate, foreign investment to expand production for the Brazilian market will also be deferred or stretched out over a longer period.

Capital inflows other than direct investment will be another major determinant of Brazil's future growth prospects. During 1972 and 1973 the inflow of financial credits was so strong that Brazil was able both to finance its capital gap and increase its foreign reserves. But with the oil crisis of 1973-74 the sources of loanable funds in international financial markets and the terms on which loans were available shifted dramatically. The oil exporting countries became major holders of loanable funds, and these funds were flowing predominantly into short-term loans and, to a lesser extent, low-risk investments in the industrialized countries.

The world oil "crisis" also created a large number of new borrowers competing for available funds. Countries such as Japan and Italy have had to expand greatly their foreign borrowing to compensate for balance-of-payments deficits arising out of the increased cost of imported petroleum. Will Brazil be able to compete effectively in international financial markets with the many countries newly seeking foreign loans? If so, will Brazil have to accept less favorable terms and shorter maturities than it has been able to get in the past?

Until 1974 Brazil had been strengthening its foreign reserve position by borrowing in excess of its current needs. But the 1974 balance-of-payments deficit was so large that Brazil had to dip into its reserves to the amount of US$1 billion even after expanding the annual influx of foreign loans and financing by about 50 percent.

On the favorable side, in late 1974 PETROBRÁS announced several major new petroleum discoveries that promise to increase domestic petroleum production and reduce the nation's dependence on oil imports. Brazil is hopeful that the new petroleum finds at the Campos field off the coast of the state of Rio de Janeiro and from offshore drilling near the states of Alagoas and Sergipe in the

Northeast will provide a partial solution to the critical petroleum problem. If the discoveries fulfill preliminary expectations Brazil should be able to save large amounts of foreign exchange, and the problems of expanding exports, attracting foreign investment, and maintaining a large inflow of foreign loans will become less difficult.

Future Domestic Economic Challenges

The domestic and the external challenges are closely intertwined. They differ, however, in the degree to which they are amenable to control. Brazilian policy makers are alert to the major domestic economic challenges they face and have revised many development strategies and proposed numerous new programs to meet them. The need to revise Brazil's industrialization strategy has been recognized. Agricultural development efforts are being expanded and strengthened. Programs have been outlined to expand domestic energy supplies, to increase employment, and to enlarge the supply of trained managers. The question for the future in all of these areas is whether the strategies are viable, and whether the implementation capability of the government is adequate to the proposed task.

Industrialization Strategy

In the industrial sector the dynamism since 1968 has come in large part from expansion in the manufacture of automobiles and consumer durables. As discussed in Chapter 6, the rate at which the domestic market will be able to absorb increased output of these products is expected to slow down. Although efforts are being made to maintain automobile production by increasing exports, the emphasis in Brazil's industrialization strategy has shifted to other product areas. The production of heavy capital goods is being encouraged to supply domestic needs. Basic intermediate products such as steel, aluminum, copper, and fertilizer have also been given priority because domestic demand for these products has been outstripping domestic production. Another industrialization priority target is to achieve a higher degree of processing of agricultural commodities, forestry products, and minerals being exported to foreign markets.

The revised industrialization strategy is impressive, and many projects that will implement the new thrust were in advanced planning stages or in construction as of 1975. The program to substitute for capital-equipment imports through expanded local production should not be seriously handicapped by short-term economic fluctuations, either domestic or external. For such types of major investment commitments, the crucial factors will be the long-range domestic growth prospects, the size of the domestic market, and governmental incentives or protection for local producers. The expansion of industries producing basic intermediate products is well under way and, again, is dependent mainly on the domestic market where shortages in most of these products already exist. The drive to process primary-product exports appears to have continuing promise. Although total exports of some items, such as iron ore, may not expand as rapidly as projected, there is still a substantial margin for increased processing of exports at present levels. The principal uncertainties, therefore, are in the short-term expansion of manufactured goods for export and in the ability of Brazil to enlarge the domestic market for consumer goods through redistribution of income measures.

Multinationals and Dependência

The multinational corporations have long encountered a friendly environment in Brazil. To be sure the amicable relations have been occasionally disturbed, such as during the Goulart presidency. But the persistent thrust of Brazilian policy for decades has been to encourage direct foreign investment, and most government officials and opinion leaders are firmly convinced that Brazil's multinationals policy has been administered imaginatively and effectively in Brazil's national interests, has contributed vitally to the nation's development success, is essential for realizing the country's ambitious development goals for the near future, and has had popular approval in the country. But with the establishment in 1975 of the Parliamentary Commission of Inquiry on Multinationals the government's long-standing policies toward the multinationals began to be challenged and at a time, in the government's view, when it was crucial that foreign investment should not be frightened away.

Brazil's II Development Plan assigned a large and multifaceted role to the multinationals. They were being relied upon to ease Brazil's balance-of-payments problems through sizeable direct investment inflows and through fulfilling a large share of Brazil's export goals; to provide a major portion of the capital needed for the many capital-intensive projects planned or underway in such fields as minerals, metal processing, capital goods, and chemicals; to be a principal source for the transfer of technology and management skills; and to contribute generally to economic growth and employment expansion through establishing advanced technology industries that have above-average expansion potentials.

As judged by the response of the multinationals since 1969, Brazil's policies have been remarkably successful—even to the point that the government's problem frequently has been to choose among, rather than to find, willing foreign investors. The economic attractions of Brazil, which varied with the business interest of the specific multinationals, have been the nation's large and growing market, the access afforded to sources of natural resources, and for a small but growing number of firms, the competitive advantage created by Brazil's export incentive policies for manufacturing labor intensive products to supply foreign markets. Added to the economic attractions have been the foreign investor's perception of a stable political environment and "enlightened" control policies.

Why have the multinationals viewed Brazil's control policies as "enlightened"? Given its propensity for pragmatism and administrative flexibility, Brazil has not followed a pattern common to many countries of trying to have a single, comprehensive law or code governing foreign investment. Some policies are written into law, such as the regulations for profit and capital repatriation and the definition of areas closed to foreign investors—mainly petroleum exploration, most public utility fields, newspapers, magazines, radio, and television. There are no laws requiring foreigners to share ownership with local partners, but joint ventures, frequently with government enterprises, are strongly recommended by government officials in such fields as minerals and petrochemicals. Of key importance to the multinationals has been the sophistication and technical competence of the government officials with whom they have had to deal, the ability to get clear-cut and reasonably prompt decisions, and the government's reputation for not changing agreements or the rules of the game abruptly and without negotiation.

If the multinationals find Brazil so attractive, does this mean that Brazil has not been maximizing its national interests? Brazilian officials reject this possibility because they accept the view that foreign investment does not have to be a "zero-sum" game in which one party loses if the other gains.[2] They feel that they have defined and anticipated the kinds of contributions toward national development goals expected from the multinationals, and have designed and implemented policies to realize these aspirations. As one example, when the development of an automobile industry was given national priority and an indigenous capability was not present, attractive incentives were afforded to foreign automobile producers. But to achieve a further goal of using the foreign automobile industry to stimulate additional local industries, local content requirements (the progressive replacement of imports by components made in Brazil) were made a part of the incentive package.

There are numerous other examples of effective policies. Brazil has induced the multinationals to become leading exporters of manufactured goods when export expansion became a national priority. It initiated in 1973 promising efforts to enlarge the contribution of the multinationals to Brazil's technological and scientific base. It has followed a policy in the operations of the National Economic Development Bank, Brazil's principal source for long-term capital, described as "creating privileges" for private national companies rather than discriminating against foreign firms. This policy has compelled the multinationals to do most of their financing outside of Brazil, thus minimizing local competition with national firms for scarce domestic sources of capital. It has reduced the political risk for the multinationals by diversifying the nationality mix of foreign investment in the country.

If the past record has been as good as Brazilian officialdom claims, why should the multinational policies suddenly be challenged? In part, Brazil has been influenced by a worldwide wave of concern in both host and home countries that the spectacular growth of the multinationals have made them a serious threat to the sovereignty of nations. President Geisel indicated that he shared this concern when, in his presidential nomination acceptance speech of September 1973, he emphasized the emergence on the world scene "of unique new protagonists, the multinational enterprises whose potential for good, or perhaps for bad, we have not undertaken to evaluate."

Most of the controversial issues that have been raised at the international level have become part of the Brazilian debate on the role of the multinationals. These include such matters as appropriate technologies, the dependência focus on having important decision centers outside of the country and the cost of and growing reliance on imported technology, "transfer pricing" and other means of excessive repatriation of funds, the potential for unwarranted political intrusion in national affairs as was demonstrated in the early 1970s by the case of ITT in Chile, and the influence of the multinationals on consumer tastes and the distribution of income.

Uniquely national elements are also involved in Brazil's reexamination of its multinational policies. The Brazilian private sector contrasts its difficulties in raising enough capital, particularly equity capital, with the much easier access the multinational (and government) enterprises have. As a result the sector has become increasingly concerned that foreign (and government) enterprises are becoming too dominant in the total Brazilian economy at its expense. Another national element is that the opposition political party with its recent political successes feels that it must become more active, and the multinationals issue has political appeal. It has long been a subject of sincere and legitimate concern to many Brazilians.

What is the likely outcome of this challenge? The parliamentary commission was required by the rules of the Congress to conclude its work in August 1975 and present its findings to the Economic Development Council, headed by President Geisel. But the challenge does not stop there. The debate has been started and will continue. If historical patterns and the Brazilian preference for pragmatic over ideological approaches are appropriate guidelines for the future, the general liberal thrust of Brazil's multinational policies is likely to continue. At the same time even more emphasis will be given to programs for strengthening domestic private enterprise. Also, control policies may be extended to restrict the acquisition of national companies by foreign firms and to expand the government's influence over the speed, cost, and kinds of technology transfers.

The behavior of the multinationals will be a crucial element in shaping Brazil's future policies. They are expected to contribute to Brazil's development as well as their own company goals. As former Minister Dias Leite warned in discussing foreign investments in the minerals field, "Foreign industries will continue to be offered the opportunity to participate in the development of Brazil, so long as their object is not to 'tutor' national enterprises or simply extend their production facilities to Brazil exclusively to resolve their own problems of pollution and energy shortages.."[3]

Agricultural Development

If Brazil succeeds in increasing the role of agricultural development in the nation's overall development strategy, any shortfall in fulfilling the industrialization goals becomes less critical. The new agricultural development strategy emphasizes a more rational use of land, raising the level of entrepreneurial capacity, agrarian land reform, expanding the agricultural frontier in the Central West and Amazon regions, improving the distribution system, and the establishment of buffer stocks.[4]

Brazil has the potential for sustaining comparatively high long-term growth rates of agricultural production. Furthermore, the relative abundance of land and labor in the rural sector should permit expansion in total national output with a lesser amount of investment than would be possible with a higher reliance on industry. The key problem in accelerating agricultural development is the need to rely on the government bureaucracy for much of the program implementation.

Traditionally, Brazil's Ministry of Agriculture has had weak leadership. In many development programs other than agriculture, Brazil has overcome the administrative weakness of the regular government ministries by creating autonomous quasi-governmental agencies or government enterprises that are not limited by low salary levels and by conventional government red tape. In the field of agriculture the opportunities for using this approach are much more restricted than for many other areas such as electric power, for example. Agricultural development programs have to deal with large numbers of participants geographically dispersed over most of the country. They are generally not revenue producing and are dependent on government appropriations. They also involve a myriad of governmental agencies at the national, regional, state, and local levels.

The aspirations of Brazilian leaders to raise productivity in agriculture, however, may not be satisfactorily fulfilled in the near future. More land is easily available, although land prices have risen as a result of speculation. The cost of agricultural inputs for modernizing agriculture, such as fertilizer, is relatively high in Brazil and prohibitively so in interior locations where transport costs must also be paid. The limited amount of agronomic research and a weak system of agricultural technical assistance and credit are other constraints.

As a reflection of the difficulties in agricultural development, the special programs for the Northeast have been handicapped by the absence of a clear definition of responsibility for overlapping agencies and a lack of central coordination. In the case of agricultural credit, colonization, and land reform, the government programs have had only modest impact. In the case of land redistribution there is considerable uncertainty as to whether the government really intends to give a high priority to the announced program. Some of of the agricultural programs have been producing impressive results, but a major uncertainty still exists as to whether Brazil can break away from a long tradition of weak program implementation in the field of agriculture.

Energy

The energy issue is characterized in the Second Plan as one of the three "Major Themes of Today and Tomorrow," along with urban development and environmental pollution. The strategy outlined for resolving the energy problem is directed to both the supply and demand for petroleum. On the demand side Brazil intends to substitute other sources of energy for petroleum, through such measures as further electrification of the railroads, expansion of "collective" transportation in metropolitan areas, and increased use of coal and nuclear energy. On the supply side Brazil is concentrating on domestic exploration programs for petroleum, is participating in a number of foreign petroleum exploration ventures, and hopes to exploit its large reserves of oil shale.

For the immediate future the energy challenge has created extremely difficult problems for Brazil. But over the medium and long term Brazil's prospects for adjusting to the changed international petroleum situation are reasonably bright, particularly through the expansion and substitution of other energy sources for petroleum. Petroleum will continue to be necessary for much of the transportation system, for industrial processes requiring heat, and as raw material inputs for the chemical industry.

Because of its climate Brazil does not consume large quantities of petroleum products for household heating, as is true in many other countries, although petroleum products are used for domestic cooking and water heating. Because of its gigantic hydro resources Brazil has one of the lowest degrees of dependence in the world (less than 10 percent) on petroleum for generating electricity.[5] Even after the hydroelectric projects now underway are completed, which will more than double Brazil's total electric power generating capacity by the early 1980s, Brazil will still have huge undeveloped hydro potential.

Over a still longer time horizon nuclear energy is expected to become of great importance. So far uranium discoveries have been minor. But both foreign and national geologists are supremely confident that major ore discoveries will be made. In furtherance of this belief Brazil and West Germany announced in 1975 a multibillion dollar agreement under which West Germany will assist Brazil in uranium exploration as well as building a uranium enrichment plant, a plant for recycling used nuclear fuel, and up to eight nuclear power stations. In return West Germany will receive long-term deliveries of natural uranium.

Employment

In employment, the issue of future jobs remains a major challenge in spite of the progress in expanding employment opportunities during the early 1970s. Over the 1960-70 decade almost 7 million new jobs became available. Of this total, agriculture contributed about 1 million new jobs, the industrial sector about 2.3 million, and the service sector about 3.7 million. During the 1970-80 decade an estimated 10 million new jobs will have to be created.[6] This challenge will have to be met almost exclusively by industry and services. Manpower needs in agriculture are likely to be reduced through the adoption of improved technology. In any event, a massive amount of underemployment already exists in the rural areas.

The principal strategy for meeting the employment challenge is to maintain high growth rates for the economy and to enlarge the education and training opportunities for workers. The official strategy has been criticized in some quarters for not giving adequate attention to the importance of "appropriate technologies"—an issue that is not unique to Brazil. Many developing countries are concerned that the technologies being imported into their countries are too capital intensive and not labor intensive enough.[7] The problem is that most technological development over recent decades has taken place in industrialized countries where the cost of labor relative to capital has been higher than in the developing countries. In contrast, the less developed countries prefer types of technology that make maximum use of their plentiful labor supply and that economize on scarce capital. In Brazil the appropriate technology debate has been particularly spirited in relation to the incentive program for industrializing the Northeast region.[8]

The dilemma that Brazil and other developing countries face in this area is that business firms must be efficient and competitive in order to stay in business and expand. In many cases this requires that the most advanced and capital intensive technology be used. The choice among available technologies is relatively limited. Neither business firms nor national governments nor international agencies have yet been willing to make the massive investments in research needed to develop new technologies that are labor intensive, small scale, and still efficient.

Along with the challenge to create new jobs, Brazil also has a critical need to expand the supply of trained personnel. In spite of an increase in the resources allocated for training and professional education, development has been so rapid since 1968 that the demand for trained people has substantially outpaced the supply. One of the most serious shortages is in experienced management personnel. The government was late in recognizing this need and has undertaken a crash program for expanding and upgrading management training. The scale of the training effort is still small in relation to the burgeoning demand, and the truncated time horizon made necessary by the force of events has resulted in a serious compromise in the quality of the training.

In other fields of professional and technical training, such as economics, science, and engineering, Brazil anticipated its needs sufficiently in advance to be able to send large numbers of Brazilians to Europe, the United States, and to programs of the international agencies so as to take advantage of foreign training resources. For training managers and professors of business administration, however, Brazil is relying almost exclusively on its limited domestic resources. The Graduate School of Business Administration of the Getúlio Vargas Foundation in São Paulo, developed through a USAID-financed cooperative arrangement with Michigan State University, has undertaken as a special project to provide more advanced training for professors of business administration from other universities in the country.

National Integration

A continuing challenge deeply ingrained in the Brazilian spirit is the goal of national integration. This aspiration encompasses the political-national security desire to populate and develop the strategic empty spaces in this vast nation. It also includes the problem of reducing Brazil's wide regional disparities in economic levels. The regional disparities question involves a complex of political, economic, and egalitarian issues. Geographical unevenness in development generates difficult political pressures on resource allocation decision even in an authoritarian political system. An economic issue is whether the less developed regions can make a greater contribution to national development goals. The egalitarian question parallels the distribution-of-income debate, except that it focuses on the need for all regions to share more equitably in the fruits of development progress.

Some government programs to occupy the "hollow interior" have been reasonably successful. The building of Brasilia, the transportation infrastructure support for the expansion of the agricultural frontier in Goiás and Mato Grosso of the Central West, the incentives and the minerals exploration programs for the Amazon are all serving as magnets to draw population to the interior.

At the same time intense emotional and military security pressures for populating the interior have created a continuing danger that inadequately planned and premature projects will be undertaken, with a resultant massive waste of scarce development resources and effort. An example of this appears to be the Transamazônica highway that was launched in 1970 with much euphoria and fanfare. It was undertaken without detailed studies of the economic base that was expected to attract and support migrants to the area and without advance preparation for relocation and colonization assistance. The accumulated construction and resettlement problems that were encountered seem to have halted the project as of 1975. It is interesting to note that the highway is almost unmentioned in the II National Development Plan.

The challenge is whether Brazil can adjust its national integration aspirations to economic realities. If the permanent base for new settlements is agriculture, there must be a growing world or domestic demand for the products to be produced, and production in these areas must be competitive with alternative areas in Brazil. If the permanent base is to be minerals, a massive highway project does not seem to be the most efficient strategy for prospecting nor a necessary condition for exploiting the more remote mineral resources in the Amazon. The recent major mineral projects in the Amazon include railway and water transportation in their plans.

Over time, many of the hollow spaces are likely to be filled. But forced pressure either from government programs that do not have a sound economic base or from high rates of population growth are not likely to be effective in realizing the national integration aspirations.

The regional disparities issue has been a recognized problem of the Brazilian government for at least a century, since the disastrous Northeast drought of 1877. For 80 years the government supported sporadic and unsuccessful programs to "fight the drought" through building dams and reservoirs. A new era in Northeast development was initiated in the early 1950s by President Getúlio Vargas, when he revised the government's approach to an economic rather than a physical solution. In support of this initiative the Bank of the Northeast was established in 1954 and the regional development agency SUDENE in 1958.

Since the new initiative began the Northeast has made spectacular economic progress relative to its own past situation. It was aided by favorable world markets for major regional agricultural products such as sugar and cacao, by large transfers of resources to the region through the 34-18 tax incentive scheme for industrial investment in the Northeast, and through the expansion of the petroleum and petro-chemical industry in the Bahia area. The gap between the region and the rest of Brazil has not narrowed in recent years, because of the extremely high national growth rate, but neither has it widened. Given the lower rate of population increase in the region, due mainly to out-migration, the rate of gain in per-capita income has exceeded that for the nation.

Yet, the Northeast still remains a major challenge. The development programs have not had sufficient impact on Northeast poverty and substandard social conditions, particularly in rural areas. Most of Brazil's pockets of absolute poverty are in the rural Northeast, and many of the national measures of poor social conditions such as illiteracy, health, and inadequate educational facilities merely reflect conditions in the Northeast.

Since 1970 the government has reoriented its programs to give greater attention and increased resources to agricultural and rural development in the Northeast. Unfortunately, the institutional and the information base needed to make these programs effective is still far from adequate. The institutional problem is being tackled through the creation of a new agency, POLONORD-ESTE, in 1974 to coordinate existing agricultural projects in that area. The basic strategy has also been improved by integrating agricultural and agro-industrial projects. The information base is being greatly enlarged through an extensive field research and analysis project assisted by the World Bank. Yet, the government has not yet been willing to face up to the matter of population policy as it relates to the problems of the Northeast and to the likelihood that a significant share of the poverty is concentrated in a rural population that has become marginal because of age or lack of education, and that will ultimately need to be assisted by direct welfare programs.

As policy makers in other countries, like the United States, are keenly aware, poverty areas are extremely difficult to eliminate. With its traditional pragmatism and innovative spirit, Brazil may eventually find solutions to this challenge that may be helpful to other countries with similar problems.

Domestic Social Challenges

In efforts to improve the quality of life, the principal challenges are to reduce poverty, increase real incomes, improve social services such as education and health, meet critical urbanization needs, and develop better environmental control programs. The issue of income distribution, though the subject of considerable political rhetoric, may actually be of less direct personal interest to individual workers and families, particularly if the growth momentum subsides, than a continued improvement in their own levels of real income and standards of living.

Income Distribution

The Second Plan discusses income distribution at considerable length and asserts that redistributive policies are required along with continued growth rates. "A solution through growth alone," the plan explains, "could take much longer than the social conscience will accept."[9] In line with the official analysis of the causal forces underlying income distribution patterns, the redistribution programs emphasized are those to expand educational opportunities and social welfare, in addition to increasing indirect benefits to workers through the Social

Integration Fund (PIS), where a form of profit-sharing places part of the employer's tax liability in restricted worker-owned deposits.

In absolute terms, the real income and living conditions of most Brazilians at all income levels should continue to improve through the forces of the market and large government expenditures for welfare programs, *if* high economic growth rates can be sustained. With a major slowdown of the economy, however, marginal and low-income workers, many of whom have only recently become part of the money economy, are likely to suffer. Another uncertainty arises out of the excessively indirect nature of the programs for reducing absolute poverty, particularly in the rural Northeast. In the social services, education programs have been reasonably successful, but the challenge to upgrade the health situation has not yet been adequately met.

Urbanization and the Environment

The urbanization challenge is particularly acute in some areas because of the unusual speed with which urbanization has occurred. In housing, the programs of the National Housing Bank have been dramatically successful, even though the housing situation is still far from being solved. In expanding urban water and sewage systems, the programs of the National Housing Bank are beginning to be effective. But Brazil still lacks an institutional structure for dealing comprehensively with the urbanization challenge.

A National Commission for Metropolitan Regions and Urban Policies (CNPU) was established in 1974 with the task of creating the necessary institutions for making urban development plans and policies operational. Broad urban development policies are announced in the Second Plan such as those to encourage decentralization through stimulating new urban centers and to design specific strategies to be followed in each major region that "reflect the peculiarities and the stage of development" of that region. The generality and the vagueness of the urban development policies reflect the early stage of Brazil's response to its urbanization challenge. Clearly, urbanization solutions are lagging far behind the problems, and Brazil may suffer the fate of most advanced countries where undesirable patterns become deeply entrenched before more rational patterns can be implemented.

The environmental challenge is a newer problem than urbanization. It is significant, however, that in contrast to the earlier and well-publicized position that Brazil had plenty of space to accommodate industries that pollute, Brazil has now decided to give emphasis to environmental and pollution problems and has established a governmental unit, called the Special Secretary for the Environment (SEMA), to undertake studies. Awareness of the environmental problem is growing, particularly in metropolitan areas such as São Paulo. The definition and the implementation of environmental control measures, however, appear to be a matter for future resolution.

Population Policy

Population policy has long been a sensitive topic on which debate was not encouraged. For decades most Brazilians have been deeply and sincerely convinced that Brazil needed a high rate of population increase and that reductions in the population growth rate should not be encouraged or tolerated. This firm conviction was due less to the fact that Brazil is a Catholic country than to the keen awareness that Brazil had vast agricultural areas which were unpopulated. The criterion was availability of land and natural resources. By this test Brazil considered itself an underpopulated country.

Beginning in the 1970s, and coincident with a growing world sensitivity to population trends, Brazil appears to have entered a transition period. A notable feature of the II National Development Plan is its extended discussion on population policy. It recognizes the traditional "underpopulation" view but then proceeds to recognize also the need to examine the population growth rate in relation to "the effective capacity of the country to expand employment."[10] Although the subject is treated cautiously, the implication is that employment opportunities are more important in a population policy than the existence of physical territory or natural resources.

Probably in pique at the aggressiveness (or effectiveness) of the international population groups, the policy statement asserts the right of Brazil as a sovereign nation to establish its own population policy. It also emphasizes the right of married couples to make their own personal decisions on family size, but with the significant qualification, when "offered the opportunity for information that permits a complete examination of the question." It is well recognized in Brazil that the affluent classes already have access to such information, but the poorer families do not.

These cautious moves implicitly recognize the reality that Brazil's population has been urbanizing rapidly and concentrating in overcrowded cities like Rio de Janeiro and São Paulo, rather than streaming to the Amazon and Central West. The treatment of the subject also reflects an awareness that, with a 3 percent annual growth rate as contrasted to 1 percent in the industrialized countries, Brazil needs an additional increment of at least 2 percent annually in its economic expansion to create adequate employment opportunities and to keep the present gap in per-capita income between Brazil and the advanced countries from widening.

Brazil takes some comfort in its official forecast that the population growth rate will continue to decline slowly because of urbanization, but the projected rate is still high. Probably a next step in policy making will be to analyze the costs and benefits of an even greater reduction in the rate of population increase. Then the question should arise as to the trade-off from an affirmative plan to increase education on family planning possibilities. A reduction of 1 percent in the population growth rate may be more helpful in raising welfare levels and probably less expensive than an increase of 1 percent in the economic growth rate.

The Political Challenge

The success of opposition candidates in the November 1974 congressional election has forced a reevaluation of Brazil's political future—a challenge both for the government and for the opposition party (MDB). Spokesmen for the military have honored the results of the election, and MDB leaders expect to use their new strength in the Congress cautiously as they test the attitudes of the military toward pressing economic and social issues.

For ten years the military authoritarian system has been enthusiastically supported by a number of Brazilians and reluctantly tolerated by others because of the phenomenal economic development achieved under its aegis. If the 1974 election provides any guidance, continued support and tolerance will heavily depend on the state of the economy and a further liberalization of the political system. Concern about inflation coupled with passions over missing prisoners could hasten the transition to a more open civilian political system. Or, it could provoke military leaders to tighten political controls.

The military leaders are publicly in favor of the idea that the government should eventually be headed by civilians. But they continue to consider most civilian politicians unreliable and corrupt and have not encouraged the emergence of a "new generation" of civilian politicians. As a result many people, especially university students, are "turned off" by politics as a desirable career, and a new civilian leadership is only slowly emerging.

The question remains, however: from which group will the next political leadership come? The younger military officers on their way up are one source. The civilian tecnicos are another. Both have acquired enormous experience in the functions of government and both are dedicated to the concept of Brazilian "grandeur."

In Summary

Despite the economic, social, and political challenges, Brazil's long-range outlook is promising. An optimistic view is supported by the country's history over the past three decades of meeting most of these difficult challenges successfully. There will be short-term interruptions in the momentum of the development drive, and Brazil has become increasingly dependent upon uncontrollable forces in the international environment. But the nation is better prepared than ever before with resources, experience, trained personnel, and self-confidence to meet future challenges. In the new international environment, it will be difficult to maintain a 10 percent annual growth rate. However, 6 to 8 percent annual growth rates appear to be feasible and should carry Brazil along the development road at a pace that many other nations would envy. Even more important, the recent movement of the political system off dead center may be what was needed to translate GNP growth rates into the general welfare of Brazilians.

Notes

1. República Federativa do Brasil, *Projeto do II Plano Nacional de Desenvolvimento (1975-1979)*, (Second Plan), Brasilia, Setembro de 1974, p. 15.

2. See Stefan H. Robock and Kenneth Simmonds, *International Business and Multinational Enterprises* (Homewood, Ill.: Richard D. Irwin, Inc., 1973) for a discussion of "Common Interests and Conflict areas" between the multinationals and the nation-state, pp. 139-67.

3. Antonio Dias Leite, *Política Mineral e Energética* (Rio de Janeiro: Fundação IBGE, 1974), p. 64.

4. *Second Plan*, pp. 33-37.

5. See Dias Leite, *Política Mineral e Energética*, pp. 9-18.

6. Rubens Vaz da Costa, *Demographic Growth and Environmental Pollution* (Rio de Janeiro: BNH, 1973), p. 34.

7. See *Choice and Adaptation of Technology in Developing Countries* (Paris: OECD, May 1974); Nuno Fidelino de Figueiredo, *A Transferência de Tecnologia no Desenvolvimento Industrial do Brasil* (Rio de Janeiro: IPEA/INPES, 1972); Francisco Almeida Biato, Eduardo Augusto A. Guimarães, and Maria Helena Poppe de Figueiredo, *A Transferência de Tecnologia no Brasil* (Brasília: IPEA, 1973); Henrique Rattner, "Desenvolvimento e Emprego," *Revista de Administração de Empresas*, June 1974, pp. 145-53.

8. Goodman and Cavalcanti, *Incentivos à Industrialização e Desenvolvimento do Nordeste* (Rio de Janeiro: IPEA/INPES, 1974), pp. 335-44.

9. *Second Plan*, p. 61.

10. *Second Plan*, p. 51.

# 11

Development Lessons for Others

What can other developing countries learn from the Brazilian experience? Obviously, many features of Brazil's development success have been shaped by its cultural, political, and physical setting and cannot be exactly replicated in a different country environment. Nevertheless, various elements of Brazil's development strategies and programs may be successfully transferred to other country settings.

Is a Military Authoritarian Government a Necessary Condition?

Although many developing countries, have authoritarian governments, a number of other nations, while recognizing that a strong government is needed for development, are not anxious to adopt a military authoritarian model. A key question for such countries, therefore, is whether the various components of the Brazilian experience require a military government in order to be used successfully or whether they can be applied effectively under other types of regimes. Because of a sincere belief that the Brazilian development success was largely due to the military government in power since 1964, foreigners have often refused to examine Brazil's strategy and policies for transferable elements. As one example, numerous Americans have brushed aside as irrelevant the Brazilian experience in handling the problem of inflation because the United States does not have a military authoritarian government.

Within Brazil the view that a military government has been an indispensable condition is also widely held. Military leaders, tecnicos, businessmen, and others testify that the military government has immeasurably improved the technical quality of decisions, the speed of decision making, and the efficiency of program implementation. Furthermore, it is argued, the absence of traditional political pressures from different regions and particular interest groups has reduced the dispersion and wastage of scarce development resources.

It should not be surprising that the military guardians of the political system and the civilian tecnicos who manage the development effort are convinced and have persuaded others that the prevailing political system has been essential. In one sense it is a fact that the specific advantages of the system noted above have existed, and the successful development results cannot be denied. But the question posed by many observers is not whether the military system in Brazil

189

was effective in achieving development results. Clearly, it was—at a price. What might have happened in Brazil with a different political system will never be known; nonetheless, there is evidence to support the view that a military authoritarian government was not a necessary condition:

1. From an historical perspective, as shown in Figure 11-1, the high growth rates achieved since 1967 can be viewed as a resumption, after the 1962-67 hiatus, of a long-run pattern of steadily accelerating growth extending over at least the last 50 yeras, rather than as a new and independent phenomenon.

2. Many key policies and programs that contributed to the development success under the military government were born, nurtured to adolescence, and in some cases brought to maturity under the preceding civilian governments. A few examples are the establishment of the automobile and shipbuilding indus-

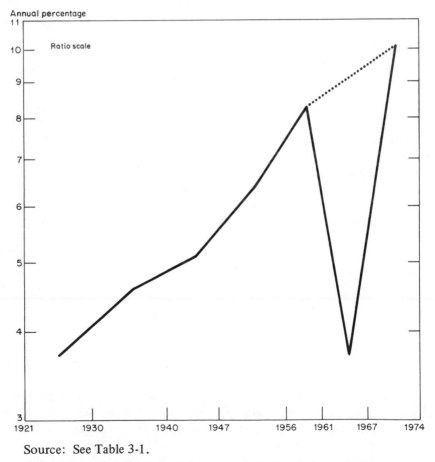

Source: See Table 3-1.

Figure 11-1. Brazilian Economic Growth Rates in Historical Perspective: 1920-74.

tries; the creation of government enterprises in steel, petroleum, mining, and electric power; and the formulation of policies for fiscal and banking reforms dating back to task forces created during the Goulart regime.

3. High growth rates have also been achieved under civilian governments. When Kubitschek assumed office in 1956 Brazil's annual growth rate was only 3.2 percent, due mainly to the collapse of international coffee prices in that year. But from 1957 through 1961 the growth rate averaged more than 8 percent annually, and in both 1960 and 1961 the annual growth rate reached 10 percent.

4. Some of the vital policy decisions made and implemented since 1964 represent a natural policy evolution that any government in power would almost certainly have made. The principal example was the evolution from import-substitution to export-oriented production.

5. External factors largely independent of the military government made important contributions to the recent high growth rates. Such factors include a sustained period of world economic prosperity during the late 1960s and early 1970s, a change in the views and policies of the World Bank and the International Monetary Fund toward lending to countries with high rates of inflation, and greatly increased availability of foreign assistance under the Alliance for Progress program initiated in the early 1960s.

A more speculative but important argument supporting the view that a continuing military government after the 1964 intervention was not essential for the recent development success is that President Goulart's failures predisposed any successor government to impose tough discipline and undertake difficult institutional reforms. The 1964 economic crisis was so severe and so disturbing that any succeeding government was almost certain to receive unprecedented popular support for austerity measures to reduce inflation and return the country to its previous path of rapid economic growth.

These arguments are not intended to minimize the necessity for the 1964 military intervention or to detract from the credit that Brazil's military government and civilian tecnicos rightly deserve for their contribution to economic development. But, it is important in considering the transferability of elements of the Brazilian development effort to other countries to recognize that many crucial internal and external forces independent of the political system have been at work over the last decade.

Lessons in Developing Strategy

Probably the most important feature of Brazil's development strategy, and the one most difficult to transfer to another society, has been the continuing dedication to pragmatism. Brazil's basic approach has been to determine its development targets and not to be constrained in reaching them by doctrinaire or ideological commitments as to means. This is not to say that Brazil's philosophy has been that the ends justify *any* means. The Brazilian approach recognizes and accepts limits in the choice of means, but, within those limits, the stress is on flexibility and imagination in "getting the job done."

Brazil's firmness on ends rather than means is well exemplified by its flexible policies in making use of private, public, domestic, and foreign enterprises. Except for a few special cases, such as petroleum and radioactive minerals, and the brief Goulart period of hostility to foreign investment, Brazil has never placed official restrictions on the types of enterprise that can operate in the various fields of economic activity.

In contrast, the government of India has long had an official industrial policy that places all industrial fields into one of three groups. Group A includes iron and steel, heavy engineering, heavy electrical, most mining, and many other types of activity, "the future development of which will be the exclusive responsibility of the state"; Group B embraces industries "which will be progressively state-owned and in which the state will therefore generally take the initiative in establishing new undertakings, but in which private enterprise will also be expected to supplement the effort of the state"; and Group C consists of the residual category of industries whose "future development will, in general, be left to the initiative and enterprise of the private sector."

Although in practice Indian officials have at times been pragmatic in applying their comprehensive industrial policy, especially in recent years, the Indian approach reflects a powerful ideological commitment regarding means. Deviations from the official doctrine do occur, but they are exceptions. Undoubtedly, this basic difference in approaches helps to explain Brazil's rapid development growth and India's sluggish economic progress.

The evolution of economic planning in Brazil is another example of the pragmatic approach. Here again, the Brazilian experience contrasts sharply with that of India. Early in the 1950s India committed itself to a highly centralized and sophisticated system of comprehensive economic planning that won renown as "a nonpareil instance of systematic economic planning in the non-Communist portion of the economically underdeveloped world."[1] The system earned India a plethora of kudos in academic circles because of its technical elegance, but those that could be given for development results were few indeed. The grand design was not in harmony with the availability in India of factual data, technical staff, and institutional capacity for plan implementation. Eventually, India began to realize these limitations and to modify its planning strategy accordingly.

In the Brazilian case during the 1950s and early 1960s, not only did the government refrain from trying to rely on a highly centralized and comprehensive planning unit, but it also recognized the limited capacity of its governmental bureaucracy to implement development programs. The early planning activity focused on defining broad areas of development priority and on the preparation of detailed investment projects in those areas, drawing heavily on foreign technical assistance. Decision-making continued to be decentralized, and incentives rather than controls or directives were used to stimulate enterprise. Quasi-independent agencies and government corporations were created to enlarge the implementation capability for development programs.

Even more important, Brazil made extensive use of the market for decision making and implementation. The market is one of the greatest labor-saving devices ever invented and the only substitute for the decision-making and -implementing capabilities that may be lacking in the government sector.

The Brazilian strategy for foreign private investment is a third important example of the pragmatic approach. Brazil shares with many other countries a deep concern over the dangers of foreign economic control, but has not been obsessed with rigid and doctrinaire measures intended to guarantee that national interests will prevail over the external interests of multinational enterprises. It has not attempted to emulate such practices as those of the Andean Common Market, which tries to achieve national goals by prohibiting foreign capital from entering designated fields and by requiring joint ventures in other designated business areas, with ownership to be gradually transferred to local interests through the "fade-out" arrangement.

The Brazilian policy has been to identify areas in which foreign investment can advance development goals and to welcome foreign firms in those areas with a minimum of entry barriers and often with attractive incentives. Brazilians have great confidence that, *after* foreign firms become established in their country, their government officials will have sufficient expertise and imagination to influence the operations of these enterprises, generally through profitable inducements, to support changes in development goals.

They recognize that a sovereign nation has many ways to exert control over foreign firms within its borders other than by insisting that a part or a majority of the ownership must be local. A striking example of the pragmatic approach to foreign investment is the electric power industry, where Brazil chose to use scarce capital to expand the country's power capacity through government enterprises rather than to buy out the foreign owners of existing facilities. It would be difficult, if not impossible, to support an allegation that its strategy has given Brazil less control over foreign enterprise within its borders than that exercised by the Andean-Bloc countries.

Lessons in Business-Government Cooperation

In the area of business-government cooperation the Brazilian experience may also have lessons for other countries. The Brazilian development effort has been fostered in many ways through a close relationship between the private and the public sector. Military personnel, tecnicos, and businessmen move easily back and forth between government service and private business activity. This means that the realities of the business world, as seen from either private or government enterprises and as experienced in commerce, banking, manufacturing, and agriculture, are understood by many persons in government service. It also means that many leaders of the private sector have extensive familiarity with the complexities and goals of government activities.

One reason for business-government cooperation in Brazil is that the value system of the social hierarchy gives roughly the same status to business managers and to government officials. Thus, no status barrier exists to movements back and forth by individuals. It would be difficult to conceive of the same thing happening in India where, with its British heritage, the Indian Civil Service officer has high social status, and most business managers have lower status.

A second factor is that military leaders, tecnicos, and businessmen have frequently shared the same educational and training experiences at such institutions as the Superior War College and the various programs of the Getúlio Vargas Foundation. The result has been a surprising harmony of views as to development strategies and goals.

Specific Development Techniques

The tools and policies that Brazil has used to implement its development strategy offer a wide array of specific techniques that might be effective in other countries. A selected list of the techniques includes the following:

Anti-inflationary Techniques. Economywide indexing, minidevaluations, price controls which stimulate productivity, and emphasis on measures that increase supply more rapidly than demand.

Use of Incentives. Tax, tariff, credit, and many other forms of incentives specifically designed to expand exports, to encourage industrial and agricultural growth in the poorer regions, to increase investment in priority activities such as forestry, fishing, and tourism, to attract foreign investment in selected industries, to encourage savings, and to stimulate the development of private capital markets.

Special Financing Techniques. The financing of massive housing and urban development programs by linking these welfare programs to a new and expanded social security system.

Effective Use of Special Training Programs. Nationwide and continuing special training programs, frequently with foreign technical assistance, to upgrade technical skills for economic planning, project preparation, management, engineering, and in many other fields.

Adult Literacy Programs. The MOBRAL program that operates outside the traditional education bureaucracy, with specially designed techniques and a system of payment based on performance.

Unique Status for Tecnicos. Reliance on technically trained people to assume major responsibility for development efforts, many of whom were called upon to serve under a wide array of different political leaders.

Concluding Comments

The transfer of development experience is hardly a science. The variables at either end of the transfer are enormous. The desire to learn from the experience of other countries is affected by the need to learn and by a reluctance to admit foreign ideas—nationalism. Even with a willingness to learn, nations may be overly conservative in anticipating what will work in their environment.

In many cases Brazilians have been almost certain that the experience of other countries was not applicable to Brazil, such as certain tax administration practices recommended by the U.S. Internal Revenue Service that, when tried, helped dramatically to increase tax collections in Brazil. The author, as a technical assistance adviser to Brazil over many years, can testify from personal experience that many recommendations based on the experience of other countries were initially viewed locally as inapplicable to Brazil but, when applied, turned out to be successful innovations.

Because the Brazilian setting is more dedicated to "doing" than to the prevention of doing things "wrong," experimentation is encouraged and a reasonable degree of failure is tolerated. In the process Brazilians have frequently discovered that many initiatives that conventional wisdom says cannot succeed in Brazil in fact do succeed with beneficial results. With this kind of tolerance for experimentation, other countries may discover that many elements of the Brazilian experience that are judged to be nontransferable can in fact be transferred and with benefit.

It must also be said that Brazil has been fortunate. As Brazilians will admit with a smile, God is a Brazilian, and he has been good to Brazil: vast resources, a blending of a variety of ethnic groups, a history that removed the stigma of colonialism, a generally non-belligerent attitude toward its neighbors. Who needs more territory? As a result Brazil can afford to experiment with the development process and accept margins of error that might not be possible for other countries. Thus, Brazil, as an economy in transition, may soon close the development gap and join the society of developed countries.

Note

1. John P. Lewis, *Quiet Crisis in India* (Washington: The Brookings Institution, 1962), p. 114.

Index

197

About the Author

Stefan H. Robock is the Robert D. Calkins Professor of International Business at Columbia University. A native of Wisconsin, he received the B.A. from the University of Wisconsin and the M.A. and Ph.D. in economics from Harvard University. He has honorary degrees from the University of Recife (Brazil) and ESTE in San Sebastian, Spain.

Professor Robock has undertaken many development assistance assignments in Brazil, beginning in 1954 with a two and one-half-year mission as United Nations Development Adviser on Northeast Brazil. He is the author of *Nuclear Power and Economic Development in Brazil* (National Planning Association, 1957) and *Brazil's Developing Northeast* (Brookings, 1963) as well as numerous other books and articles on international business and economic development. His most recent book is *International Business and Multinational Enterprises* with K. Simmonds (Irwin, 1973).

Related Lexington Books

Benoit, Emile; *Defense and Economic Growth in Developing Countries*, 335 pp., 1973

Casadio, Gian Paolo, *The Economic Challenge of the Arabs*, In Press

Morgenstern, Oskar, and Thompson, G.L., *Contracting and Expanding World Economies*, In Press

Morley, James, ed., *Prologue to the Future: The United States and Japan in the Postindustrial Age*, 256 pp., 1974

Owens, Edgar, and Shaw, Robert, *Development Reconsidered*, 208 pp, 1972

Singh, S.K., *Development Economics: Some Findings*, 320 pp., 1975